The 33rd

This book is dedicated to the memory
of Professor F. Elaine DeLancey,
respected colleague and friend in
the Department of English and Philosophy.

Editor-In-Chief	Scott Stein
Senior Editors	Albert DiBartolomeo
	Kathleen Volk Miller
Layout Editor	William Rees
Graphic Design	Randi Dean
	Laura DiSanto
Editorial Co-ops	Amy Jacob
	Dan Savage
Design Co-ops	Matthew Garrity
	Catherine Lewandowski
Student Interns	Wendy L. Childs
	Bridget M. Gawinowicz
	Giby George
	Humza Ghori
	Laura A. Knoll
	Adria Leeper-Sullivan
	Margaret Leoffler
	Dori Malozonov
	Christopher Manzi
	Carolynn M. McCormack
	Sara Parysz
	Francisco Santoni
	Samantha Slusarczyk
	Jasmin Sosa
	John D. Suozzi
	Justine Wan

Sponsors

Drexel University
The College of Arts and Sciences at Drexel University
The Department of English and Philosophy at Drexel University

Dr. Donna M. Murasko, Dean, College of Arts and Sciences,
Drexel University
Dr. Abioseh Michael Porter, Department Head, English and Philosophy,
Drexel University

The 33rd Volume 4
Drexel University
Department of English and Philosophy
3141 Chestnut Street
Philadelphia, PA 19104
www.drexelpublishing.org

Cover photo by Laura DiSanto

Copies of this volume are available for $10 by writing to the above address.

ISBN 978-0-9820717-3-1

Thank you, thank you, thank you and thank you to: Dr. Donna M. Murasko; Dr. Abioseh Michael Porter; all the judges from the Drexel Publishing Group Essay Contest, the Week of Writing Contest, and the Freshman Writing Contest (Ben Poletta, Robert Gilmore, Rebecca Hoffman, Scott Warnock, Anne-Marie Obajtek-Kirkwood, Ronald Bishop, Rebecca Ingalls, Alexander Friedlander, Barbara Hoekje, Emmanuel Koku, Maria Hnaraki, Rakhmiel Peltz, Jonathan Seitz, Leonard Finegold, Donna McVey, Eric Schmutz, Henry Israeli, Harriet Levin Millan, Genevieve Betts, Lynn Levin, Cassandra Hirsch, Miriam N. Kotzin, Dan Driscoll, Emilie Passow, Karen Nulton, Valerie Fox, Fred Siegel, Stacey Ake, Kathy McNamee, Albert DiBartolomeo, Jan Armon, Ken Bingham, Valerie Booth, Anne Erickson, Michelle Kline, Deirdre McMahon, Donald Riggs, Gail Rosen, Marshall Warfield); Department of English and Philosophy, especially Mary Beth Beyer, Eileen Brennen, and Nicole Kline; contest participants; Drexel Publishing Group staff.

Distributed by the Drexel Publishing Group
The fonts used within this publication are Archer and Avenir

Credits:

Betts, Genevieve. "Fault." Rev. of *Fault*, by Katherine Coles. *Western American Literature* Volume 44, Number 1, Spring 2009: pp. 86-87. Print.

Cohen, Paula Marantz. "Counter Argument" was first published in *The Smart Set* <*the smartset.com*>.

Fox, Valerie. "Teacher" and "How the river had invited her down for a serious talk" both appeared in *The Glass Book* (2010 Texture Press).

Hirsch, Cassandra. "Ghosts" was first published in *Parlor Journal* in December 2007 and was nominated for a Pushcart Prize.

Ingalls, Rebecca. "The Trilemma Revised: Harry Potter and a Landscape of Moral Uncertainty" was originally published in POROI in January 2011.

Knowles, Scott Gabriel. "Phantom of the Fair" was first published in *The Smart Set* <*the smartset.com*>.

Kotzin, Miriam N. "Magic Act" and "Collection" are in *Taking Stock* (Star Cloud Press, forthcoming 2011)

Lee, Jeffrey E. "After she said 'You can work around me / somehow he knew" was a finalist in the James Hearst Poetry Prize Competition, published in *North American Review*, March-April 2006.

Levin, Lynn. "On Going to the Playboy Club with My Father" was first published in *Michigan Quarterly Review* in 2010.

Millan, Harriet L. "She Walked in Late" was originally published in *Drunken Boat*, 10th Anniversary Issue, Spring 2009.

Millan, Harriet L. "Swimming in a Glass" was originally published in the *Harvard Review*, Issue 37, Fall/Winter 2009-10.

Miller, Kathleen Volk. "A Haunted House" was previously published in *Opium Magazine*, 2011.

Objatek-Kirkwood, Anne-Marie. "American and French Voices Telling/ Re-telling September 11" was first published as "Diverses voix sur le 11 septembre : celles de Vinaver et Lang" in *Romance Studies*, Vol. 28 No. 3, July 2010, 206-216.

Riggs, Don. "Inventio of Poetry" was part of the series "Making Things out of Words," published in *Press 1*.

Credits:

Rosen, Gail D. "Joan Rivers: Serious About Comedy" originally appeared in *When Falls the Coliseum* *<whenfallsthecoliseum.com>* on June 23, 2010.

Siegel, Fred. An earlier version of "Doug Henning Can Fly" originally appeared in *When Falls the Coliseum* *<whenfallsthecoliseum.com>* in October, 2010.

Thorpe, Elizabeth. "William Tell" was originally published in the "Punishment" issue of *Painted Bride Quarterly* in 2010.

Warnock, Scott. "The Song Might Have Never Been: Zeppelin in the Age of Helicopter Parents" originally appeared in *When Falls the Coliseum* *<whenfallsthecoliseum.com>* on December 3, 2010.

Welcome

This has been an exciting year for the humanities at Drexel. The Week of Writing has continued to grow, with new events and some exciting—and famous!—guest speakers. Notable author Sir Salman Rushdie graced our campus in May, serving as the inaugural speaker in the College's Distinguished Lecture series. And our remarkable students have taken home prestigious awards including the Fulbright and Jack Kent Cooke scholarships.

The 33rd continues to be a visible expression of the College of Arts and Sciences' commitment to writing excellence. Within its pages you will find an eclectic mix of faculty and student writing, from thoughtful essays to entertaining short stories, from moving poetry to scholarly articles on scientific topics. This volume is a reminder that good writing is vital to the success of students and professionals in all fields, not only in the humanities, but also in the social and natural sciences. Let these pages motivate you to do more than you ever imagined.

Donna M. Murasko, Ph.D.
Dean
College of Arts and Sciences

Preface

As is often noted, the Department of English and Philosophy has established a well-deserved reputation not only as a place where instructors of all ranks are passionate about teaching and learning—derived from classroom and other such experiences—but also as the one locale at Drexel where excellent writing is seen as a daily, achievable goal. Because our ultimate objective is to make excellent writing a defining characteristic of a Drexel education, we will continue to help our students understand that a fine blend of traditional literary skills and modern thought and practice will help to make them excellent, even outstanding, writers. We, the faculty in our department, have therefore set as our primary goals the achievement of the highest academic standards, the creation of a congenial atmosphere for our students, and a dynamic teaching and scholarly environment.

It is thus with immense pleasure that we present the fourth volume of this yearly anthology. In *The 33rd* 2011, we aim to encourage our students to fuse insights derived from their varied experiences and knowledge to create a document that truly should impress readers because of the complex web of writing the authors present, even with an occasional undergraduate self-consciousness.

Using varying approaches that, even in these early stages, reveal the complexity, density of texture and meaning, and the richness of vision and artistry that often characterize good quality writing, the students—guided by their very able instructors—have carefully demonstrated in print some famous words of wisdom by Diane Stanley, author and illustrator: "Good writing is clear thinking." What I now hope the students, again with guidance from all of us, will continue to do from this point on is to apply the other half of Ms. Stanley's statement: "Reading is how you learn what good writing sounds like."

My personal congratulations—as well as those of the whole department—go to all who participated in this laudable and practically useful project. To those whose selections were published, I would like to conclude by offering some more words by the writer Enrique Jardiel Poncela: "When something can be read without effort, great effort has gone into its writing." Bravo!

Abioseh Michael Porter, Ph.D.
Department Head
Department of English and Philosophy

Table of Contents

Zelda Provenzano Endowed STEM Writing Award

Graduate

Week of Writing
Introduction

Poetry

Fiction

Non-Fiction

Humor

Opinion/Editorial

Faculty Writing
Introduction

Freshman
Writing

Introduction

Each year, students enrolled in the Freshmen Writing Program sequence at Drexel write thousands of projects and papers. These texts represent the extraordinary perspectives of our students, and they are composed over weeks of reading, research, discussion, drafting, and tapping into their diversity of experiences. Here at Drexel, our hope is that students will start to make their work "count" beyond the boundaries of the classroom: in publication, in the crafting of proposals for change, in the building of ideas that lead to innovation. The Freshman Writing Award hopes to recognize student excellence and to provide them with a gateway toward visibility to a broader audience.

The contest process is rigorous. In the fall of 2010, faculty members from the 140 freshman writing courses nominate the best examples of student writing. These papers and projects are distributed to a panel of faculty judges. This year these judges narrowed down 61 initial entries to a finalist list of 18. A smaller panel of faculty judges then re-read the final group and ranked them to make the final determination of the top three prize winners and honorable mentions. The awards for this contest are given at the English Awards Ceremony in the spring term, and for years this contest has been generously supported by Ingrid Daemmrich, one of our faculty members.

We continue to be amazed each year at the array of academic disciplines represented by the winning entries. This variety emphasizes the importance of writing in the careers and lives of all of our students. In addition, this contest, with its winners from across Drexel's curriculum, helps us recognize our students as writers; that is fitting, because we believe that is exactly what they are.

Rebecca Ingalls, Ph.D.
Incoming Director of the Freshman Writing Program

Scott Warnock, Ph.D.
Director of the Freshman Writing Program, 2007-2011

Kevin Biallas

Home Is Where the Mine Fire Is

While I was growing up in the heart of Pennsylvania, my dad always enjoyed exploring the towns and sites of our area and took me along to be his co-pilot. Often he would take side trips on our way to destinations. Although it would involve a longer and winding route, my dad would justify his actions by quoting Robert Frost: "Two roads diverged in a wood, and I took the one less traveled by, and that has made all the difference." One of the most memorable places my dad took me to was the town of Centralia. The word "town" is used very loosely because Centralia is slowly vanishing from the maps. In fact, Larry King and his ex-wives now outnumber the residents of Centralia. Why residents remain in the dying town is a question that I wanted to explore.

Centralia is a borough located in the heart of Pennsylvania's coal region, an area covering the northeastern part of the state. The main commodity that led to the growth and development of this area was anthracite coal. Anthracite is the highest quality of coal and burns slowly and at a high temperature because of its high carbon content. Unfortunately these characteristics would ultimately prove to be disastrous for Centralia. Centralia was founded in 1862 and became home for the miners who worked in the nearby mines. The town grew into a thriving community, but in May of 1962 its fortunes changed for the worse. As part of the town's spring cleanup efforts a pile of trash was burned in an abandoned strip-mine being used as a dump. Residents were unaware of an exposed seam of anthracite coal behind the trash and soon enough it caught fire (Nolter and Vice 99). The citizens were also unaware of the danger, as the fire spread and moved into a vast network of abandoned mines below Centralia. The years that followed were marked by a series of failed attempts by the government to control or extinguish the fire. In fact, the *Washington Post* reported that by 1982 "$4.5 million had been spent by the county, the state and the federal government in projects to extinguish, trap or simply locate the fire" (Fishman). In a 1980 study it was estimated that it would cost $85 million to excavate and put the fire out. Eventually the government concluded that it would be more cost effective to buy out the town and relocate the residents. As a result only seven people remain in the town to this present day (Fishman).

Ever since my first visit to Centralia, I have been interested in the history of the town and the mine fire that has destroyed it. When visiting family, I often drive through the coal region, making sure not to bypass Centralia. Every time

I visit there, the town has fewer houses standing as the population continues to dwindle. Even more interesting to me is the group of residents that refuse to leave the ill-fated town. The residents have fought numerous efforts by the government to get them to leave their homes. I have always wondered what their motivation and reasoning is for refusing a government buyout to remain in a town that has signs reading, "Warning—Danger Underground Mine Fire. Walking or Driving in This Area Could Result in Serious Injury or Death. Dangerous Gases are Present. Ground Is Prone To Sudden Collapse."

In order to get an understanding of why some Centralians remain in their homes, I wanted to learn about the lives of the people who lived and remain in the town. With the decline of the coal industry in the earlier half of the 20th century, Centralia had fallen on hard times. Much like all the neighboring towns in the area, Centralia was experiencing significant population loss and the young were leaving the area in search for work. According to Fishman's article, the homes in the town were mostly "filled with retired miners and their families. Depending on whom you ask, between 60 and 80 percent of the town lives on a fixed income: black lung benefits, disability, Social Security" (Fishman). Furthermore, the *New York Times* reported in 1981 that "the median income here is about $9,000, a good $12,000 below the national figure" (Kalson). The fact that the population of Centralia was aged and living on fixed incomes as retired mine workers suggests that the people remaining in the borough have a strong attachment to the community they live in. This strong attachment to community leads to different perceptions on the aesthetics of the land and the health risks of living next to a mine fire.

Even without the mine fire I wondered what appeal the residents of Centralia see in the area they live in. The anthracite coal located in the mountains of this region may have been responsible for the growth and prosperity of the region, but it came at a heavy price for the environment. The landscape has endured decades of intensive mining operations that have carved away hillsides and left black scars on the mountains. Many streams in the area have been stained burnt orange thanks to uncontrolled acid mine runoff. In Centralia, the aesthetics of the place are made even worse by the mine fire. Instead of seeing children playing in the streets from their front porch, the residents of Centralia see white plumes of smoke rising from the ground. The abandoned grid of streets and smoking hillside give the impression that the town was caught in a war and became a victim of the scorched earth policy. Recently in my visits to Centralia, I have observed that a string of windmills have been constructed on a ridge overlooking the town. While this may be a sign of progress for the region as we attempt to transition from fossil fuels to renewable energy, the windmills tower ominously over Centralia and are a slap in the face to a town that was created and destroyed by coal. Few outsiders would consider the landscape of Centralia to be scenic or inviting, but to my surprise the locals actually view the scars on the mountainside as a symbol of the region's heritage and former economic power.

When driving to Centralia from my home I drive through the neighboring city of Shamokin. One of the first views welcoming visitors to the city is a man-made mountain of anthracite mining by-product, called culm. The pile of mining waste is somewhat of an eyesore, but as Ben Marsh states, "It is actually, as people tell with a certain pride, the world's largest pile of anthracite mine waste" (345). What is a perceived symbol of the destructive mining operations by outsiders is seen by locals as a source of pride. Shriver and Kennedy write about a rural Oklahoma town that has been contaminated by nearby zinc mining operations. Locals who didn't want to be relocated viewed the mountain of zinc mining by-product "as important landmarks in the community" (507). This perspective from another town with its own similar situation helps me understand why Centralians would actually look to the scars on the mountainside as a testament to the hardworking miners who lived in the borough.

I also wondered why Centralians would continue to live in an area that can have negative consequences on their health. My research shows, however, that it is all a matter of perceived risk. As Shriver and Kennedy explain, "While residents may be confronted with similar environmental conditions, they often use different sets of criteria for making their assessments of environmental harm" (493). This different interpretation of the risk of living with a mine fire led to two conflicting groups consisting of those who wanted to relocate from the borough and those who wanted to stay.

Younger residents like 21-year-old Catharene Jurgill did not want to take the risk of any harm being done to her two young children. In a 1982 article in the *Washington Post* she said, "I have trouble sleeping at night because I'm worried about the children. I worry when the gas levels are high..." (Fishman). Since she is younger it is likely that she did not have as strong of an attachment to Centralia as older members of the population and like many of the younger citizens in the anthracite region she was willing to give up her residence in Centralia for more opportunities.

Other residents like 73-year-old Thomas Gerrity saw no harm in the fire even though he lived only a block away from it. When asked if he was afraid of the fire, he responded, "Noooooo. We sleep. We don't feel any gas. We don't worry about it. We're living in the coal region all our lives" (Fishman). Even though the harmful gases like carbon monoxide being vented from the fire are odorless and colorless and need a monitor to detect, Gerrity wanted visual evidence that the fire posed a risk to his health. Because of his old age, Gerrity most likely had a strong attachment to Centralia and was willing to deny the health risks in an attempt to save his community.

Those who remain in the borough today are older and continue to debate the health risks of living next to the fire. Local news reporter Kena Vernon interviewed a lawyer, representing the remaining holdouts in an ongoing case, who wrote that, "They have not seen proof the fire is a hazard or is increasing in condition and may have never been a problem." While I would be worried about my health living in such close proximity to a mine fire releasing sulfurous gases and carbon monoxide, it is clear that those who have lived there for years and have a strong community attachment have never seen the fire as a risk to their daily lives in Centralia.

Another reason that the remaining residents resist relocation is the belief that they are victims of a government conspiracy. Centralia is unique in the fact that it owns the mineral rights to the coal that is beneath the borough. The town lies directly above the nation's largest vein of anthracite coal, so potentially there could be hundreds of millions of dollars worth of coal that could be mined. Many past and present residents believe the government delayed attempts at putting out the mine fire so that it could obtain the mineral rights to the coal. In a *New York Times* article, Centralia resident Tom Larkin claims that the government has purposefully stalled on efforts to extinguish the fire. "This fire got this big by design," says Larkin. "Every time they were ready to pull it out they mysteriously ran out of money" (Kalson). Former resident Helen Womer expressed a similar point of view in a Charles Fishman article: "They're letting the fire burn so they can condemn the community and get the coal!" It is believed by some that once the last resident leaves and Centralia ceases to exist as an entity, the state will open the town up for deep mining operations. If the residents feel that they are being pushed out of their homes for other reasons than their safety, it is understandable that they would resist relocation and refuse to leave. Perhaps the remaining holdouts feel they are the last line of defense against the government takeover of their community. In the spring of 2010, Kena Vernon reported that the last remaining holdouts in Centralia filed a lawsuit against the Commonwealth of Pennsylvania in an attempt to keep the state from forcing them out of their homes.

Before my research I may have been one of the many who view the residents as being crazy for wanting to stay in their homes in a town that has very little life supporting aspects remaining, but after researching and understanding the reasons and motivations for staying in their homes, I have a new appreciation and admiration for the remaining residents who have tried so hard to keep the last bit of their town alive. As the final residents of Centralia live out their stay, nature has already begun to reclaim the area. Streets have become narrower each year as vegetation slowly engulfs the pavement. It is my hope that when the last remaining resident has left, the people and heritage of Centralia will live on and not be forgotten, especially those tenacious residents that fought to keep it alive.

Works Cited

Couch, Stephen R. and J. Stephen Kroll-Smith. "Controllability, Social Breakdown and Technological Disasters: The Case of the Centralia Coal Mine Fire." *Natural and Technological Disasters: Causes, Effects and Preventive Measures*. p. 337-349.

Fishmen, Charles. "The Long, Slow Burning Of Centralia; A Community Divided and the Government Stymied by a Fire That Smolders in a Pennsylvania Coal-Mining Town." *The Washington Post*. September 5, 1982. LexisNexis. Web. 30 October 2010.

Kalson, Sally. "Slow Burn in Centralia, PA." *The New York Times*. November 22, 1981. LexisNexis. Web. 30 October 2010.

Marsh, Ben. "Continuity and Decline in the Anthracite Towns of Pennsylvania." *Annals of the Association of American Geographers*, 77. 3 (Sep., 1987): 337-352. JSTOR. Web. 30 October 2010.

Nolter, Melissa A. and Daniel H. Vice. "Looking back at the Centralia coal fire: a synopsis of its present status." *International Journal of Coal Geology*, 59 (2004): 99-106. ELSEVIER. Web. 28 October 2010.

Shriver, Thomas E. and Dennis K. Kennedy. "Contested Environmental Hazards and Community Conflict over Relocation." *Rural Sociology*, 70.4 (Dec. 2006): 491-513. WILEY. Web. 18 October 2010.

Vernon, Kena. "Centralia Residents Sue to Remain in Homes." *WNEP-TV*. March 9, 2010. Web. November 9, 2010.

Tom Ben-David

Unfolding the Past

A book. A bunch of pages bound together can make a huge difference in one's life. Every year Israel has a weeklong national holiday dedicated to books, involving many events revolving around these magnificent fountains of knowledge. One Book Week, when I was in the first grade, my father got me—what else—but a book. That book changed my life entirely. It was not a typical book filled with literature. The book contained instructions for an ancient Japanese art—an art of dedication, patience, precision, accuracy, and concentration. It was an origami book. At the time, I did not comprehend the colossus of the gift and did not know that this simple hobby would soon become an integral part of my life. I was excited, though, to receive such a practical gift from my beloved father.

My father and I hardly ever got to do things together. Managing a company and working for many hours each day, he barely had any time to spend time with me as a child. That book he gave me became an excuse for us to spend time together. We bought special origami paper and sat together to fold it according to the instructions—fold; crease; mountain; valley; sink; squash... the various commands became synonymous with quality father-and-son time. We created some wonderful designs together: a house, a bird, a frog... the endless possibilities of paper folding were in the palms of our hands. I soon received another instruction book, and another, and another, and soon my collection included thirteen books diagramming hundreds of different paper models ranging from very simple to complex.

Due to my father's busy schedule and my excess of free time as an elementary school student, I started folding paper by myself, without my father's explanation of each and every step. He grew busier with his work, and I grew more skillful with origami. I really wanted to spend the time with him, but the old excuse was not strong enough to keep my indefatigable father away from his work schedule. I learned a lot of skills I now possess from my father: he taught me how to draw; as a construction manager, he taught me about the various building processes; we used to play chess together. My folding ability grew advanced faster than he could keep up, though. But even though our origami relationship had ended, we have retained our intimate father-son relationship. I enjoyed paper folding so much that, even without my mentor, I kept doing it religiously as an independent hobby. I became more experienced and could soon enough handle models labeled "intermediate" and "complex" by myself. As much as I wished my father were still there to fold with me, I enjoyed folding quietly without any distractions. It was relaxing, therapeutic, and even, in some senses, enlightening; a whole new world revealed itself before my eyes. I started recognizing patterns, discerning mathematical concepts, and seeing beyond the actual folds. Memorizing a hundred-step diagram had become an easy task, as the process merely "makes sense." I could, all of a sudden, see things better: everything felt like an enormous piece of paper folding and unfolding itself, revealing its structure, its secrets, its relation to the space. My perspective, my mathematical abilities, and my attention to details had all become very keen. I discovered the truthfulness of all the popular, wise Oriental statements through this timeless art. And yet I missed folding with my father.

My father, despite the lack of time, was always very supportive of everything I did, namely origami. He was a self-taught artist when he was in high school, which certainly augmented this appreciation. The support was one reason for which this obsession had become progressively more and more intense. The other reason was my addiction to folding. As some are addicted to drugs or alcohol, I was addicted to creasing pieces of paper. It was like a gene commanding me to fold was inscribed in my DNA. I often found myself just folding aimlessly with no memory as to why and when I even started. I was not able to hold a piece of paper—or any foldable material—for an extended period of time and keep it free of creases. In effect, it really helped me to concentrate on whatever else I was doing at the time. I actually received special permission from my middle school teacher to fold in class for that exact reason after my parents had met with her and discussed the situation. One would think that I had a serious problem, but I would say I was just exploring space and the endless possibilities paper folding contains.

In high school I started attending a monthly origami group, whose membership representation consisted of some very respectable members of OrigamiUSA—the largest group in the world dedicated to the art of origami. People like Doctor Robert Lang (a renowned mathematician and physicist, considered the father of modern origami) had become my idols. I started looking more closely into some practical applications of the art. I studied the mathematics behind it and read about some incredible problems that were solved thanks to paper folding principles. I even wrote an extensive paper explaining how one can solve cubic equations using origami. I was completely mesmerized by the beauty of origami both from an artistic and from a mathematic perspective. It has become such an important part of my life and it is impossible to imagine myself living without folding. Paper folding patterns are now an integral part of my cognition. Origami, for me, is an inexplicable compulsive obsession that was generated from a simple pastime. All this started with a book, a book my father bought me one day when I was in the first grade. A book filled with pictures of various creatures and objects and instructions that tell the reader how to create them by applying simple folds on a square piece of paper. I will treasure this book and the opportunity that it gave me my whole life, for it is priceless.

Divya Sreenivasan

The Dancer in Me

When I was about three years old I was learning "Bharathanatyam," a form of South Indian classical dance. But my issue was that I always had a hard time sticking to a single teacher. I switched back and forth between three or four dance instructors, until I met Ramaa Ramesh through family friends. "Ramaa Aunty," as I used to call her, was not like the other dance teachers I had. In the process of deciding whether or not to join her academy, my parents and I observed her class; it was pretty obvious that she was not trying to impress us with her teaching skills. In fact, it didn't even matter to her if we enrolled in her dance academy or not. She just wanted to make sure I was interested in what I would be learning. The first thing she told me was, "This can be a 'trial' class. If you like what you see, then welcome to Nardhana Academy of Dance. If you're still not interested, then please don't push yourself to be interested in something you won't enjoy. Either way it's a free class. I want my future students to get a feel of what true dance is like." As I watched Ramaa Aunty teach new pieces to her students, I realized that I never enjoyed dancing before because my other instructors never explained the meaning of the pieces I learned. To me it was just gestures and movements that made no sense. Joining Nardhana Academy of Dance taught me so much about my culture and religion, and sure enough it was one of the best decisions I've ever made.

I was eleven years old when I started my lessons with Ramaa Aunty. To be honest, I was very nervous on my first day because she was very intimidating. My other dance instructors taught dance once a week as a "side job." In my opinion, dance was not a big part of their lives other than the fact that they too learned as children and decided to teach what they still remembered. On the other hand, Ramaa Aunty had a Master's Degree in Bharathanatyam and devoted her life to this career. Since I had a basic background of dance from previous lessons, I knew she held high expectations for me. I was first taught *Namaskar*, which was what we were supposed to do before and after a lesson or performance. It was a gesture where we respectfully touched the ground with both hands and then touched our eyes, asking Mother Earth for her blessings and to pardon us while we stomped on her during our classes or performances. Ramaa Aunty next taught me the beginning steps of Bharathanatyam. They were taught in "sets" starting with just simple feet movements that progressed into combining hand gestures and feet motions together. For the first set, I had to be in a "half-sitting" position with my toes pointed outwards, my knees slightly bent along with the back of my hands on my hips. This was called *"araamandi"* position. She explained to me that it was a basic position we would be using in all the pieces and routines we would soon learn. Once we were in *araamandi* position, we had to stomp our feet (starting with the right foot) one at a time, in a rhythmic pattern always ending the sequence with the right foot. Along with the feet movements, we learned hand gestures that represented different things like the sky or earth and wrote them down in our dance notebooks. After a year of learning all the beginner sets and hand gestures, Ramaa Aunty said I was ready to move onto the actual dance pieces. These pieces usually depicted different stories about the many gods and goddesses in the Hindu religion, while the lyrics were in Sanskrit.

Ramaa Aunty's teaching style was unique and effective. Before learning a piece, she would sit us down and explain what we were about to learn. Then, we learned the Sanskrit lyrics, what they meant word for word, and finally the hand gestures that went with them. We always jotted down the lyrics with their meanings in our notebooks. She did this to help us clearly understand what story we were portraying and so we could thoroughly show the emotions of the character. For example, if the character was sad, Ramaa Aunty would constantly repeat, "Sita is miserable because she's been kidnapped and is locked away from her husband! You look like you just hit the powerball! Show me what real misery looks like!" Times like this often caused us to giggle during rehearsals, but her point was made. After understanding the combination of gestures and lyrics, Ramaa Aunty incorporated the footsteps with it. It was a simple process of teaching, yet so beneficial. We learned the pieces in a way that made us want to perform them as best as we could.

There was one piece in particular that I was very fond of called *Chinna Chinna Padam*, which was about the childhood days of Lord Krishna. In this piece, the dancer portrays Lord Krishna's naughty antics such as stealing butter or hiding the girls' clothing while they bathed in the river. The dancer also portrays Yashoda, who was Lord Krishna's mother, and how she put up with his mischief. Even though Yashoda could not keep up with Lord Krishna's pranks and had to hear the complaints of her neighbors, she never showed frustration and always showered her son with love. This piece would have no meaning to it if the dancer did not incorporate the facial expressions. The audience would know what the dancer is trying to tell from the combination of hand gestures, movements and facial expressions.

My first on-stage performance was a piece called *Anjali*. Although it did not depict a story, it consisted of fast-paced movements, many of which were from our beginner sets. *Anjali* was a piece performed at the beginning of a recital to welcome the audience. Even though I was performing with a group, I was very nervous, especially since it was my first recital. Backstage, Ramaa

Aunty told us to relax and to dance with a flow, not by memorization. By flow, she meant that she wanted us to dance as gracefully as we could. Even if we made mistakes we shouldn't freeze up; instead we should incorporate the mistakes into our performance. Either way the audience most likely wouldn't know if we made errors. She told us that mistakes were natural and we were to dance freely so we could perfect our pieces for the future. She wanted the dance to come to us instead of our nervously trying to remember what comes next. This made me feel more confident because I knew I would get better with practice even if I did not do so well on stage. After the show I was really happy because Ramaa Aunty's advice worked! This really boosted my confidence and helped me set a goal for the kind of dancer I wanted to become.

Being Ramaa Aunty's student taught me a lot about self-confidence, endurance and team-work with my fellow dance girls. As a child I know I honestly hated Bharathanatyam, mostly because I didn't understand it. Now, I know that giving dance another shot with Ramaa Aunty has really changed my view of it. It is obvious that there was something about her that made me actually stick to her for five years. She made me want to learn more, immerse myself in the movements and feel that I was the character I was portraying. Unfortunately, I had to quit dancing during my junior year of high school because it was getting hard to balance my school work and activities. It has been over two years since I have learned new dance pieces, however I still remember mostly everything Ramaa Aunty has taught me. I also perform some of them for cultural events at my temple. Even though I am not Ramaa Aunty's student anymore, I still cherish the memories and the lessons I learned while being her student for five years. I learned how to be self-confident, to take joy in what I am learning, and to make the most out of dancing. I learned about so many stories that were a part of my religion and culture which helped me grow spiritually. Most of all, I learned how to be a good student by embracing Ramaa Aunty's teaching style and what Bharathanatyam had to offer me.

Allison Brophy

Breast or Bottle?

From the halls of the Children's Hospital of Philadelphia's maternity ward, glimpses into the rooms of new mothers holding their babies, fawning over them, so clearly enamored with their new little bundles of joy, reveal the special bond between mother and child. Far from mind at the time, in a few short days those mothers will be discharged with their newborns from the security of the hospital, left to tackle the many challenges of parenthood, including the all-important choice to breastfeed their infant or use bottled formula.

Many years ago, mothers did not have a choice whether or not to breastfeed. Times changed approaching the 20th century when an alternative infant formula was introduced, giving mothers the option not to breastfeed. Before the modern infant formulas available today, mothers that were incapable of or opposed breastfeeding resorted to other options. "In the early 1900s, the majority of American women breastfed their infants...mothers who could not or chose not to breastfeed used a wet nurse, fed animal milk to their babies, or made do with crude mixtures of flour, rice, and water called "pap". The newborns' chances of survival decreased significantly as a result" (Meek).

Today's new mother has much to consider in the decision to breastfeed or formula feed her infant. Some of the same considerations that drove mothers to alternative methods in the 1900s are still present—health limitations, convenience, and the lack of desire to breastfeed. These valid rationales are what drive some mothers today to opt not to breastfeed their infants. Looking into the reasons mothers may have for choosing to formula feed their infant versus breastfeeding shows that to some, breastfeeding is simply not feasible. Some mothers face specific health circumstances that limit or prevent them from breastfeeding. A mother may be unable to produce the milk needed to breastfeed her infant, a condition known as prolactin deficiency (Klibanski). Mothers with health conditions requiring specific medications that can be harmful to infants are often warned not to breastfeed for the medications can be passed to the baby through the mother's breast milk and cause lasting damage. In those cases, alternatives to breastfeeding are necessary.

Convenience seems to be a more recent reason for mothers to opt out of breastfeeding. For some, the maternal time commitment required of breastfeeding is too challenging. All newborns require feedings every few hours and according to William Sears, in his book *Keys to Breastfeeding*, breast milk is more easily digested in infants' stomachs than formula, causing them to be hungry more frequently than if fed formula. For a young mother, this constant need for feedings can be simply too exhausting. Diet is another aspect of breastfeeding that can pose an inconvenience on a mother. While breastfeeding, a mother has to consistently be aware of her diet because what she consumes, her baby consumes as well. For example, breastfeeding is not recommended for mothers who live a lifestyle of frequent social drinking, because the alcohol consumed will be passed through the breast milk to the baby. Lastly, a mother's simple desire to breastfeed impacts her decision. Not all women desire to breastfeed for reasons all their own.

Around the 1950s, modern commercial infant formula was slowly gaining popularity and by the mid 1970s it was named the new standard for infant nutrition. By that point, the new, scientifically manufactured infant formula was considered as good, if not better, for the child than breast milk (Schuman). Understandably, mothers would opt to formula feed their infant versus breastfeed, decreasing the rate of breastfeeding across the country. According to Schuman, during this time the percentage of women breastfeeding their infants reached an all-time low of 25% due to the common belief that formulas were "medically approved" to provide optimal nutrition for young infants.

As of late, researchers have conducted various studies on the benefits breastfeeding has for infants and mothers compared to those of formula feeding. Evidence supports breastfeeding as the optimal choice of infant nutrition, benefiting both mother and child. Their findings can generally be categorized into several parts: nutritional health, developmental, psychosocial, and immunological advantages.

Apart from the findings of numerous research studies, recent scientific breakthroughs have uncovered components of breast milk that shed light on countless nutritional health benefits of breastfeeding for infants. Between the nourishing aspects and its mysterious ability to dynamically adapt to the changing needs of infants, a mother's breast milk is truly "the perfect nutrient" (Sears). According to the American Association of Pediatrics (AAP), breast milk is the ideal source of nutrients for infants, for it contains every element of nutritional value essential for the optimal health, growth, and development of a child. In fact, "breast milk is such a rich, nourishing mixture, that scientists have yet to identify all of its elements; no formula manufacturer has managed to or will ever be able to fully replicate it" (Meek), proving that there is something so biologically special about a mother's breast milk that no other concoction can ever measure up.

Looking into the biology of breast milk, it could be said that breast milk is a continuation of a mother, linking her with her infant as the umbilical cord did when in utero. A mother's breast milk is not simply a substance containing the vital nutrients for an infant's well being, but is a dynamic living tissue containing living cells that has the ability to alter its nutritional content at any point in time, in order to meet the changing needs of the infant (Sears). There are five fundamental components of breast milk that mothers naturally pass on to their infant; fats, proteins, carbohydrates, minerals, and vitamins.

Fats and fatty acids account for the majority of calories found in breast milk since fat is arguably the most crucial nutrient for an infant's growth and development, especially immediately following birth. As said by the AAP, after birth a mother's body produces its first milk called colostrum. Colostrum has a high concentration of protein and fat, giving the newborn essential immediate nutrients (Meek), while also acting as a natural laxative, clearing out any sticky meconuim or fetal waste from a newborn's digestive tract during the first few days (Sears). Two aspects of fat, unique in human breast milk, are enzymes and cholesterol. Fat enzymes in breast milk enable infants to easily and completely digest fat and fatty acids, whereas formula-fed infants can only partially digest them. According to Sears, as breast milk contains cholesterol and formula does not, questions have been raised regarding whether or not the exposure of an infant's liver to cholesterol in breast milk protects them from suffering high cholesterol later on in life.

In keeping with Sears's findings, fats and fatty acids found in breast milk play a significant role in optimal brain development of infants. In fact, the human brain develops most rapidly during infancy and early childhood, therefore it is crucial that a child receives the necessary fats found solely in breast milk. In studies by the AAP, regardless of a mother's socioeconomic or intelligence levels, children who were breastfed as infants scored higher on IQ and various cognitive-ability tests than children who were fed formula (Meek).

Protein plays an influential role in the health of an infant starting only a few short moments after birth. When many think of protein, they imagine a piece of steak or chicken filet, however, the protein found in breast milk is a curd that is smaller and more easily digested by infants versus the protein found in formula. There have also been recent findings by allergists showing that "breast milk is naturally less allergenic because it strictly contains human proteins" (Meek).

According to Sears, when studying the carbohydrates found in breast milk (which is predominantly the sugar lactose) researchers discovered that mammals with larger brains have larger amounts of the sugar lactose in their milk. This explains why human breast milk tastes sweeter than that of mammals with smaller brains, such as cows. In order for formula manufacturers to replicate the sweetness of a mother's milk, they add cane sugar and corn syrup to their formulas (Sears). Infants digest these unnatural sugars far more rapidly than the lactose found in breast milk, resulting in frequent bothersome diarrhea and diaper rash. The diarrhea caused by an infant's ingestion of unnatural sugars like cane sugar and corn syrup could be prevented by the growth of certain beneficial bacteria in an infant's intestines. However, the lactose found in breast milk is what catalyzes the development of that very bacteria needed to ward off other bacteria that causes diarrhea. These and other factors weigh heavily on infants' fragile, developing body systems, making them more susceptible to other health risks, posing threats to their overall health.

Similar to the way cane sugar and corn syrup can disrupt the digestive system, excess amounts of minerals digested can disrupt infants' kidneys. Stated by Sears, because cow bones grow at a much higher rate than humans, their milk has much higher levels of the minerals calcium and phosphorus. When fed formula, the excess mineral salts from the cow's milk pose an extra load on the infant's immature kidneys, preventing the development of proper kidney function at a healthy rate. "The mineral iron is essential for life and is present in every living cell" (Sears). Understandably, iron is incredibly important in meeting the needs of an infant's health. From the words of Sears, in order for infants to produce new blood cells as they grow, iron is required. While developing in the womb, infants receive their necessary iron supply directly from their mothers' blood by way of the placenta. After birth, alternative methods are needed to ensure they receive adequate amounts of iron, either by breastfeeding or formula feeding. Through numerous studies, it was found that the amounts of iron found in formula and in breast milk have entirely different effects on infants. "Your infant can absorb only ten percent of the iron in iron-fortified formulas compared to at least fifty percent of the iron in breast milk...and infants who are fed breast milk very rarely become anemic, whereas infants fed formula or cow's milk often become anemic between one and two years of age" (Sears).

In the United States, taking daily vitamin supplements has become a fairly common occurrence among adults and children. Infants too require essential vitamins for their proper development and health. A mother's breast milk contains every essential vitamin an infant needs in just the right amount, which makes it unnecessary to supplement an infant with any other vitamins. Formula on the other hand, contains manufactured vitamin supplements in order to meet the needs of infants.

Benefits of breastfeeding impacting physical development of infants have been found which emphasize that some of the most rapid physical development occurs during the early stages of infancy. An infant's physical development outside the womb begins immediately following birth. Research by the AAP found that during the critical first few weeks after birth, the composition of a mother's breast milk adjusts specifically to the infant's needs through each stage of development. For example, a mother's colostrum or first milk is packed fill of nutrient-rich protein and fats in order to provide the infant with a boost of nourishment, allowing the proper development to begin outside of the womb. Fewer calories per pound of body weight are needed for the physical development of infants as they grow older (Sears). As a result, a mother's milk adjusts and gradually becomes lower in fat as her infant grows. A benefit of breastfeeding that is often overlooked is how breastfeeding aids in infants oral facial development. "Orthodontists believe that breastfeeding contributes to the proper alignment of the infant's jawbone, whereas bottle-feeding may result in malocclusion" (Sears). For this reason, breastfeeding can prevent the need for orthodontic intervention later in a child's life.

The psychosocial developmental benefit that breastfeeding has on infants is staggering. According to the AAP, the sheer closeness of mother and infant while nursing is proven to have lasting effects on an infant. Infants that are breastfed come to feel love and protection while being nursed in their mother's arms, which allows for adjustment to the strange new world outside of the womb. "Scientists now tell us that infants learn best in the context of emotional closeness with an adult. Breastfeeding promotes a growing attachment between the two of you [mother and infant] that will continue to play an important role in your infant's development for years to come" (Meek). The emotional bond and closeness created between mother and child through breastfeeding is just as vital as the nourishment passed to the infant through its mother's breast milk. Infants who are bottle-fed miss out on this special bonding. According to Laurence Gartner, medical professionals encourage that healthy infants should be placed and remain in direct skin-to-skin contact with their mothers immediately following birth.

Breastfeeding adds a level of protection to the immune system that is not available with formula feeding. One of the most vulnerable aspects of infants is their immune system and noted by AAP, breast milk is unique in that it protects an infant's immune system in ways that no formula can. The protection provided by a mother's breast milk is not limited to the time while breastfeeding, but long after the infant is weaned. According to the United States Government Accountability Office (USGAO), infants who are breastfed are less likely to contract infectious diseases and chronic health problems. In addition, the AAP found that "infants who are breastfed were more resistant to disease in the environment" (Meek). This resistance to environmental disease observed in breastfed infants can be attributed to the transfer of crucial antibodies, enzymes, and white blood cells from a mother to her infant, through her breast milk. The transfer of a mother's antibodies to her infant is especially important.

"If you [mother] develop a cold while breastfeeding, you are likely to pass the cold germs on to your baby—but the antibodies your body produces to fight that cold will also be passed on through your breast milk. This defense against illnesses significantly decreases the chances that your breastfeeding infant will suffer from ear infections, vomiting, diarrhea, pneumonia, urinary-tract infections, or certain types of spinal meningitis." (Meek)

The list of conditions preventable or minimized by breastfeeding is ever growing as new studies continue.

As for mothers, breastfeeding yields its own health benefits. It was found by the AAP that mothers who breastfed their infants recovered from childbirth more quickly and easily. As stated by Sears, research found that the hormone oxytocin released during breastfeeding triggers the contraction of the uterus back to its normal shape more rapidly. The AAP also found that women who breastfeed tend to lose their pregnancy weight more quickly than women who do not. In addition, startling research has found evidence linking breastfeeding to the rate of cancer contraction. "Studies show that women who have breastfed experience reduced rates of ovarian and breast cancer later in life...and breastfed daughters are at a reduced risk of developing breast cancer as adults" (Meek). Results of studies performed by the AAP suggest that breastfeeding may lead to an increase in bone mineral density after weaning. This increase can potentially protect a mother against suffering from osteoporosis and bone fractures in older age.

With the all-too-common struggles of deciding whether breastfeeding or formula feeding is the right choice for you and your infant, you must take into consideration the vast amount of information that has recently been made available. Through the numerous studies and research regarding the advantages of breastfeeding versus formula feeding, there is evidence that singles out breastfeeding as the best choice. "The AAP firmly adheres to the position that breastfeeding ensures the best possible health as well as the best developmental and psychosocial outcomes for the infant...the promotion and practice of breastfeeding is essential to the achievement of optimal infant and child health, growth, and development" (Gartner). In each aspect, nutritionally, developmentally, psychosocially, and immunologically, breastfeeding is the best way of nourishment for infants. Overall, current thought supports what Mother Nature has offered all along. Breastfeeding is the optimal choice.

Works Cited

Gartner, Lawrence M., and Arthur I. Eidelman, MD. "Section on Breastfeeding." *Breastfeeding and the Use of Human Milk*. Pediatrics ed. : American Academy of Pediatrics, 2005. N. pag. American Academy of Pediatrics. Web. 16 Nov. 2010.

Klibanski, Anne. "Neuroendocrinology." *Endocrinology and Metabolism Clinics of North America* 30.3 (2001). Print.

McDowell, Margaret M., Chia-Yih Wang, and Jocelyn Kenedy-Stephenson. Breastfeeding in the United States; findings from the National Health and Nutrition Examination Surveys; 1993-2006. NCHS Data Brief ed. Vol. 5. : n.p., 2008. N. pag. Web. 16 Nov. 2010. http://www.cdc.gov/nchs/data/databriefs/db05.pdf

Meek, Joan Younger, and Sherill Tippins. *American Academy of Pediatrics New Mother's Guide to Breastfeeding*. Bantam Mass Market Ed. Westminster, MD: Banton Books, 2005. Web. 16 Nov. 2010.

Schuman, Andrew J. *Blue Sky Global Network*. Ed. Krista Clark. N.p., n.d. Web. 26 Nov. 2010.

Sears, William. *Keys to Breastfeeding*. New York: 1991. N. pag. Web. 29 Nov. 2010.

United States. Government Accountability Office. *Breastfeeding: some strategies used to market infant formula may discourage breastfeeding; state contracts should better protect against misuse of WIC name: report to congressional addressees.* Washington, D.C.: U.S Government Accountability Office, 2006. Web. 18 Nov. 2010.

Zachary Geesey

Totalitarianism in Society

The United States government has grown immensely powerful over the last two centuries. It has developed as the nation's industrial system became the largest and most powerful in the world. The nation's power climaxed after World War II, at which time a prominent author named George Orwell was busy writing books that criticized Stalinism and totalitarianism. At this time in history, Orwell wrote his most famous novel, *1984*, which described the most dramatic form of totalitarianism resulting from a massive and powerful government. Orwell's novel was not only a criticism; it was also a prediction of how modern governments were going to evolve given the opportunities after WWII. His prediction is surprisingly accurate when making comparisons to the modern world. Even modern scholars like Gary Cirelli think that *1984* has a valuable impact on society. He commented on *1984* by saying:

> "As we look towards the future, dystopic novels like
> *Nineteen Eighty-Four* do a valuable service as they remind
> us that if something so horrible can be conceived on
> paper, then it could one day be actualized in the real world.
> When combined with knowledge of history and/or current
> events, novels like *Nineteen Eighty-Four* prove their worth
> as devices that foster greater understanding and increased
> critical thinking." (Cirelli 2)

Several major world powers, like the United States, Great Britain and China, have begun to bring about some of the same techniques and methods as the oppressive totalitarian dictatorships presented in George Orwell's *1984*.

Orwell's novel describes a futuristic dystopia where three major nations control most of the world. The story takes place in one of the nations called Oceania where the government controls the thoughts of its citizens by manipulating every piece of information that is published and killing anyone who appears to be a threat to the nation. The government, run by the mysterious Big Brother, finds a way to monitor their people at all times during the day by creating a device called the telescreen. This device forces people to watch the propaganda Oceania broadcasts, and it is a continually observing camera which allows the government to monitor people. Big Brother, the mysterious and godlike figure, is portrayed as a perfect being that is always right. However, toward the end, the novel suggests that Big Brother may not actually exist, as if he were an imaginary fairy tale solely used to inspire and manipulate people. Whenever Oceania publishes a piece of information that conflicts with something previously published, there are government workers who change the original records so that everything Big Brother says is "true." The three nations of Oceania, East Asia, and Eurasia are constantly trading alliances and fighting each other in order to keep their respective countries in a state of war hysteria. This makes the people much more willing to accept the strange and restrictive policies of the government. This war-frenzied behavior drives the citizens of Oceania to turn in anyone who appears to be disloyal to Big Brother. These people are then branded as traitors and "disappear" from society in order to be placed in a torture camp until they are brainwashed and killed. The governments also keep themselves completely isolated from one another, preventing people of the lower classes from attempting to contact any outsiders. Oceania also prevents people from having sex unless the sole reason is to procreate according to the limits put forth; this means no joy or emotion is allowed to be a part of sex. Unfortunately, some modern governments have actually put forth restrictions on published material, the ability to travel, and sex, which are limiting people's rights and desires.

The process of controlling people begins with having the capability to monitor them at all times. This has become much more feasible and widespread across the world with the use of cameras and the development of the internet. One perfect example of people being monitored is an article on a website called "What does the Internet know about you?"(Monies) Within this website, you are able to type in a person's name, and the website looks through the internet in order to find any information about that person. When a name is put in, the website looks for any online web profiles related to that name. This includes anything that a person posted in the past. Even if something was deleted, Google bots and spiders are able to trail back to whatever may have been posted; so no information is ever truly gone (Monies). This is one of the reasons why colleges tell students to be careful about what they post because it can deter a company from giving a position to someone. According to Tracy Miranto, a college student posted about the size of a certain male body part on Facebook. Consequently, when this student went to his first job interview he was turned down because the employer looked the student up on Facebook and saw his inappropriate post. The student tried to remove the post, but had a difficult time doing so because of the elaborate procedure he had to follow in order to remove it. This is just an example of how a seemingly harmless piece of information could damage a person's ability to get a job. Information can be monitored with extreme ease nowadays, and privacy has started to disappear. People are unknowingly and willingly giving away personal information, which is different from *1984*, but the result is still the same because personal information is visible to the public. This could help deter extremely unruly behavior on the internet, but it can also ruin a person's life by holding a sword over their head that is impossible to remove.

People are also starting to be monitored in public places. This is mostly prevalent in the United Kingdom where there is approximately one camera for every fourteen people (Britain). The article, "Britain is 'Surveillance Society,'" discusses why the British government is increasing its level of monitoring citizens' credit card transactions, working rates, telecommunication, and traveling plans. The article also predicted that by 2016 shoppers could be scanned as they enter stores, schools could bring in cards allowing parents to monitor what their children eat, and jobs may be refused to applicants who are seen as a health risk. These measures are very intrusive and have the potential to blacklist a person, thereby preventing him or her from getting a job or medical insurance because of a pre-existing medical condition. The government states that it could help prevent criminal behavior or improve its detection thereof, but any action taken can be monitored and traced back to a person with ease. These actions are very extreme because people do not need to be constantly monitored like cattle. People should not have to live in fear that anything they say or do in public could get them in trouble with the law.

One of the most apparent and prevalent examples of totalitarian governments of the modern day is China. The Chinese government has created a "great firewall of China," which keeps Chinese citizens completely unaware of any outside sources of information. It is similar to a school's internet censorship which prevents people from looking up distractions, like pornography, online games or hate speech sites (Marsan). This also allows the government to control the entirety of information that is kept from the public and released to the public. A perfect example of the Chinese government controlling information on the internet is the story about a Chinese woman named Cheng Jianping. This woman was arrested and sentenced to a year in labor camp for resending a Twitter message from her fiancée that mocked young nationalists who held anti-Japanese rallies all over China (Jacobs). The Chinese legal system allows the police to send people to labor camps for up to four years without having a trial. This is a complete parallel of Oceania because the Chinese government has the ability to control online information without having people attempting to challenge it. People can be arrested and punished without having a chance to appeal their case, which forces them to be especially careful about anything they post. This firewall does have benefits in that it helps keep people productive, but it also keeps people unaware of many outside countries and their cultures.

China has also implemented a very strict child birth law in order to reduce the population of the country. China's one child policy is designed to limit the number of children a couple can have to one (Rosenberg). The law also makes sterilizations, IUD's, and abortions legal in order to help restrict the population. It is possible for a couple to have two children, but the couple would have to pay a tax for having more than one child. This policy is not necessarily bad because it restricts the growth of the already overpopulated country. However, this law demonstrates how the government is involved in such a personal and important aspect of a Chinese citizen's life.

The United States government has begun to lean towards policies that resemble a totalitarian government similar to Oceania. This has been shown by the government's great deal of media and public disapproval for its use of torture on foreign prisoners. The problem arises from the torture of prisoners who may or may not be involved in terrorist forces, like Al Qaeda, who are being tortured and abused. A former U.S. interrogator commented on some of the overseas prisons, and how the other interrogators used methods of psychological and physical torture. The interrogator said that a majority of the prisoners had nothing to do with Al Qaeda, but they were tortured anyway (Cole). Sometimes, the United States can choose to torture anyone who is deemed to be a threat to the country. This is a parallel to *1984* because if the government of Oceania discovered anyone who committed a "thought crime," they were deemed as a threat and disappeared in order to be tortured and ultimately killed. Cruel and unusual punishment is not only one of the major pieces of the Bill of Rights, it is also banned by the Geneva Convention, which states that prisoners of war must be treated humanely (Geneva Convention). These policies must be followed so that America does not resort to torture in order to get any piece of information from a prisoner.

Despite the media and public disapproval of torture, applying physical pain to criminals has become much more tolerated after the terrorist attacks of September 11 (Cusac). This stems from the nightmarish idea that there are people who want to hurt American citizens, which was encouraged and played again and again on television. This fear of attack led to a large number of rash arrests of Arab and Muslim immigrants. Many of the people who were rounded up claimed they were beaten, locked in solitary confinement, injected with substances against their will or denied blankets, food and toilet paper (Cusac). Even though it is easy to accuse people who are associated with a horrible and catastrophic event in history, it does not excuse the inhumane treatment of innocent people. The war hysteria brought upon the country after September 11 encouraged the sort of panic and fear that the governments of 1984 used to persuade its citizens to report anyone who was suspected of being a traitor to the country, and they used the fear to justify the torture and harsh treatment of prisoners.

A problem in the United States government is that so many people in Congress are re-elected year after year. The average reelection rate for a member of the House of Representatives has stayed over 90% for the last forty years, and the reelection rate for a Senator is on average around 82% (Reelection Rates). These rates strangely contradict the incredibly low Congressional approval rating of 11% (Saad). Even in the 2010 midterm election, which had a record low re-election rate, over 86% of the incumbent candidates were re-elected in the House of Representatives and 94% of the incumbent candidates were re-elected in the Senate. Even though people do not approve of what Congress is currently doing, they are not willing to replace the Senators and Congressmen who they disapprove of. If people are unwilling to change the things that they do not want, then they will have to live with the consequences.

The major world powers are beginning to parallel the ones that were described in George Orwell's *1984*. They have taken large political steps which limit or hinder the rights of their citizens. These steps have benefits, but the benefits from their actions do not outweigh the limitations and problems. If people's rights are not respected in society, then governments are not adequately performing their duties, and they must be changed.

Works Cited

"Britain is 'Surveillance Society.'" BBC. 2 November 2006. 10 November 2010. <news.bbc.co.uk>

Cirelli, Gary. "Why Nineteen Eighty-Four Still Matters, Preliminary Thoughts." ECCCS 1.2(2009): 1-13. Scribd. 3November 2010. </www.scribd.com>

Cole, Juan. "Former US interrogator recounts torture cases in Afghanistan and Iraq." 15 December 2007. 22 November 2010. <www.juancole.com>

Cusac, Anne-Marie. *Cruel and Unusual*. New Haven, CT: Yale University Press, 2009.

"Election 2010: Senate Final Results." Real Clear Politics. 30 November 2010. <www.realclearpolitics.com>

"Geneva Convention: an Introduction." Learn Peace. 22 November 2010. <www.ppu.org>

Jacobs, Andrew. "Chinese Woman Imprisoned for Twitter Message." The New York Times. 18 November 2010. 21 November 2010. <www.nytimes.com>

Marsan, Carolyn Duffy. "Chinese Internet censorship: An inside look." Network World. May 12 2008. November 7 2010. <www.networkworld.com>

Mitrano, Tracy. "Thoughts on Facebook." April 2006. 6 November 2010. <www.cit.
cornell.edu>

Monies, Paul. "What does the Internet know about you?" 4 September 209.Data Watch.
3 November 2010. <blog.newsok.com>

Orwell, George. *1984*. New York: The New American Library Inc., 1977.

"Reelection Rates Over the Years." 2010. November 7 2010. <www.opensecrets.org>

Rosenberg, Matt. "China's One Child Policy."14 June 2010. 7 November 2010.
<geography.about.com>

Saad, Lydia. "Congress Ranks Last in Confidence in Institutions." Gallup Polls. 22 July
2010. 7 November 2010. <www.gallup.com>

Devon Laughlin

A Dark Place

Ever since I was a little girl, I remember being enthralled with extremely dark and violent aspects of humanity. Not a normal hobby, but one that kept me interested throughout my middle and high school years. In a sociology class earlier this year, I was assigned an essay by Mark Colvin on the New Mexico State Prison Riot of 1980 and my interest was immediately piqued. Before I even began reading, I wanted to know why the riot happened and what could have been done to prevent it. Was it a careless guard or a well-organized force of nature that couldn't be stopped? Were there hostages and were they hurt? I wanted all the details of what happened. I got them.

"The riot at the Penitentiary of New Mexico on February 2 and 3, 1980, is without parallel for its violence, destruction, and disorganization ("Descent" 183). This is the opening line to the assigned reading. I was hooked. From there the article went on to describe in semi-graphic detail how the prison dissolved into madness. By the end of the riot, 33 were dead and over 400 of the remaining inmates were injured (Useem 680). According to Mark Colvin's first article, of the inmates that were killed, over a third were tortured for hours with blow torches, pipes, shovels and other objects found in the prison. No specific motives for the violence have ever been discovered. Twelve prison officers were taken hostage during the riot by different groups of inmates. Some groups tried to protect the officers from the violence, giving them prison jumpers to disguise themselves, while other groups tortured, but did not kill, the guards ("1980" 449). One murdered inmate's cell bars were cut open with a blow torch by the murderers to get to the prisoner after he jammed the door shut. I was disgusted as I read the details of the torture and at some points almost became physically ill but I still wanted to know why. The level of violence exhibited during that riot has never occurred in any prison riot in the entire history of the U.S. penal system (Useem 677). The riot in New Mexico was special; there had to be something different in that particular prison.

According to several sociologists, all prisons are maintained through formal and informal controls by both guards and prisoners (Fox 13). The means of guard control range from the obvious, such as physical restraints and power over privileges, to more dubious forms like threats of exposing an inmate as a 'snitch' to other inmates ("Descent" 185). Vernon Fox also suggests prisoners control others through violence as well as non-violent tactics such as using power to influence others to do what is in everyone's best interests. If inmates are given a measure of control in their environment, such as having an inmate government or appointing some inmates to act as official guards over others, the prisons are very stable and reports of violent episodes are extremely rare (Fox, 13). In a way, these tactics of maintaining control do make sense. When children are younger and they misbehave, one of the easiest ways of redirecting their attention is to ask for their help. Almost immediately, the child will stop the bad behavior and encourage others to behave as well because they feel that they have a measure of control over what is going on. It is their decision to do the right thing and in return they will be rewarded for helping the adult regain control of the situation.

According to research completed by Mark Colvin, ten years prior to the riot, New Mexico had abnormally low violence rates and guard turnover when compared with the national average, which makes what happened in 1980 even more surprising and reinforced my opinion that something was indeed special in New Mexico ("1980" 451). During the early '70s, inmates were allowed to participate in "outside contact" programs which included college and college prep courses and volunteering opportunities outside of the prison. Since inmates with good records were chosen to participate, these programs promoted cohesiveness among the inmates; plus participation increased the likelihood of transfers to minimum security prisons or parole, both important incentives from an inmate's point of view ("1980" 453). Although the prison didn't have a specified inmate government, convicts were put in positions of authority in some of the "outside contact" programs. As a result of their positions, these men had a lot of contact with prison authorities and the administration had faces instead of being seen as a faceless bureaucratic organization, which I believe had the same effect as inmate governments.

Another aspect of Mark Colvin's research showed that during the early '70s, a large amount of heroin was being smuggled into the prison by different groups of prisoners. As improbable as it sounds, this actually helped keep order in the prison because disruptions might have prompted authorities to start investigating the drug trafficking ("1980" 453). In many organizations I have been exposed to, if something is against the letter of the rule, but it isn't seen as a disruptive force, authorities will overlook the transgression. As a result, it was in the best interests of drug dealers, traffickers, and users to keep their heads down and not cause trouble for the guards.

In the mid-'70s, political pressure forced the warden and chief of security for the prison to transfer to different, lower positions within the state penal system when the high-volume drug trafficking in the prison was exposed ("Descent" 185). Mark Colvin also found that when the new administration was put in place, they began changing several of the prison's longstanding policies so they wouldn't also be seen as corrupt. The newly appointed staff began taking away incentives for the prisoners such as shortening length of yard time as well as cutting many of the "outside contact" programs ("1980" 454). The "new guys" must have felt that they had to show they were different and were going to stop the drug flow into the prison and stand up to the inmates. By taking this stance, the administration removed many of the incentives for good behavior that were seen in the previous years. The drug traffickers no longer had any influence over others, nor did they care whether disruptions occurred because they had no product to protect. The legitimate programs were also shut down so the inmates' social structure was completely rearranged over the period of a few months (Useem 682).

A nonviolent sit-down strike was organized by the prisoners to protest the removal of these programs in 1976 but, because the prison authorities felt like they couldn't concede to the inmates, tear-gas and batons were used to end the strike, causing several injured protesters ("Descent" 185). After the strike ended, the alleged leaders were removed from the main population; some were placed in extended solitary confinement and many were transferred to different prisons in the state ("1980" 454). The use of force to end a nonviolent strike clearly showed the inmates that they had absolutely no control over their environment. The men that everyone looked up to were suddenly taken away from the general population, resulting in confusion and chaos for the rest of the inmates.

It is also logical to believe that the previous sequence of events fostered a feeling of mistrust between the prisoners and the guards. Whatever the reason, after the 'changing of the guard' occurred, the number of voluntary informants decreased and the staff was forced to go to prisoners for information ("Descent" 186-87). Since the inmates wouldn't voluntarily give out information to the staff, threats were made against the inmates if they didn't supply information. Uncooperative prisoners would be outed as snitches to fellow inmates; this soon became known as 'the snitch game' ("1980" 455). The snitch game further fragmented the inmate population into very small, distinct groups of inmates ("Descent" 187). The snitch game is certainly one of the most brutal tactics that could be used in a prison. Men who are labeled as informants to any type of authority figure are outcasts whether they are in prison or on Wall Street. The added pressure of being in a prison environment where violence can be a part of daily life adds a sadistic twist on the part of the guards. Consequently, the inmates were put in a "damned if you do, damned if you don't" type of situation. If the inmate does not provide information, they will be labeled a snitch and have to face the consequences.

Mark Colvin also discovered that inmates who did provide information were usually found out because the guards were extremely careless about protecting the informants' identities from the general population. Another consequence of the snitch game was a lot of the information received was unreliable because many of the inmates chose to lie to the guards instead of tell them the truth ("Descent" 189). The consequence of this is evident in the context of the riot. Two days before the riot broke out, there were several rumors that a major disturbance in cell block E-2 was imminent; the riot started in cell block E-2 ("1980" 458). In this respect, the snitch game can be compared to the torture of suspects. It has been shown by many different institutions that men and women will say anything to make the pain go away. In the same respect, inmates in New Mexico told guards what they wanted to hear to make the threat go away.

In part because of the snitch game and also because of the removal of the prison leaders after the protest, the prison became increasingly violent over the last four years leading up to the riot (Useem 681). After the leaders were taken away, others at the prison aimed to take control of the prison and many inmates tried to gain control through violent reputations ("1980" 455). The phrase 'violence begets violence' seems particularly appropriate when describing the late '70s in the New Mexico State Prison. Those wanting to take control were violent in order to increase their reputations but many other inmates became involved in violent acts because a willingness to engage was a major defense against assault from other prisoners ("Descent" 188). In other words, no one messed with inmates who were able to defend themselves, but in order to prove that, the inmates would have to incite fights. According to Mark Colvin, convicts labeled as snitches or inmates who wouldn't fight back were the most common victims of unprovoked attacks. As violence became an integral part of prison life, the inmates divided themselves into small, protective groups. The cliques pitted themselves against one another or joined forces to beat suspected informants. Attacks on suspected informants almost never provoked retaliation. However, attacks on other inmates were met with retaliation, further perpetuating the already rampant violence ("1980" 455-56).

Mark Colvin also found that because the level of violence in the prison during the late '70s hadn't been seen in the prison before, higher level administrators were replaced constantly, with 4 different wardens between 1974 and 1980. The high turnover rate in the upper levels of the administration caused a lot of confusion in the inmates' day-to-day lives. With every new warden, new policies and directives were issued while others were disregarded. Both guards and inmates had a difficult time keeping track of the policies of the prison, so many mid-level prison supervisors began disregarding orders from the top and began running the prison as they saw fit. Some supervisors were extremely lenient while others would impose solitary confinement on inmates who committed minor offenses ("Descent" 186). The lack of consistency from supervisor to supervisor created a lot of confusion among the guards and inmates because the supervisors worked in shifts, so at every shift change new policies came into play. Inmates were never sure what would and wouldn't be tolerated, further destabilizing the prison environment.

Any one of these causes, or a mixture of all of them, finally blew up on February 2, 1980 in the New Mexico State Prison. The riot that occurred is unlike any other riot that has ever occurred in U.S. history. Vernon Fox's proposal that riots follow a five-stage pattern is generally accepted by many sociologists. The first stage is characterized by "unbridled violence" followed by a regrouping stage on the inmates' part, then negotiations with authorities, surrender, and finally state investigations (Fox, 10). The prison riot of 1980 did not follow this pattern. The extreme violence definitely occurred during the riot but the inmates never unified or formed demands to give to authorities. Although negotiations were held with several inmates, they never had control of the riot or were in any position to make demands in order to end the riot ("1980" 459). Stage four and five were applicable to the New Mexico riot because state police eventually stormed the prison and afterwards state appointed investigators, such as Mark Colvin, were sent in to determine what happened (Useem 679). The stages that were skipped had to do with inmate solidarity. The cohesiveness of the prison inmates had been destroyed by changes during the years leading up to the riot. Since the inmates didn't trust each other before the riot, there was little chance they would trust each other after the riot began.

Many factors were involved to create the level of violence seen in New Mexico in 1980. Although none of the articles I found specifically stated that the change in administration was the cause of the riot, it seems clear that the initial change as well as the subsequent changes in leadership at the prison played a key role. Had the men and women at the top known how to curb the increasing violence between inmates, the riot could have been completely avoided or at least more humane. Instead it was total chaos, which resulted in no net gain for any of the parties involved.

Works Cited

Boin, Arjen R., Menno J. Van Duin. "Prison Riots as Organizational Failures: A Managerial Perspective." *The Prison Journal* 75.3 (1995): 357-379. Web. 9 Nov. 2010.

Colvin, Mark. "Descent Into Madness: The New Mexico State Prison Riot." Mapping the Social Landscape: Readings in Sociology. Ed. Susan J. Ferguson. New York, NY: McGraw Hill, 2010. 183-196.

Colvin, Mark. "The 1980 New Mexico Prison Riot." *Social Problems* 29.5 (1982): 449-463.
Web. 9 Nov. 2010.

Fox, Vernon. "Why Prisoners Riot." *Federal Probation* 35.10 (1971): 9-14. Web. 9 Nov. 2010

Gover, Angela R., Deanna M. Perez, Saskia D. Santos and Kristin M. Tennyson. "Individual
and Institutional Characteristics Related to Inmate Victimization." *International
Journal of Offender Therapy and Comparative Criminology* 54.3 (2010): n. pag.
Web. 9 Nov. 2010.

Useem, Bert. "Disorganization and the New Mexico Riot of 1980." *American Sociological
Association* 50.5 (1985): 677-688. Web. 9 Nov. 2010.

.

Tuyet-Nhung Nguyen

To Eat or Not to Eat

"Mmmm...that smells so good," I say as the scent of pork congee wafts through the room.

"It's almost ready," calls my grandmother from the kitchen.

"What's in it today?" I ask.

"The usual—coagulated pig blood, intestines, liver, heart..."

"The intestines are my favorite. I love how they slide around the inside of my mouth."

"Mine, too," agrees my grandmother.

Congee is a type of thick soup made with rice. Various ingredients can be cooked with the rice to create different kinds of congee, including mung beans, eggs, and pork innards. Most Americans would cringe at the thought of eating coagulated blood, but for the Vietnamese, it is a part of everyday life. What exactly makes a food taboo for a culture? Why would some Americans be willing to eat scrapple but not stewed pig liver? I believe that the answer is different for every individual, depending on his upbringing, geography, and religious and cultural beliefs. And while many taboos protect the individual from sickness and disease, some reflect preexisting social hierarchies.

Over the course of history, man has become more and more proficient at survival. He has learned how to create fire, build shelter, and grow crops. He has also learned what foods to eat and what foods to avoid based on their health implications (McLaughlin 1). Rats, for example, were the primary vessels of the fleas responsible for the Black Plague that killed a third of the medieval European population ("Bubonic Plague"). Naturally, "'Europeans... [have] form[ed] a real prejudice against bug and rat dinners'" (McLaughlin 1). Similarly, the high toxicity of the tropical fish in their waters has led to several food restrictions on pregnant Fijian women, including moray eels and barracuda (Henrich and Henrich 4). As a result of these taboos, the mean corresponding fish poisoning rate of women during pregnancy per year was found to be 4.3%, which is almost three percent less than the normal rate

(Henrich and Henrich 6). The dangers of consuming these foods outweighed the potential nutrients that they may have offered these peoples.

The availability of sufficient food sources must also be taken into account when studying what people eat and do not eat. Insects are a good source of protein in much of the world, but Europeans tend to avoid them ("Edible Insects"). Due to their lesser numbers and size, eliminating European insects from their diet was no great loss ("Edible Insects"). Conversely, countries that face difficulty feeding large populations will make use of whatever energy sources they can obtain (McLaughlin 1). Some developing countries simply cannot afford to turn down insects for domesticated beef.

In Vietnam, for example, the prices for beef are much higher than that of chicken or pork. Most people are too poor to buy meat on a regular basis, so they resort to trapping wild animals and cooking insects. My father speaks constantly of catching mice in the fields for dinner. He claims that since these mice eat only rice, they are extremely fat and nutritious. Likewise, my mother reminisces about the milky sweetness of fried bee larvae. Moreover, when the Vietnamese obtain any food source, they need to limit waste. They utilize the entirety of the animal in their cooking, from its ears down to its feet.

In areas with enough safe foods for people to pick and choose, people's dietary decisions may be based on personal emotions (Meyer-Rochow 8). Some empathize with the animals killed for their consumption (Meyer-Rochow 8). This holds especially true for animals held as pets (Meyer-Rochow 9). Eating dog in the United States is taboo because many Americans are dog owners and see them as vital parts of their families. Such humanization makes consuming dogs appear barbaric and almost cannibalistic. Taking this idea a step further can lead to the avoidance of animal products altogether, as in Meredith's case.

Meredith was one of my best high school friends. A passionate animal lover, she bred about twenty guinea pigs in her barn and dreamt of owning an animal sanctuary in Scotland. She never used products tested on animals and proudly championed animal rights. However, up to her senior year, her parents forced her to eat meat so that she could obtain enough protein. Every so often, she would talk to me about the sweet big-eyed cows that died to make her hamburger or the adorable pigs that were mercilessly slaughtered to make her bacon. She felt like a murderer whenever she thought about eating a defenseless animal. Fortunately, she managed to convince her parents that she could find other nutrient sources and became a vegetarian.

Swearing off meat was Meredith's own choice, but several religious faiths have strict restraints on diet. Hinduism is an excellent example of such a religion. The Hindu faith is centered on the idea of reincarnation and social divisions known as castes (Meyer-Rochow 4). Hindus believe that souls are reincarnated into different forms based on the lives they led; therefore, "by eating an animal, a Hindu could...be eating a deceased relative" (Meyer-Rochow 9). Hindu food taboos help to further emphasize divisions within their society. At the top of the Hindu social hierarchy are the Brahmins, or priests (Meyer-Rochow 4). Under the Brahmins are the Kshatriya warriors, Vaisya farmers and merchants, and Shudra laborers (Meyer-Rochow 4). Brahmins are not allowed to consume meat under any circumstances, but members of lower castes are only restricted from eating cow (Meyer-Rochow 4). Since they do not consume the souls of others, the perceived holiness of the Brahmins is preserved.

Cow is considered especially sacred to the Hindus, and its consumption is prohibited (Meyer-Rochow 4). Red meat is a significant dietary component in numerous other societies. It is used to make hamburgers, steaks, and various other hearty dishes. In fact, the United States devoured 26.9 billion pounds of beef in the year 2009 alone ("U.S. Beef and Cattle Industry: Background Statistics and Information"). The value of this animal as a foodstuff draws into question why its consumption is forbidden in the Hindu faith. Rejection of such a rich protein source seems physically unreasonable.

Clearly, deciding what to eat and what not to eat is quite subjective. Biologically, there is no real reason why Philadelphia restaurants do not offer chocolate-covered ants; they are incredibly nutritious ("Edible Insects"). Likewise, rejecting meat is senseless from a physical standpoint due to its protein content. However, people throughout the world continue to pick and choose their foods every single day. If there is no true biological basis for much of this behavior, how can it be justified?

Like choosing what to eat, many of the activities that we find most natural are often the most culturally influenced and structured. They are arbitrary and have little basis in fact. Take general attitudes towards homosexuality, for instance. Women can hug and kiss each other in public, but if men were to do the same, they would be considered "gay" in most American circles. In our culture, we tend to jump to conclusions based on what is considered acceptable behavior, so we are judging others based solely on our perceptions of this behavior. Two men who hug in public might not be gay, but two girls who kiss in public may be. We cannot read what goes on in other people's minds or what happens in their bedrooms. Even if we were able to do so, we have no right to suggest what people can or cannot do in public. Besides, why is homosexuality regarded in such a negative light? Oscar Wilde, one of history's greatest playwrights, was gay (Adams). Leonardo da Vinci was also suspected of engaging in intimate activities with members of the same sex (Adams). A person's sexual orientation is not a reflection of his worth or intelligence. Yet, our cultural prejudices towards homosexuality have driven countless people to commit suicide out of despair. One of the most recently publicized incidents was that of Tyler Clementi, a Rutgers freshman who killed himself on September 22, 2010, after his roommate revealed his sexual orientation over the Internet (Mauriello 1). If our society were more accepting of his choice, Clementi's death could have been prevented.

It is wrong and dangerous to assume that our preconceived notions are natural or even logical. Prejudices hurt. Even prejudices towards food. When I was in middle school, my cousin raised a chubby black cat in our backyard. We named it "Tham An," which literally means "Glutton" in Vietnamese. My cousin fed Tham An the most expensive canned cat food and treated him just like a regular pet. One day, Tham An was run over by a car. To our dismay, our neighbors accused us of eating Tham An for breakfast. They believed that all Asians ate cats and dog (which they deemed barbaric). To us, their ignorance towards our dietary habits translated into general discrimination against our culture as a whole. Their assumptions were absolutely unfair and painful.

If we can all learn to be more open-minded about food, we can train ourselves to be more open-minded about the cultures from which these foods develop.

Works Cited

Adams, O. R. "How Homosexualists Redefine Homosexual Child Molesting." *American Traditions Magazine.* 2009. Web. 17 Nov. 2010. <http://www.americantraditions.org/Articles/how_homosexualists_redefine.htm>.

"Background Statistics: U.S. Beef and Cattle Industry." *USDA Economic Research Service.* 10 July 2010. Web. 17 Nov. 2010. <http://www.ers.usda.gov/news/BSECoverage.htm>.

"Bubonic Plague." *Loyola University Chicago.* Loyola University Chicago. Web. 07 Nov. 2010. <http://www.luc.edu/faculty/ldossey/bubonicanov6.htm>.

"Edible Insects." *Food-Info.* Wageningen University, 1 July 2010. Web. 07 Nov. 2010. <http://www.food-info.net/uk/products/insects/intro.htm>.

Henrich, Joseph, and Natalie Henrich. "The Evolution of Cultural Adaptations: Fijian Food Taboos Protect against Dangerous Marine Toxins." *Proceedings of the Royal Society Biological Sciences* (2010): 1-10. *The Evolution of Cultural Adaptations: Fijian Food Taboos Protect against Dangerous Marine Toxins.* The Royal Society, 28 July 2010. Web. 31 Oct. 2010. <http://rspb.royalsocietypublishing.org/content/early/2010/07/26/rspb.2010.1191.long>.

Mauriello, Tracie. "Campus Climate for Gays At Issue After Rutgers Suicide; PA. Students Say Hate Still Rises To Surface." *Pittsburgh Post-Gazette* 2 Oct. 2010, Sooner ed., State sec.: A-1. LexisNexis Academic.Web.17 Nov. 2010.

McLaughlin, Katy. "Mixed Grill." *Wall Street Journal - Eastern Edition* 31 Oct. 2009: W10. *Business Source Premier.* EBSCO. Web. 31 Oct. 2010.

Meyer-Rochow, Victor B. "Food Taboos: Their Origins and Purposes." *Journal of Ethnobiology and Ethnomedicine* 5.18 (2009): 1-10. *Journal of Ethnobiology and Ethnomedicine.* BioMed Central Ltd, 29 June 2009. Web. 31 Oct. 2010. <http://www. ethnobiomed.com/content/5/1/18>.

Dickens Omondi

My Mission to Travel the World

Back in Kenya I live with my family in a two-story townhouse on a hillside in a small town. From the balcony the biggest lake in Africa and the second biggest in the world, is visible in the distance. Between us and the lake is a rich diversity: a high-cost private primary school, a 'free-education' public school, modern houses, huts, a shopping center and kiosks. A highway crosses this diversity right at the middle, which connects our small town to one of the biggest cities in the country.

Our townhouse, painted in white with a red roof, standing in an acre surrounded by a perimeter brick wall, stands out due to its location on a hill, and I am aware as I stare at 'the world' from the balcony, that it is staring right back at me, though I can see it better than it can see me.

I did the first three years of my schooling in the public primary school, then did the remaining five years in the high-cost private school—my dad's school. Obviously, that got me and my classmates good grades, and we were admitted to some of the best schools in the country. Sadly, most of our colleagues in the 'free education' public schools, as is the norm, barely got half of the pass mark in the same national exam that all candidates took countrywide. The brightest of them made it to district or provincial schools, while most of them never made it to high school, and for them that was the end of schooling and 'life' had started, 'life' meaning hustling for income to support themselves. They fell victim to the decline of quality education in public schools, which is a problem not just in Kenya, but worldwide, including in the United States. The problem takes different dimensions in different countries but in Kenya it has mostly to do with economics. Primary education was made free in public or government-funded schools in 2003. This was a relief to poor households that had no means to pay the fees for their children previously. Immediately there was a high increase in the rates of enrollment, which led to overpopulation in public primary schools.

What followed was a string of problems: there was a strain on the school facilities such as classrooms, teachers and books, leading to decline in the quality of education offered. Parents who were able to pay the fees withdrew their children from public schools, citing the decline in quality of education, increasing rates of indiscipline and the problem of overpopulation. This led to a segregated education system where public schools were left for the poor as the rich took their children to private schools. As the performance of students in public schools worsened due to shortage of teachers and resources and low motivation levels among teachers and students, many other parents took their children to private schools where they paid high fees to have them get personalized attention in small classes, with highly trained, highly paid and hence highly motivated teachers, and abundant modern learning resources.

In Kenya, all students take the same national exam to graduate from primary school, regardless of which school they attended, be it public or private. This definitely disadvantages the unprepared students from public schools. As admission to high schools is done at a national level based on the results of the national exams, the students from private primary schools take up the best schools while a few students from the public schools make it to high school. I got admitted to one of the best high schools in the country. That was my first venture out of home into 'the world,' as the school was in the capital city Nairobi, an eight-hour bus ride from home. That means for four years I lived with students from all corners of the nation. I got to learn more about and appreciate the diversity in our country at large. I met some students from the most remote corners of the country, some of which had only a few schools scattered over several miles. These students were admitted to the best high schools in the country despite their marks that were relatively lower than the rest of the incoming class, based on the quarter admission system where a certain number of students have to be admitted from each district in the country. So despite their low marks, if they were the best in the district, they qualified for the admission. And they turned out to be very bright in high school and most of them graduated with higher scores than their classmates who had come from private primary schools with the highest marks.

Then there was the other group of students from very rich families, some of them being children of top ranking government officials. We all had to eat the same food, sleep in the same dorms, go to the same classes and do the same cleaning and community work. But our differences were exposed in other areas; for example, those from the rich families would be visited in school by relatives driving big cars, the middle class like me would usually take a bus ride home during school breaks, while those from poor backgrounds would normally stay in school for the whole term due to lack of means to travel home. All Christians had to attend a weekly chapel service in the same service where we sang, prayed and were inspired and shaped from boys to men by talks from guest speakers all across the nation.

Four years went by like half a day and after graduating from high school, I joined the best private university in Nairobi for a one year post-high school diploma. For the first time in my life I had the independence to make big choices in life, like where I was going to stay, my career path, what to eat daily, my dressing and how to spend my time. This is the freedom that comes with graduating from high school and joining college, as before high school my parents were in charge and in high school there were the time tables to tell us what to do at what time, the bells to wake us up and drive us to bed, the school diet that left not much choice over what to eat, and the teachers on duty. I took up a diploma course in business as I waited to start my degree work, because I wanted to experience college life, a college class and a field different from engineering, my main career path. It was a very high-cost college so it was a preserve for the relatively wealthy, but it was also known for the high quality of education, student discipline and respect for religion and ethics. I interacted with many students who were also fresh from high school and we were slowly led to start thinking critically and learn with an objective of applying the knowledge to daily life and in the business environment.

Ideally, I was awaiting admission to a public university, which is done by a national joint admissions board based on the results from the high school national exam. However, as during my time in college I was more exposed to the world, given free access to high-speed internet, took classes where we discussed international case studies, and had an opportunity to interact with other students and professors who also had big dreams and a diversity of life experiences, I gradually developed an interest in the world at large and a drive to go beyond borders and experience what the rest of the world has to offer. I started musing over the idea of doing my first degree studies in another country. One day I was going over the papers and came across an advertisement about Drexel University coming to Nairobi for an informative session about the university. I attended the presentation on a day which coincidentally was my birthday. I was persuaded that Drexel was the right college for me. I gave it a shot, and the rest as they say is history.

I graduated from Strathmore, left the city and went back to the small town, to the white house on the hill. I was going to have my longest stay ever at home since I joined high school, because high school breaks usually lasted a month or less, and for the first time I could just sit back, enjoy the company of my parents and watch months pass by. Having got my yellow envelope and gone through the stressful visa process, I booked my flight and decided to put everything aside for a while and have a well-deserved break as I prepared to take on 'the world' again.

My break was mostly spent on a couch in our living room, next to a window and the nearest to the television that rests in an entertainment unit. As I tried to let everything outside pass me by, this TV brought me more of the world than I could possibly see outside, and so it became 'the world.' And as I threw my legs in the air, coffee or juice in hand depending on the time of the day, Haiti was reduced to rubbles, Toyota recalled cars, there were a couple of plane crashes, one of which claimed the life of the Polish president alongside several top government officials, there was a massive oil spill in the Gulf of Mexico, a volcanic eruption brought air traffic over Europe to a standstill, there was a world cup in South Africa, and Kenya got a new constitution.

On several occasions, especially when there was a storm, the TV would be turned off due to a blackout and I would be left staring at the silent world, wondering, do we actually understand how big the world is? When we call something a worldwide concern, do we have any idea of the concerns of a starving child in a slum in Nairobi, who can't go to school because her parents can't afford to buy her a uniform? Does my grandfather know the world when he thinks that the rest of the world out of Africa is one country? Do the leaders have in mind the widow whose unarmed husband was killed Afghanistan, leaving her with two kids she has no idea how she will provide for, when they debate sending more troops?

Most of us tend to create our own little worlds, our places of comfort, and consciously or subconsciously ignore what goes on around us that we feel do not affect us. As long as we are comfortable and safe, what happens in the news is not much of our concern. For example, the debates over the war in Afghanistan make little sense to us compared to a mother whose son is a marine on duty in Afghanistan. This detached attitude is also partly caused by a subconscious feeling that there is nothing that we can do about the situation, or that our individual contribution, for example speaking out about tax cuts or donating to charities, would be too little and too insignificant. And as Michael Jackson sings, we expect someone to solve the problem, to make a change.

But each of us is part of that picture that we think is too big for us; together we form the world. If we all appreciated the fact that every contribution from us counts, just the same way votes from each of us add up to the millions of votes that give politicians the mandate to public office, we would change the world and solve our problems. We should take an interest in what is going on around us and make it a moral responsibility to contribute to solving our problems. Given our diversity and different gifts, we can contribute to solving a problem in an almost countless number of ways. Some of us can lead, journalists can collect the news and enlighten the rest, some can write, some can start charities and all of us can contribute to the charities.

On one such occasion when the power failure persisted and 'the world' went silent for a long time, I went upstairs to the balcony. There I was safe as I watched the storm hit roofs, shake trees, chase people towards shelters, and cover the ground with running pools of water as the lake in the far distance turned to near black. And I decided to travel the world and find out as much about people, places and culture as I can.

Daniel Sullivan

Text Messaging and Conflict Resolution: What Does That Emoticon Mean?

Dan: What do you think; is text messaging a viable means for conflict resolution?

World: No, text messaging is for short messages only, not confrontations or debate.

Dan: I agree that was the intended purpose, but it has progressed over time. What are people using it for now?

World: According to a survey in 2004, people are asking questions and sending reminders, not having conversations (Faulkner).

Dan: From my research in 2010, I've found the most common uses to be event planning and gossip/casual conversation, categories with a "back and forth."

World: Argh, I'll give you that. But what about people using texting as a security blanket? It's destroying the closeness of mankind! (Pressner)

Dan: What about people using texting for "romantic interactions?" And who's to say people can't be close over non-verbal communications?

World: Or what about the fact that it's difficult for people to get their meaning across in text? (Pressner)

Dan: Actually, people think they get their meaning across.

World: Wah? But whole relationships have fallen apart from misunderstandings! (Pressner)

Dan: Then maybe it depends on other factors?

World: Well, like what?

That is the question. In my daily life, text messaging is a core component of my communications with others. I use it for everything from planning events to casual conversation and getting help on homework; but I also use it to flesh out issues with my partner and others close to me. Recently, I have wondered why we have turned to text messaging for the majority of our conflicts. Prior to doing outside research, I created a few theories as to why, for some, text messaging is a more accessible means of conflict resolution. Due to text messaging's limit of 160 characters, people have to make their arguments concise and to the point. It might also be easier for people who are shy, since they have time to formulate what they want to say, instead of feeling intimidated by a face-to-face conversation.

To see how texting can be used, we must first look at how it has been used. A 2004 study at London South Bank University examined who used texting, and why. Their results showed that those who are younger tend to send and receive a greater number of messages than those who are older (Faulkner). The study also looked at what kinds of messages were sent and found that the majority of texts were asking questions, sending farewells, and sending personal information.

In order to gain a broader perspective, I conducted my own study, in the form of an online survey. There were a total of 389 responses. After analyzing the data, and comparing it to Faulkner's survey, there are drastic differences. The first is the percentage who text. According to their collected data, 16% of their result set said they did not text. In my data, only 8% did not text, a reduction of half. Another extrapolated comparison to Faulkner's data is that texting activity declines when age increases, a fact that remains true.

When looking at the types of messages sent, we see a contrast. The two most popular uses for texting are event planning and casual conversation. The key distinction is "conversation"—not simply reminders or single questions. So text messaging has become more of a dialogue between people, rather than "fire and forget."

Armed with the information that a sizeable percentage of people have text message conversations, the next step is to see who has arguments over text messaging. Of the 360 people who use texting, 51% have had arguments. They all say it happens rarely or very infrequently. Due to the non-confrontational nature of the medium, an assumption could be made that people who are less outgoing might prefer texting to other means of communication. A study at the University of Plymouth by Reid examined the general use of text messaging vs. other mediums, looking to see if those persons who are shy and socially anxious would prefer it more. The results of the study coincided with their hypothesis; socially anxious individuals are more likely to resort to text messaging. I looked at this idea more deeply, seeing if their conclusion correlated with arguments over text as well.

My survey shows that there is no real correlation between someone's personality, and whether or not they have an argument over text. Returning to Faulkner's study however, and looking at the ages instead, there is a trend. As age increases, the amount of people who say they have arguments over text decreases. This agrees with Faulkner's thoughts: "It might be that the teenage users having grown up with text messaging are far more comfortable with it and therefore see it as just another means of communicating with their circle" (14).

The reasons for the arguments differ, but a consensus among analysts seems to be that misunderstandings due to the medium are a large cause. Etiquette expert Ceri Marsh, in an interview for *USA Today*, had the following to say: "Couples have arguments over text because of a simple misunderstanding in wording or tone. They'll say 'What exactly did you mean by that emoticon?'" (Pressner). From my research, it appears that those who say they've been in an argument agree that it is usually a misunderstanding. However, if we look at how often people feel that they got their meaning across, we see that 51% of people feel that nine out of 10 times they do indeed transmute their thoughts effectively into text. Despite this, however, there is no correlation between getting their meaning across and how often they have arguments. This goes against Marsh's thoughts and texters' own thoughts as well.

Let's take a step back and look over what we've examined so far. Texters are nowadays comprised of a broad range of ages. They primarily have conversations and plan events. Only half of them have arguments. This half is comprised of a variety of people, though, only barely separated by age The next step is—are these arguments being solved, and by whom? The short answer is—generally not. My survey shows that most people find that their arguments go unresolved.

"But what about people who effectively use texting," I thought. Looking at the data from my survey, there is once again no correlation. Those who rarely get their meaning into text solve conflicts at the same rate as those who constantly articulate their thoughts accurately. This is interesting, because if someone can get their meaning across, what is preventing them from using the same tools they use verbally in text effectively?

With these results, I was compelled to look at my own experience again. Text messaging works for me as a means of conflict resolution, but why? With the prior question in mind, I thought about what I know about solving conflicts. My experience is unique; I spent the majority of my youth volunteering at an organization called The Peace Center, in Langhorne, Pennsylvania. There I learned (and subsequently taught) the tools needed to effectively resolve conflicts. The major points are to be clear about your own feelings, listen to the other(s), and to be open to compromise. Is applying these guidelines to text arguments the difference in their success or not? The research conducted did not look at this, but future research should consider it, as it might just be the magic factor for resolving text arguments. With the collected data, however, it almost seems as though the medium has no effect on people's ability to solve conflicts. There is, however, one more factor to consider; does the "disconnect" of the situation aid people in solving conflicts?

Reid's study, which looked at social anxiety, concluded "SMS [allows] users to disengage from the demands of immediate interactive involvement, releasing time and attentional resources to compose and edit messages" (11). Meg Hallissy, a student from Fairfield University, thought similarly, "[We] are constructing our arguments, or manipulating them. We rough-draft what we really mean to say; then edit, cut, paste, or fit it into 160 characters. The final draft is often the nicer version of our original statements, without the swearing and name-calling" (Hallissy). This was one of my hypotheses, and even after all of the data showing that there are a very small number of conflicts resolved over text messaging, I still think it is true.

Based on my own positive experience, there must be a set of factors that allows someone to effectively use text messaging as a means of conflict resolution, but I have not narrowed them down. If anything, this exploration of the subject shows that it requires a significantly deeper insight into the individual than a quick survey could possibly hope to show. More questions have been raised, and their answers might hold the key to a better understanding of how we can effectively resolve arguments.

Works Cited

"Conflict Resolution - Resolving Conflict Rationally and Effectively." Mind Tools. 10 June 2010. Web. 28 Oct. 2010. <http://www.mindtools.com/pages/article/newLDR_81.htm>.

Faulkner, Xristine, and Fintan Culwin Culwin. "When Fingers Do the Talking: a Study of Text Messaging." Interacting with Computers 17.2 (2005): 167-85. 25 Dec. 2004. Web. 1 Nov. 2010.

Hallissy, Meg. "Y R U Mad? Mediated Conflict Resolution | The Fairfield Mirror." The Fairfield Mirror. 21 Oct. 2009. Web. 01 Nov. 2010. <http://fairfieldmirror.com/2009/10/21/y-r-u-mad-mediated-conflict-resolution/>.

Kasallis, Theresa. "Text Messaging Affects Student Relationships." Universe. 5 July 2005. Web. 27 Oct. 2010. <http://newsnet.byu.edu/story.cfm/60307>.

Pressner, Amanda. "Can Love Blossom in a Text Message?" USATODAY.com. 29 Jan. 2006. Web. 28 Oct. 2010. <http://www.usatoday.com/tech/news/techinnovations/2006-01-29-love-texting_x.htm>.

Reid, Donna J., and Fraser J.M. Reid. "Text or Talk? Social Anxiety, Loneliness, and Divergent Preferences for Cell Phone Use." CyberPsychology & Behavior 10.3 (2007): 424-435. Business Source Premier. EBSCO. Web. 1 Nov. 2010.

Sullivan, Daniel. "Text messaging and Conflict Resolution." Web Survey. 07 November 2010.

Publishing Group
Essays

Introduction

Researching, thinking, and writing are at the core of the College of Arts and Sciences. No matter what field they're in, students must be able to research, to find and evaluate the best evidence and information on a topic. They must be able to think, to formulate original ideas and take a fresh approach to a problem or question. And, of course, they must be able to write—excellent research and thought must be communicated to others to have value. After all of their reading and thinking about the work of others, students must make their own contributions to the field by writing.

The constant exposure to accomplished works published in their field of study can intimidate students when they sit down to write. Or inspire them. It may do both as students struggle to bring their own vision to the subjects they study and find the right words. Fortunately, this struggle often yields remarkable writing. The following works, selected from student submissions to the fourth-annual Drexel Publishing Group writing contest, exemplify a firm grasp of subject matter and a facility with language.

The essays in this section of *The 33rd* cover a host of subjects from a range of disciplines in the arts and sciences, including the cutting of funding for Planned Parenthood; the problem with physician-assisted suicide; the potential benefits and risks of synthetic biology; the similarities between an ironic love poem and a Vietnam War story; and an evaluation of the 2010 Healthy, Hunger-Free Kids Act. The topics are as diverse as the students who wrote about them, but the essays all demonstrate originality and boldness as well as great skill in researching, thinking, and writing.

Charles Falone
I Will *Not* Be a Murderer

On February 18, 2011, the United States House of Representatives decided, in a vote of 240 to 185, that we are a nation of murderers. On that day, in House vote 93, the legislative body that is intended to most closely reflect the will of the American people approved an amendment to H.R. 1, which was put forth by Representative Mike Pence of Indiana, that would "eliminate 'any and all' federal funding to Planned Parenthood Federation of America" (Wetzstein). Personally, I have no desire to kill women; the House of Representatives, it would seem, *does* have that desire.

You may be confused, at this point, as to how stripping federal funding from Planned Parenthood amounts to murder. Your mind may immediately connect the name "Planned Parenthood" with abortion. However, the vast majority of Planned Parenthood's budget does *not* go toward abortions; as was pointed out in an article in the *New York Times* that commented specifically on Planned Parenthood in southern New England, abortions are provided in "fewer than 10 percent of visits" (Eckholm). Indeed, only 3% of all services provided by Planned Parenthood nationally in 2008 were abortions. In contrast, 34% of services involved testing and treatment of sexually transmitted diseases, while 17% involved cancer screenings and prevention (Planned Parenthood Annual Report). These services are overwhelmingly provided to low-income women, for whom Planned Parenthood is the only viable option for health care. Ron Pollack, executive director of the nonpartisan health care consumer advocacy group Families USA, adds that "[t]his amendment will harm the health of millions of low- and middle-income women by eliminating their access to essential preventive health care, including cancer screenings, breast exams, STI and HIV testing." He also points out that "[f]or many low- and middle-income women, these health centers are their only source of women's health care."

Taking away funding from Planned Parenthood means taking away life-saving medical care from these women. Imagine, if you can, being in that situation. All the pain that comes with a devastating illness, an illness of such a personal nature. And you have no means to pay for medical care. *That* is what Mike Pence of Indiana would inflict upon these women. *That*, in my eyes, is murder.

If you label yourself as "pro-life," the statistics regarding Planned Parenthood may not be enough to sway your opinion on this amendment. Three percent, in your opinion, might be far too much. You certainly do not want to fund abortions with your tax dollars. Fortunately for you, you are *not* funding abortions. In an examination of public reactions to the Pence amendment, the *New York Times* pointed out that "Congress has long barred the use of federal money for abortion, but it provides more than $75 million a year to Planned Parenthood affiliates to support family planning for low-income women" (Eckholm). In fact, in 2008, Planned Parenthood prevented approximately 621,000 unintended pregnancies, thereby *preventing abortions* (Planned Parenthood Annual Report). Your tax dollars are being used to provide sexual education and low-cost birth control; preventing unwanted pregnancy prevents abortion.

As I have said, I will *not* be turned into a murderer by my Congressional representatives. But it seems there are those who would like that. In an article from the *Washington Times*, Andrea Lafferty of the Traditional Values Coalition was quoted as saying, with regard to the Pence amendment, "I couldn't be happier" (Wetzstein). An article from the *New York Times* that examined H.R. 1 as a whole cited Mike Pence himself as calling the amendment "a victory for abortion opponents" (Herszenhorn). Victory! The man attempts to commit murder in the name of the American people and calls that a *victory*!

This has nothing to do with victory, and this is not the time to strive for hollow political gains. It is also not the time for cheap-shot sound bites. The *New York Times* article that examined H.R. 1 quoted Representative Nancy Pelosi's response to the Pence amendment. She pointed out the inherent inconsistency in expressing a goal of reducing or eliminating abortions and simultaneously taking funds away from family planning services. Then, in a news conference, Ms. Pelosi scathingly commented that "[p]erhaps we have to have a lesson in the birds and the bees around here for them to understand that" (Herszenhorn). Mike Pence might want to turn you into a murderer, but Nancy Pelosi would rather crack jokes about her fellow Congress-people than directly confront the reality of this amendment.

Politicians have an almost preternatural tendency to make decisions based on the absolute worst aspects of human nature. Demagoguery, it would seem, is much easier than rational thinking. Michael Gazzaniga, of Dartmouth College, tried to alert the nation almost a decade ago when human prejudice was threatening human well-being. Dr. Gazzaniga served on President Bush's panel on bioethics, which was intended to discuss somatic cell nuclear transfer, a method of biomedical cloning which has the potential to lead to lifesaving medical discoveries. Unfortunately, the full discussion never took place. In an opinion editorial for the *New York Times*, Gazzaniga stated, with a sense of both reproach and melancholy, "I only hope that in the end the president hears his council's full debate." President Bush never heard that debate; before the council issued its final recommendation, he decided to ban all forms of cloning, both reproductive and biomedical. Then, as now, divisive politics drowned out rational thought and endangered human life. But this time, there is not even a hint of a moral gray area. Even if you love every blastocyst that ever existed, whether it was formed within a woman or in a lab dish, there is no moral or logical ground from which you can defend the Pence amendment. If you have any compassion whatsoever, the prospect of killing women should disgust you.

Mike Pence is responsible for this amendment; there is no one who could deny that. Indeed, all 240 Representatives who voted "yea" to this amendment are responsible for it. But the House Democrats who turned this into a debate over the "role of government" or who used it as an opportunity to take a shot at those across the aisle are responsible for it as well (it certainly is not the "role of government" to kill women). Every citizen of the United States who voted for those 240 Representatives in 2010 out of anger over the policies of President Obama without critically examining the positions of those Representatives is responsible for this amendment too, as are those who voted for these Representatives *because* of their positions. Every American who has the audacity (or is it cognitive dissonance?) to label themselves "pro-life" while advocating for an amendment that would kill women is responsible for this amendment. Every ACLU advocate who wants to make this about "liberty" or "reproductive freedom" is responsible for this amendment (you can't have liberty if you are dead).

For now, we are not a nation of murderers. This first shot in the war on women was deflected by the U.S. Senate, but not in the name of saving lives. Partisan politics did one thing right, albeit unintentionally. On March 9, the *New York Times* reported that "[t]he Senate on Wednesday dismissed competing plans to impose new spending cuts and finance the government" (Hulse). But is that the climate you want to see in Washington? The only thing preventing the House from developing a policy of murder is a margin of 16 votes in the Senate. If you want to ensure that you will never be turned into a murderer, if you do not want to be responsible for this amendment, or any like it, you must do what the politicians seem to be incapable of doing: you must always base your decisions on reason rather than preconceptions. When you vote, do not vote for a murderer. And when something like this happens, when our representatives in Congress no longer represent our interests—indeed, when it seems they are actively working against us—speak up. Write to, call, or email your Congress people and Senators. Silence, in such situations, is murder. And I will *not* be a murderer. Will you?

Works Cited

Eckholm, Erik. "Planned Parenthood Financing Is Caught in Budget Feud." *New York Times*. 17 Feb. 2011. Web. 03 Mar. 2011. <http://www.nytimes.com/2011/02/18/us/politics/18parenthood.html>.

Gazzaniga, Michael S. "Zygotes and People Aren't Quite the Same—Op-Ed—NYTimes.com." Editorial. *The New York Times - Breaking News, World News & Multimedia*. 25 Apr. 2002. Web. 7 Mar. 2011. <http://query.nytimes.com/gst/fullpage.html?sec=health&res=9C04E5D8143EF936A15757C0A9649C8B63>.

Herszenhorn, David M. "As House Votes to Cut $60 Billion, Standoff Looms." *New York Times*. 19 Feb. 2011. Web. 03 Mar. 2011. <http://www.nytimes.com/2011/02/20/us/politics/20congress.html?pagewanted=1&_r=1>.

Hulse, Carl. "Rival Bills to Keep the Government Running Fail in Senate." *New York Times*. 9 Mar. 2011. Web. 11 Mar. 2011. <http://www.nytimes.com/2011/03/10/us/politics/10congress.html>.

"Planned Parenthood Federation of America Annual Report 2008-2009." Web. 3 Mar. 2011. <http://www.plannedparenthood.org/files/PPFA/PP_AR_011011_vF.pdf>.

Pollack, Ron. "Pence Amendment Defunding Planned Parenthood Seriously Endangers Women's Access to Needed Health Care." *Families USA: The Voice for Health Care Consumers*. 17 Feb. 2011. Web. 07 Mar. 2011. <http://www.familiesusa.org/resources/newsroom/press-releases/2011-press-releases/pence-amendment.html>.

Wetzstein, Cheryl. "For Planned Parenthood, a GOP Shot across Bow." *Washington Times*. 20 Feb. 2011. Web. 03 Mar. 2011. <http://www.washingtontimes.com/news/2011/feb/20/for-planned-parenthood-a-gop-shot-across-bow/?page=1>.

Arhama Rushdi

The Burden and Facilitation of Path Dependency: A Historical Institutional Analysis of Political Development in India and Pakistan

Parting Ways

British Raj started in 1858 and had a stronghold on India for almost a century. It was only after the outbreak of WWII in 1939 that the subcontinent (pre-partition India) demanded complete, immediate independence. Indians, both Muslims and Hindus, were outraged that the British had dragged them into war without any consultation. Furthermore, British troops were abusing their extra coercive powers as a result of the ongoing war. Indians had finally had enough (Pardesi 46). Long before this, another, internal conflict, was brewing. By 1906, separate electorates for Hindus and Muslims had become institutionalized, Congress, a secular party led by upper caste Hindus, had been established, and the Muslim league was created. These three events caused a deep Hindu-Muslim divide within Indian politics (Pardesi 44). As revolution fervor grew, so did this divide. On midnight of August 14-15, 1947, the subcontinent was divided and two independent nations, India and Pakistan, were born.

Half a century later, while their conflict remains the same, it is hard to believe that Pakistan and India were ever one nation. Freedom House gives India a combined average rating of 2.5, categorizing it under the "free" category, and Pakistan a rating of 4.5, categorizing it under the "partly free" category. Indian citizens enjoy many more political and civil liberties than Pakistani citizens. The two countries have drastically different political regimes. India has managed to maintain a relatively stable liberal democracy while Pakistan has failed to do so, despite its numerous tries. This leads us to an intriguing question: what accounts for this difference? How could two countries with the same underlying factors—they were literally the same country—end up on such different political paths?

Historical Institutionalism

A historical institutionalist approach can be used to explain the matter at hand. This approach basically follows a fundamental principle: countries are path dependent, history matters. Barrington Moore, one of the most influential historical institutionalists of our time, theorized on this subject in relation to revolutions. In his book, *Social Origins of Dictatorship and Democracy* (1966), Moore says that countries are path dependent. The type of revolution a nation has ultimately results in the type of regime a country has. Bourgeois-led revolutions result in liberal democracy; conservative-led revolutions result in fascism; and peasant-led revolutions result in communism. As this book was written in 1966, Moore wasn't sure that India had followed any of these types of revolutions and was therefore worried whether or not liberal democracy lay in India's future. However, today we have a clearer picture of what happened during the revolution and can thus use his theory to assess present outcomes.

Barrington Moore's theory of path dependency is very useful in analyzing the reasons India and Pakistan have ended up with different political regimes. According to him, the reason Pakistan and India have different political regimes depends on the type of revolutions each country had: whether it was either bourgeoisie- or elite-led. Today, it is much more clear the type of revolution each nation had and the end results. India's revolution, especially during Gandhi's time, was a grassroots movement, involving much of the middle class, while Pakistan's revolution was spearheaded by mostly political and economic elites. Therefore, India's revolution led to democracy while Pakistan's revolution led to semi-authoritarianism.

Kapstein and Converse also studied path dependency. In their work, *Why Democracies Fail* (2008), they studied 123 modern cases of democratization and concluded that poor economic performance is not in fact the most important factor in democratic stability. Rather, the formations of strong democratic institutions in the early years of a country are important for democratic survival. They emphasized that the balance and constraints on executive power rather than the institutional features (whether the regime is parliamentary or presidential) is what is most important to a regime's survival.

This fits the Indo-Pak case study because from the beginning India had strong (though symbolic) democratic institutions with relatively strong constraints on executive power while Pakistan had weak institutions with very weak constraints on executive power, which has led to its repeated failure to establish a successful liberal democracy.

Initial Conditions

Using path dependency to analyze the Indo-Pak case first requires analyzing each country's path toward such different destinations. Looking back, pre-partition, we can see two major differences: the ideology and orientation of the two country's nationalist movements.

The differences in scope and reach of the Indian nationalist movement, led by the Indian National Congress, and the Pakistani nationalist movement, led by the Muslim League, help explain the different political regimes they have today (Pardesi 39). Under the leadership of Mahatma Gandhi the Indian nationalist movement became a grassroots movement. During the Gandhian phase, the national movement's base was socially deepened to include active incorporation and support from all social classes, especially the bourgeoisie. As a result, both Congress and the Indian nationalist movement "enjoyed considerable popularity and legitimacy" (Kohli 6). This helped Congress establish a legitimate democratic regime after the partition. Another way to analyze this is through Moore's theory of revolutions and path dependency. Since the bourgeoisie led India's revolution it was likely to result in a democracy.

On the other hand, the Pakistani nationalist movement was not a grassroots movement. It was spearheaded by Muslim elites and lacked fundamental tenets of a political organization including a grassroots following. Ahmed summarizes this point well: "The Muslim league, which basically headed the partition and the newly formed Pakistan, was a loose collection of Muslim politicians with regional support bases. It did not represent a cohesive or coherent political party with grassroots organizations throughout the country. Under such circumstances, the civil service and the military came to dominate the state" (Ahmed 6). As a result, neither Pakistan nor its political regime ever gained true legitimacy. Furthermore, "Pakistan was won, round the table and not by the people, and for the people; hence democracy has never taken root in the foundations of Pakistan" (Khan 2). Thus, one can clearly see that the Pakistani revolution was headed by elites and therefore, according to Moore, it was very unlikely to result in democracy.

The ideology of the Pakistani nationalist movement was not based on freedom or democracy but rather evolved from the fear of being downgraded in a united India. Pakistan meant different things to different people. To the Muslim fundamentalists it meant an Islamic state, to the peasants it meant freedom from the Hindu moneylender, and to the bureaucrats, military and elites it meant an opportunity to secure quick promotions (Ahmed 49). Everyone had personal interests in Pakistan and as a result the nationalist movement did not have a true sense of nationalism. "The movement for Pakistan was essentially negative in its orientation: it had come into being in opposition to a perceived fear that in a United India the Hindu majority would be a permanent political majority thus reducing Muslims to the positions of second class citizens" (Ahmed 50). The Muslim League used students from Aligarh Muslim University to spread the message of Pakistan. They highlighted the atrocities of Congress to establish hatred for Hindus in Muslims around the country. Democracy failed in Pakistan because its foundations were laid negatively, on hatred for the Hindus, rather than positively on progress and solidarity (Khan 6).

On the other hand, India's nationalist movement had a positive orientation with one major goal: "to keep the diversity of a subcontinent afloat in a democratic ark" (Kesevan 2). Unlike Pakistan, India was founded on the basis of freedom and democracy. From even before the partition the Indian National Congress ensured that "[t]he political culture of the republic [would consist] of the balancing of special interests, procrastination, equivocation, pandering, tokenism and selective affirmative action: in a word, democratic politics" (Kesevan 7). They ensured that Congress remained secular and represented the Indian populace. The foundations of India were laid in a democratic mortar with progress and reform in mind, not with hatred for the British.

Early Politics

Certain early choices made by political elites, during and after the partition, have paved the paths each country has followed. The fact that Pakistan has failed to become a successful liberal democracy and has lived under military dictatorship for most of its existence can be partly attributed to the specific choices made by the Muslim League. Firstly, the League itself was not a democratic institution. Apart from a few notable members, including Muhammad Ali Jinnah and Liaqat Ali Khan, it was made up of political and social elites who had little or no interest in democracy. They consisted of wealthy landlords or tribal leaders whose interests lay in maintaining their positions of power. Thus, when Pakistan was established the Muslim League "utterly failed to transform itself from a nationalist movement to a national party which could serve as an effective political machine for aggregating national interests and identities into a plural and participatory framework" (Mukherjee 72).

The Muslim League (ML) itself maintained less than democratic practices. Though the League did hold regular elections, leadership would never change and many people reported seeing discriminatory politics. For example, during the 1946 elections ML members deliberately sabotaged opponents by causing havoc and beating attendees at their public events (Yousaf 3). From the start, the Muslim League made undemocratic decisions and failed to provide the backbone the country needed. It failed to institutionalize any form of government, something we can still see in Pakistani politics. As a result the Muslim League could not maintain legitimacy and eventually deteriorated. Authoritarian regimes took over to provide the stability the struggling, new nation needed and have not left ever since.

On the other hand, India's successful democracy can be attributed to Congress's organizational strengths and the political skills of its members. From the beginning, Congress was established as a democratic institution with the purpose of representing the Indian population's views. Post-partition, the "Indian Congress party quickly moved to a dominant position in politics" (Mukherjee 72). Thus, after the partition the Indian National Congress was able to make choices that laid the foundations for democracy in India. It carried out a number of functions that were pivotal to democratic political development. For example, Congress was governed by democratic rules and procedures and members showed tolerance toward adversaries. Referring to this specific trait a historian writes, "even though Congress's democratic procedures were more symbolic than substantive, they indicated a commitment both to representative institutions and to an accommodation of India's pluralism in a future Indian constitution" (Gupta 223). It also provided a platform to discuss conflicting goals and priorities for the nation, something the Muslim League failed to do.

The Burden of History: Pakistan

Pakistan's history has proven to be a burden on its chances of stability and democracy. Pakistan came into being under extremely difficult conditions. During the partition, over 8 million Muslims fled India, leaving their homes, belongings and jobs, to take up residence in Pakistan. The violence caused by the partition separated families and killed hundreds of thousands of people. (Zagorski 306). Hindu-led Sikhs attacked entire flocks of migrating Muslims, killing the men and kidnapping the women. The partition of the province of Punjab was especially involved in high levels of organized violence from the Sikhs, costing at least half a million Muslim lives (Waseem 41). As India had inherited most of the developed cities, Pakistan had to start from scratch. They had no capital city, no government buildings, and no national level administration. As a notable historian puts it, "in these circumstances it is perhaps not surprising that it took some time for the Pakistani establishment to build an infrastructure" (Mukherjee 70).

Furthermore, both economically and strategically, Pakistan got the bad end of the bargain. Pakistan ended up with a mountainous region in the north and west and desert in the south, making agriculture cultivation, the original livelihood of most Muslims, very difficult. This made it harder to develop a stable economy, which could have possibly led to modernization and democracy. Pakistan also inherited some frontier areas where local governance was very weak. This could also help explain Pakistan's tradition of military involvement. While the ongoing dispute over Kashmir was a problem for India, it was a survival issue for Pakistan. As pressing matters like sovereignty, security, and mere survival took over, the military assumed greater responsibility, resulting in a more authoritarian regime (Mukherjee 70). Put boldly, Pakistanis had better things to worry about than establishing democratic roots.

During such hard times, the loss of a strong charismatic leader didn't help. Qaid-e-Azam (Muhammad Ali Jinnah) spearheaded the Pakistani nationalist movement and was the face of a united democratic Pakistan. He was practically the only politician at the time with legitimacy and a mass constituency. The movement was woven around his dream of the perfect Muslim nation of Pakistan but on its own lacked firm organizational and institutional structure (Ganguly 26). Jinnah's sudden and early demise left Pakistan without any true leadership. He died before he had the chance to formally institutionalize any regime. Without Jinnah, the Muslim League proved incapable of coping with the unstable state. Furthermore, without his leadership, the Muslim League members "were busy in resettling themselves through just and unjust claims of lands, houses, and factories... Instead of establishing the roots of democracy our leaders have been busy in establishing themselves" (Khan 4).

Soon after Jinnah's demise, his right hand man and the first Prime Minister of Pakistan, Liaqat Ali Khan, also died. This left the army-general-turned-president Iskender Mirza in charge. General Iskender Mirza failed to stabilize the country so he shared his leadership with his commander-in-chief, General Ayub Khan. Within 21 days General Ayub Khan overthrew General Iskender Mirza and established a military coup. This was the first blow to Pakistan's already weak democracy. General Ayub drew up Pakistan's first separate constitution which basically said the president ruled for life or until he wanted to. This paved the path for Pakistan's tradition of authoritarian regimes. When leaving office 10 years later he handed power over to his commander-in-chief, General Yahiya Khan, thus also starting the tradition of de-facto military power (Khan 6).

The early tradition of de-facto military power in Pakistan can help explain the differences between Pakistan and India's very different political regimes. It can also help explain why Pakistan has failed to establish a liberal democracy despite its many tries. Throughout Pakistan's history there have been three military coups, each followed by a failed attempt at democratic transition (Bhave 56). This seemingly odd phenomenon can be explained using Kapstein and Coverse's approach to democratic reversals. As mentioned before, they emphasize the importance of constraints on executive power for a successful democracy. From its start, Pakistan has had a tradition of giving too much power to its executives. As long as this tradition remains, so will the ongoing rule of semi-authoritarian and military-run regimes.

The Facilitation of Democracy through Path Dependency: India

India's history, especially its inheritance from the British Raj, helped facilitate democracy in the country. India and the Indian Congress party inherited almost all of the major cities, including the capital and all of the ministry buildings. Most of the British structures, including administration and education, were left on the Indian side. This gave Congress a head start as they could just use the existing government infrastructure and apparatus. The inherited structural institutions provided strong foundations for India's future democracy. Furthermore, India inherited both the Indo-Gangetic plain and the soil of the Deccan, fertile land that some scholars credit for India's successful and stable economy (Mukherjee 69). Simply put, India's favorable inheritances allowed them to focus on laying democratic foundations within their political structure, resulting in the liberal democracy they have today.

The legacy of the British Raj was more than good soil, buildings and cricket; India also inherited much of the modern British ideology. As one historian notes, "the struggle for self-rule was actually part of a process that helped build Indian institutions and reshape Indian political and social culture" (Zagorski 133). A democratic constitution based on federalism was quickly drawn up. Traditional practices of oppressing women and discrimination based on the caste system was outlawed. Human rights and freedom of speech and religion were established. India also inherited a military establishment that was committed to civilian control of the armed forces. This prevented the military from gaining too much power as in Pakistan's case and resulting in a tradition of military coups (Zagorski 135).

Historically Locked-In

As this paper shows, from their very inception, the two countries have, partly because of fate and partly because of their own choices, followed two different paths that have led them to the very different destinations they are at today. Once again, history matters. One comparativist summarizes this theory very well: "The two countries created different politico-military frameworks around the time of their independence and have been 'historically locked-in' along two separate politico-military paths" (Pardesi 39).

Pakistan's path had started being paved at the birth of the Muslim League. The Muslim League lacked fundamental organizational and democratic structure, something still lacking in the nation of Pakistan today. Muhammad Ali Jinnah brought Muslims together out of fear of a united India and ironically Pakistanis have never been united since. "Pakistan was not a democratic dream but a Muslim aspiration, based on a political reality. It was established as an independent country as a result of a political movement of Muslims in South Asia, but those Muslims were not politically organized" (Mukherjee 68). Furthermore, their early instability led to an above average involvement of the military, resulting in the tradition of military coups.

India's path started during British Raj, and the British sociopolitical inheritance still dominates Indian politics today. Its positive-oriented foundations, laid on unity and progress, have led to both political and economic progress. The democratic roots and procedures of the Congress and Indian nationalist movement can be seen in Indian political institutions today. Its bourgeois-led revolution has, in fact, resulted in democracy. Though its democracy has dwindled in the past, the strong constitutional safeguard against usurpation of executive power has prevented it from taking a path similar to Pakistan's.

Works Cited

Ahmed, I. (2008). Pakistan's National Identity. *International Review of Modern Sociology, 34*(1), 47-59.

Bhave, A., and Kingston, C. (2009). Military coups and the consequences of durable de facto power: the case of Pakistan, *Econ Gov, 11,* 51-76.

Converse, N., & Kapstein, E.B. (2008). Why Democracies Fail. *Journal of Democracy, 19*(4), 57-68.

Ganguly, S., (2008). The Burden of History. Journal of Democracy, 19(4), 26-31

Gupta, J.D. (1990). India: Democratic Becoming and Combined Development. In L. Diamond & J.J. Linz & S.M. Lipset (Eds.), *Politics in Developing Countries: Comparing Experiences with Democracy* (219-269). Boulder, CO: Lynne Rienner Publishers.

Kesevan, M. (2007). India's model democracy. Retrieved from http://news.bbc.co.uk/2/hi/south_asia/6943598.stm

Khan, A.A., (2001). Why Democracy Failed in Pakistan. Retrieved from http://www.mediamonitors.net/ashraf23.html

Kohli, A. (2001). *Success of India's Democracy.* Cambridge, England: Cambridge University Press.

Moore, B. (1966). *Social Origins of Dictatorship and Democracy: Lord and Peasant in the Making of the Modern World.* Boston, Massachusetts: Beacon Press.

Mukherjee, K. (2010). Why Has Democracy Been Less Successful In Pakistan Than In India? *Asian Affairs, 41*(4), 67-77.

Pardesi, M.S., & Ganguly, S. (2010). India and Pakistan: The Origins of Their Different

Pardesi, M.S., & Ganguly, S. (2010). India and Pakistan: The Origins of Their Different Politico-Military Trajectories. *India Review*, 9(1), 38-67

Waseem, A. (2005). Causes of Democratic Downslide in Pakistan. In V. Kureja & M.P. Singh (Eds.), *Democracy Development and Security Issues Pakistan* (36-51). UK: Sage Publications

Yousaf, N. (2007) Why Democracy Failed in Pakistan. Retrieved from http://www.allamamashraqi.com/images/Why_Democracy_Failed_in_Pakistan.pdf

Zagorski, P.W. (2009). *Comparative Politics: Continuity and Breakdown in the Contemporary World*. New York, NY: Routledge.

Alexis Kerri Burns

Paralyzed Men

One would never think that an ironic love poem and a Vietnam War story would have anything in common. However, after one reads T.S. Eliot's "The Lovesong of J. Alfred Prufrock" and Tim O'Brien's "The Things They Carried," one can recognize that the protagonists J. Alfred Prufrock and Lieutenant Jim Cross are very different individuals plagued by self-doubt and relationship issues that greatly impede their lives. Eliot and O'Brien use objects and the surroundings to depict these two characters and reveal their internal struggles with self doubt and feelings of emasculation as well as difficulties in maintaining a healthy, normal relationship. After understanding these protagonists and their situations, the reader realizes that both men are experiencing an existential crisis proceeding from their physical and emotional disconnect with women. To then cope with the terrible sense of indecision and emasculation, they retreat to their own personal fantasy worlds.

Eliot and O'Brien use a similar technique for characterization: they project the characters' lives onto objects and surroundings. The reader can infer much about the characters from the descriptions of the objects and surroundings. In "The Things They Carried," O'Brien basically constructs the story by the objects the soldiers possess. These objects are in fact the vehicles through which the story is told. Two examples of these items are Lieutenant Cross's pebble and photographs of Martha (his girlfriend). These two objects prompt the narrator to discuss the emotional plotline: Lt. Cross and Martha's relationship or lack thereof. Through the objects, Cross remembers his times with Martha. They in fact reveal his love and obsession with Martha, for he projects his fantasies onto the objects, such as in his pretending the pebble in his mouth is Martha's tongue. Likewise, O'Brien uses it as a symbol of Cross's distress over his failure to make a romantic connection with Martha.

Eliot utilizes this technique of externalizing the character's internal state but in a slightly different manner, allowing the reader to infer Prufrock's personal history and current situation through the oppressive milieu of his world. Eliot, for example, writes "Of restless nights in one-night cheap hotels/... Streets that follow like a tedious argument/Of insidious intent" (Eliot 3). Now, a street can never literally be an argument, so really the description of the streets is colored by Prufrock's emotions. The poem's stream of consciousness technique allows the reader to see into Prufrock's mind in this indirect manner. One can easily discern, through the description, that Prufrock, like Lt.

Cross, is having difficulty with relationships. Prufrock has had relationships that possess all the emotional shallowness of a one-night stand and the destructive nature of an argument; in other words, they never come to fruition of a mature and stable relationship. Obviously, both poems use the objects and surroundings to describe the unfulfilling romantic relationships Cross and Prufrock have had and their relationships with an unattainable woman and women in general, respectively.

Both writers allow the reader access to the characters' minds and opinions of themselves. Eliot also is able to incorporate the surroundings into Prufrock's frame of mind and perspective (Bloom 17). Prufrock has a terrible self-esteem which is manifested in the description of his surroundings. "When the evenings are spread out against the sky/Like a patient etherised upon a table" (Eliot 3) is an example of Prufrock's inverting a conventionally romantic scene into a morbid symbol of sedation and self-doubt. The opening lines "invite us to imagine strolling ... but our expectation of romantic reveries [is] quickly undercut by the macabre image of 'a patient etherised upon a table' – the world out cold" (Bloom 17). As shown by his choice of description, Prufrock has a negative outlook on his life. He feels like the patient: sedated. His life remains repetitive and stagnant from his inhibitory self-doubt; he cannot bring himself to act out of extreme anxiety and insecurity. In addition, he, like the patient, is supine, almost trapped like being "pinned and wriggling on the wall" (Eliot 5) like an animal. Likewise, Prufrock, most likely in some restaurant in London, incorporates coffee spoons to describe his life as being "measured out ... with [them]" (Eliot 5). He views his life as so romantically lacking and so repetitive that it can be measured with tiny spoons, unlike Hamlet and Michelangelo who had illustrious lives. This is just mundane and repetitious like "the cups, the marmalade, and the tea" (Eliot 6).

Lt. Jim Cross shares a similar outlook but in different way. For the American soldiers, the days all blend together since "otherwise it would be one day layered upon all the other days" (O'Brien 631). The impetus that keeps Cross going is his unrequited love for Martha. The reader, through Cross's fantasies about Martha, also gets a glimpse of his psyche. Unfortunately, he misinterprets Martha. When he gazes at the photo of Martha against a brick wall, Lt. Cross quickly focuses on the shadow of the picture taker. Consumed by questions, he asks: who is this person, is this one of Martha's boyfriends, and is Martha a virgin? His obsession stems from the fact that Martha does not reciprocate his love. He states that even through the letters "were signed 'Love, Martha,' ... 'Love' was only a way of signing and did not mean what he sometimes pretended it meant" (O'Brien 616). Likewise, the pebble stirs up many questions. Martha had sent the pebble since it had "this separate-but-together quality" (O'Brien 621). Cross consciously misinterprets Martha's gift as a symbol of love instead of its true meaning of friendship. Cross's intense jealousy emasculates him as he devotes himself to the unattainable ideal that is Martha. He rejects all other possible relationships due to this extreme and unhealthy obsession.

These two characters, J. Alfred Prufrock and Lieutenant Jim Cross, are both portraits of emasculation. They have experienced and are experiencing relationship issues with women, specifically an unnamed woman and Martha, respectively. Within Eliot's poem a multitude of prostration images appear. As previously mentioned, the etherized patient and the "pinning down and wriggling on the wall" are two of the most literal images of prostration. A third exists in the biblical allusion to Lazarus of Bethany. Jesus did not reach the ill Lazarus in time to cure his ailment before Lazarus died; consequently, Jesus raises him from the dead. This poem conveys the images of death and prostration. Collectively, these prostration images can be interpreted as Prufrock's passivity in life. He places himself as unimportant as an individual and unworthy of attention and recognition. The meaning of the prostration images fits nicely with Eliot's allusion to Hamlet. Prufrock denies himself the role of Hamlet, the ultimate character of indecision, in his own life. He cannot take center stage of his life since Prufrock recoils into the role of "an attendant lord, one that will do/ To … start a scene or two …/At times, indeed, almost ridiculous–/Almost, at times, the Fool" (Eliot 7). He but says a few words and at times seems ridiculous. No one, however, forced him into this embarrassing and lowly role; Prufrock, despite despising his life, embrace his role and does nothing to break from it. The images of prostration and Hamlet converge and display how Prufrock is emasculating himself. His inability to communicate with the woman and his submissiveness translate to his low self-esteem. He is full of indecision and questions that in turn lead to more anxiety and even ridiculous questions such as "[does he] dare eat a peach" (Eliot 7). Prufrock remains firmly planted in a never-ending cycle of indecision and inability to romantically interact, creating a pedestrian, repetitive life. All of these in combination with his aging (for he has a bald spot and "[he] grows old … [he] grows old" (Eliot 7)) produce the perfect condition for his feeling vulnerable, weak, and emasculated.

Lt. Jim Cross also produces this same situation within "The Things They Carried." His emotional and social issues are exacerbated by the war and culminate in his intense fixation with Martha, unlike Prufrock, whose problems arise from his personality. Cross's anxieties about Martha stemmed from previous events like the movie theater incident before arriving in Vietnam. Cross had been dwelling on his relationship, although most likely not to the extent he does while marching and "hump[ing]" (O'Brien 17) his things. Metaphorically interpreting the title, one can say he and his men "all carried [the] ghosts" (O'Brien 621) of memories; for Lt. Cross, his was Martha. This "emotional baggage of men who might die … had their own mass and specific gravity, they had tangible weight" (628-629), as O'Brien states. O'Brien then points out that they "all got [emotional] problems" (O'Brien 629). These problems are added to the already heavy and burdensome pile of physical and psychological things to carry; to deal with this, Cross focuses on his futile love for Martha, which ironically makes him feel even worse. He feels emasculated since he is being sexually rejected by the object of his affection, Martha. Likewise, he feels like that he cannot perform his duty because "he was just a kid at war, in love" (O'Brien 623). He blames himself for the death of Ted Lavender even though he couldn't have prevented it. Yet, he will always blame himself because he was consumed by his fantasy of Martha during Ted's death.

> While Kiowa explained how Lavender died, Lieutenant Cross found himself trembling. He tried not to cry. With his entrenching tool, which weighed five pounds, he began digging a hole in the earth. He felt shame. He hated himself. He had loved Martha more than his men, and as a consequence Lavender was now dead, and this was something he would have to carry like a stone in his stomach for the rest of the war. All he could do was dig. He used his entrenching tool like an ax, slashing, feeling both love and hate, and then later, when it was full dark, he sat at the bottom of his foxhole and wept. (O'Brien 625)

As one can see, he interprets Martha's rejection and Ted's death as his own fault. Lt. Cross cannot reach his expectations and dreams; thus, he feels emasculated. However, the ending of the "The Things They Carried" is rather ambiguous since it does not give Cross's absolute course of action.

Lt. Cross and J. Alfred Prufrock isolate themselves and retreat to their fantasy worlds. As shown in the previous paragraph, Cross spends the majority of his time, even while performing his duties, dreaming of Martha and his encounters with her. He isolates himself by not communicating his internal strife with his fellow soldiers. In fact, rarely do any of the soldiers speak to one another of the difficulties they face. That explains why openly speaking of relationship problems would not be acceptable. Lt. Cross and his men deal with the hardships and terrible events by using their own jargon and jokes. They attempt to make the very real and visceral events seem fake: in other words, a world of pretend. For example, O'Brien writes:

> They were actors and the war came at them in 3-D. When someone died, it wasn't quite dying, because in a curious way it seemed scripted, and because they had their lives mostly memorized, irony mixed with tragedy, and because they called it by other names, as if to encrypt and destroy the reality of death itself. (628)

Since they cannot speak of their hardships, all of them, especially Cross, create their own personal fantasies and collectively create an unreal situation. Lt. Cross uses both his fantasy of Martha and his company's pretending to help cope with the horrors of wars, the sudden "boom, down" (O'Brien 631) nature of death. However, this fantasy world is easily destroyed by the sudden injection of Ted Lavender's death. Lt. Cross sobers up to the realness of the situation and vows to not live in his fantasy world and neglect his duties; nevertheless, he might not stick to his resolution and might just "shrug and say Carry on" (O'Brien 632).

Prufrock employs use of his fantasy world in a different manner and far less successfully. He lives in three worlds, according to Robert Canary: the yellow fogged-covered London, the tea and cakes filled restaurant, and his own personal world (94). He has a different time in the first two realms. By his disturbing imagery of the street, he does not find that world as welcoming and a timid, anxious man like Prufrock cannot live in such a world as that. The second world does not suit him either because it is where most of his anxiety stems from: the world of women. In this place, "the women come and go/Talking of Michelangelo" (Eliot 4). He cannot even say a sentence without feeling like he is not communicating exactly what he wants. so he cannot live in that world either. Thus, he must construct his own sanctuary in his mind; in spite of his attempt, he cannot live in this world either. Eliot references this world in the last few stanzas of the poem with the mermaids. The image of mermaids implies fantasy. Prufrock has been to this world since "[he has] heard the mermaids singing, each to each" (Eliot 7). However, instead of being accepted by the women and finding solace, he is rejected in his own fantasies since "[he does] not think that [the mermaids] will sing to [him]" (Eliot 7). He cannot even accept himself in his dreams, showing how pathetic Prufrock's situation really is. Now, like Cross's world, it is quite fragile. When reality like losing virility and aging hits Prufrock or when "human voices wake us" (Eliot 7), the fantasy world and the possibility of acceptance is destroyed and "[Prufrock and his fantasy] drown" (Eliot 7).

As shown, Prufrock and Lt. Cross share many similarities. After finding out from the writers'externalization of the characters' psyches, the reader sees these emasculated men suffer from the inability to have a meaningful relationship with the women from either extreme self-consciousness or jealousy. The lack of those romantic relationship damages their self-esteem and their outlook on life. Unable to directly face the issue, they produce fragile fantasy worlds. However, their creations cannot solve the root of the problem: the inability to deal with reality and the truth of their own flaws.

Works Cited

Canary, Robert H. *T.S. Eliot: The Poet and His Critics*. Chicago: American Library Assocation, 1982. 94. Text.

Eliot, T.S. "The Lovesong of J. Alfred Prufrock." *The Complete Poems and Plays*. New York: Harcourt, Brace and Company, 1950. 3, 4, 5, 6, 7. Text.

O'Brien, Tim. "The Things They Carried." *The Best American Short Stories of the Century*. Eds. John Updike and Katrina Kenison. New York: Houghton Mifflin Company, 1999. 616, 617, 621, 623, 625, 628-629, 631, 632. Text.

"Thematic Analysis of 'The Lovesong of J. Alfred Prufrock.'" *T.S. Eliot: Bloom's Major Poets*. Ed. Harold Bloom. Broomall, PA: Chelsea House Publishers, 1999. 17. Web. <http://www.netlibrary.com/Reader/>.

Clinton Burkhart
The Extended Mind of a Modern Cyborg

Abstract

In this paper I present and argue the idea that we all have extended minds, and that these extended minds make us cyborgs. I contend that the extension of our minds has come as an evolutionary adaptation to surviving in the modern technological world, and that it is because of this adaptation that we have become cyborgs.

A World of Technology

The technical advances of our society have steadily been gaining steam over the past few decades, and to some this represents a decline in human society as a whole, similar to the fear Socrates had of the invention of the written word (Carr 2010). This fear that our way of life is changing and is becoming unrecognizable is, by no means, a new one. In his 1970 publication of *Future Shock*, Alvin Toffler expressed his fear that the continuing development of technology would cause a mental breakdown among the future population that could not adapt to the rate at which technology was increasing (Toffler 1970). Freud also had a similar feeling in his *Civilization and Its Discontents*. Freud claimed that people would become neurotic because of the pressure placed on them by society (Freud 1930). Toffler and Freud bring up a similar point in that eventually, as society advances, technological advancement will outpace the rate at which humans will be able to adapt to it.

Toffler's views of society, for the most part, have come true. In his book, he describes a growing obsession with novelty as society seeks to be continuously stimulated by increasingly novel things (Toffler 1970). Toffler argues that we continue to seek these novel stimuli due to an "orientation response" (OR), and that in this response to stimuli, certain brain changes cause alertness. Toffler argues that as novelty continues to increase, the ORs occur more and more frequently. In considering the question of what would happen if this level of alertness brought on by the OR did not subside, Toffler contends that this would force an "adaptive reaction" that would "tamper with the chemistry and biological stability of the human race" (Toffler 1970). The only way to eliminate this problem is to slow the pace of change to a grinding halt, but what kind of life is that? No life at all, Toffler argues. We need to adapt to survive, but adaptability has limits. "Each orientation response, each adaptive reaction wears down the body's machinery...a biosystem with limited capacity for change. When this capacity is overwhelmed, the consequence is future shock" (Toffler 1970).

Toffler proposes that adaptation can indeed occur, but that it does so only in a limited "adaptive range" which is established when the amount of change or novelty in the environment is neither too low nor too high, and when an individual's coping needs fall beyond this range they experience future shock (Toffler 1970). Toffler describes future shock as something similar to culture shock; when abroad a traveler may feel unusually drained because the way the individual is used to handling problems is no longer applicable, and in response becomes tired more rapidly than usual. The same can be said of future shock except people experience it within their own society and watch the world change around them. Toffler proposes that certain actions can occur for one to adapt to experiencing future shock—specialism and the establishment of enclaves, both past and future, can allow for people to adapt to a pace of life suited to them and their adaptive range.

Toffler's idea of specialism is such that a single person may continue to adapt in certain areas, a specialty, and allow the rest of their being to lay behind. By doing so, the specialist is able to keep within their adaptive zone and avoid future shock. Enclaves of the past and future are also ways Toffler proposes to deal with this problem. Enclaves of the past allow people who cannot adapt to the quickening pace of life a place to live where the pace of life is slowed down. Enclaves of the future, on the other hand, provide people who need to adapt a way to do so gradually, similar to how an astronaut training for a space mission first spends time in a pool to simulate weightlessness. Thus, enclaves of the past and future can also help humanity adapt to the changing pace of society (Toffler 1970).

Similar concerns were launched by Nicholas Carr in his 2010 book, *The Shallows*. Carr supports Toffler's view that technology can be detrimental to the human condition, especially to the human brain. Carr cites a 2006 memoir by Eric Kandel, *In Search of Memory*, in which Kandel states that brain synapses may be altered and changed in response to stimuli like learning, and that so long as the anatomical configuration was maintained, so too would the memory (Kandel 2006). Carr goes on to quote T.S. Eliot, "Composing on the typewriter I find that I am sloughing off all my long sentences," with the point being that the technology we interact with can, and does, affect the way we think and the way we construct our thoughts. Carr cites a Richard Foreman quote, which perhaps sums up his fears: "[W]e risk turning into 'pancake people—spread wide and thin as we connect with that vast network of information accessed by the mere touch of a button'" (Carr 2010). Carr's main fear is that with all the information the development of technology has placed at our fingertips, we risk losing our humanity as we dive into this vast cyber world of information and, as Toffler feared, novelty.

A Novel Adaptation: the Extended Mind

Perhaps Toffler and Carr underestimate the resiliency of the human mind or perhaps they overestimate our importance; regardless, they ignore the amazing ability of the human mind to evolve and adapt to new circumstances. Evolution has been around for billions of years, and Charles Darwin's theory of natural selection states that organisms adapt to survive in their environments. They do this on an individual genetic basis and subsequently propagate such adaptations into the population, whereby selection pressure can act upon them, determining which gene is fit, or incurs a benefit to the individual, and eventually makes its way throughout the population until the species evolves. Humans are no different and are equally subject to the same laws of natural selection as is the rest of the animal kingdom. The idea proposed by Toffler and Carr is therefore an absurd one, as humankind will adapt as it always has, albeit to a new world of technology, but the process is still the same. Humans that are able to thrive in a technological society will thrive with the advancement of technology, and those who are unable to will fade into the memory of yesteryear. Why? Evolution and adaptation.

This can be seen in studies done by Ophir and colleagues. Their experiment was designed to test the attention and memory of high media-multitaskers (HMMs) and low media-multitaskers (LMMs). The test was designed to see what chronic media multi-tasking does to our brains. In the experiment, subjects are shown a set of blocks for 0.1 seconds. In this set two blocks were a different color, and the subject was asked to pay special attention to the orientation of these two blocks. The subject was then asked 0.9 seconds later whether the next array of blocks matches the previous one or not. In conclusion, they found that LMMs fare much better at this test than HMMs (Ophir et al., 2009). Is that a surprise? If indeed the HMMs are better, as they claim, at multitasking would it not be the case that they would be easier to distract by showing them more blocks? By the definition of multitasking, doesn't this prove that they are capable of paying attention to more than one thing at a time? This simple experiment seems to suggest that humans among us are already adapting to our new world of technology. How are they doing this? By increasing their interaction with the world, because after all they are high multitaskers, and so they interact with the internet and technology much more than an average person. Again, as Carr quoted T.S. Eliot, "Composing on the typewriter I find that I am sloughing off all my long sentences"; so, as the typewriter changed T.S. Eliot's sentence composition, so does the internet shape our brain's ability to use technology (Carr 2010). Toffler worried that the growth of technology would outpace the rate of human evolution, but as long as there is an evolutionary niche there will be an organism to occupy it.

If we admit that there is adaption occurring, can we pinpoint what this adaptation is? This novel adaption to excess novelty is the extended mind. The concept of the extended mind has been a debate for over a decade. Toffler suggests that in a future-shocked society, future humans will crave novelty, and Carr writes that we will become so spread out with all of the connectedness that the internet provides, that we will become "pancake people." How can this be avoided? By creating room in the brain for more information. How is that accomplished? Using tools like the Internet, computers, PDAs, cell phones, notebooks, anything that can carry an idea, and then subsequently use it as an external storage device to free up space within the internal mind.

Clark and Chalmers argue in their 1998 paper, "The Extended Mind," that a notebook, when reliably accessible, in a patient with long-term memory loss, is indistinguishable from the way the long-term memory functions in a normal human (Clark & Chalmers 1998). Isn't it true? It can function in the same way, but more importantly, however, the two people can function in the same way. The memory-loss patient and a normal human will be indistinguishable. Both can function in everyday society. How can this be? The patient with his notebook and the normal individual with his long term memory function as complete systems, which are irreducible, and should be referred to as such.

Phenomenology of the Extended Mind

If one agrees that a notebook indeed can function in a capacity equal to that of a long-term memory, provided that it is equally reliable (if not more) and accessible, than one cannot deny the existence of the extended mind, and it is this phenomenology of the person-notebook system that makes this possible.

The concept of emergence is crucial to the understanding of phenomenology. Emergence states that the complexity of the whole cannot be predicted from the sum of the parts, and phenomenology is just this concept applied to the mind. To stick with the notebook-human memory system, the notebook is just a notebook and the human with long-term memory loss is just that, but together they both function as something more. In a 2002 paper, "Intelligence Without Representation – Merleau-Ponty's Critique of Mental Representation: The Relevance of Phenomenology to Scientific Explanation," Hubert Dreyfus stated that through an intentional arc, learned behaviors aren't merely stored information accessed within the brain as needed, but instead, when mastered, actually create a change in the way the person views the physical world around them (Dreyfus 2002). Dreyfus specifically cites the game of chess as an example of learned behavior that when mastered can actually be represented visually to the chess expert (Dreyfus 2002). Certainly a phenomenal claim, but where is the proof?

In 2010, a study was conducted by Dotov and colleagues in which the test subjects were tasked to keep a ball within a target zone by corralling it with the movement of a computer mouse (Dotov et al. 2010). The test subjects where then asked to do the same task but with a delay in the response of the mouse to their movements, breaking the smoothness of the system. After the subjects were comfortable with this task, they were asked to perform a second task to count backwards by threes, at which point their ability to perform the second task was measured with and without the disruption of the delay in the mouse response to their hand movements (Dotov et al. 2010). The results showed that when the delay in mouse response was created, there was a drop in performance of the counting task, and that when the delay was removed, the task returned to the level it was at before the introduction of the delay (Dotov et al. 2010). The implications of this are that when there is no interference or delay in the system, the test subject is not aware of the first task and can perform it well. When the interference is introduced into the first task, the test subjects needed to shift their focus from the second task to the first because of this interference. The system no longer functions because of the discord between hand movement and mouse response, suggesting that when behaving as a fluid system, the subjects didn't notice the mouse. It was as if it were part of their bodies because it was part of the system, and as though they were not forced to pay attention to or think about it.

If we follow the phenomenological argument that the system as a whole is the thing that should be addressed, because parts cannot function in isolation, then we must accept that the mind can be extended into objects in our lives, and that the extended mind is an adaptation to the technological world we inhabit.

The Modern Cyborg

To understand a cyborg, one must first understand the origin of the term "cyborg." The term was created by Manfred Clynes, and the following quote is how it was originally printed in *Astronautics*: "The cyborg deliberately incorporates exogenous components...in order to adapt to new environments" (Clark 2007). The gravity of this definition is that when an organism adapts itself to exist in a new environment, it is a cyborg, and the modern human qualifies.

In direct response to the novelty over-stimulus, and rapid pace of life that comprises the modern world of technology, we find that for the modern human to thrive, one must adapt to survive in such an environment. A novel adaptation to cope with the future shock caused by the technological world is the extension of the mind, and it is this adaptation that creates the modern cyborg. Adaptation to the modern world of technology has occurred through the use of tools like a cell phone, computer, PDA, and the Internet, as the mind becomes extended into these objects as a mechanism of coping with the future shock envisioned by Toffler. Through the exercise of phenomenology, these tools literally become extensions of the human system, and as such serve as the adaptation that defines the modern cyborg.

Logical and Ethical Ramifications

When one accepts the idea that the modern human being is a cyborg or cybernetic organism, one must also consider that perhaps more literal cybernetic organisms could exist. A.M. Turing. in a 1950 publication, "Computer Machinery and Intelligence," proposed that if a computer could fool a competent judge that it was human, then quantitatively the computer and the human were the same (Turing 1950). The problem with this argument arises from a standpoint that the test, which would become known as a Turing test, was weighted towards the computer; and, also, in order for the test to work, the judge must be secluded from seeing either the participant, the person or computer, and that the participants can only communicate with the judge through typed word, with the idea being that one can discern the difference between a human and a computer in both sight and sound. Excluding this bias, the logic of the Turing test is sound, but what if the bias didn't matter?

With the idea that the modern human is a cybernetic organism, perhaps we can ignore the physical appearance of the computer because it is composed of cybernetic components, and if we accept this premise, then the voice should follow, since the body of the organism isn't really of grave importance, but instead it is whether or not the organism has a mind, and can think. This being said, the phenomenological objection is that being able to replicate and fool a judge in human conversation doesn't make something quantitatively the same as a human, as conversation is merely one aspect of humanity. It should be noted that Turing published his paper over 60 years ago, and computer intelligence has certainly evolved since then, and the day might not be far off when the sentient machines should be granted rights, just like any other cyborg.

The rights of sentient machines are addressed by Isaac Asimov in his short story, "Robot Dreams." In this story, robots live in society to serve humans, treated almost as slaves and are programmed—essentially brainwashed—into following the three laws of robotics, whereby a robot must: (1) not harm a human being, nor through inaction allow a human being to come to harm, (2) obey orders given by a human except where they interfere with rule (1), and a robot must protect its own existence except where it interferes with rules (1) and (2) (Asimov 1986). In this story, a robot is destroyed because it becomes self-aware, and, as such, is a threat to the society that the humans have established with robots as their slaves (Asimov 1986). The destruction of this sentient machine is not deemed unethical in the story, but certainly if the modern human is a cyborg then any sentient cybernetic organism should be granted the same rights as a human, and certainly with the growing rate in the development of technology and with the current state of robotics, this isn't a future that is very far off.

Conclusion

In the future-shocked world imagined by Toffler, humans are forced by the limitations of their brains to stay in their adaptive zone to avoid the consequences of future shock. They can do this by joining an enclave of the past or future or by becoming a specialist (Toffler 1970). Carr also worries that this world of ever-advancing technology will destroy our humanity and turn us into interconnected "pancake people" (Carr 2010). The evolutionary adaptation of the extended mind in modern humans provides an alternate route allowing us to avoid the pitfalls of a future-shocked existence, as well as creating new ways for humans to interact in our world of growing technology.

The phenomenological argument put forth by Dreyfus and supported by Dotov and colleagues demonstrates that the adaptation of the extended mind creates within humans a complete system that cannot be reduced. It is this system and adaptation to the world of technology that qualifies modern humans as cyborgs, under the definition of the term's creator, Manfred Clynes. One who subscribes to this view must also take into consideration that if humans are cyborgs, then other cybernetic organisms like sentient or thinking machines proposed by A.M. Turing and Isaac Asimov may indeed be granted the same rights. It makes one wonder whether or not science fiction will become the future of philosophy.

Works Cited

Asimov, I. (1986). Robot dreams. In S. Schneider (Ed.), *Science fiction and philosophy: from time travel to superintelligence.* (pp. 117-121). Oxford, UK: Wiley-Blackwell.

Carr, N.G. (2010). *The shallows: what the internet is doing to our brains.* New York: W.W. Norton.

Clark, A. (2007). Cyborgs unplugged. In S. Schneider (Ed.), *Science fiction and philosophy: from time travel to superintelligence.* Oxford, UK: Wiley-Blackwell.

Clark, A. & Chalmers, D. (1998). The extended mind. *Analysis,* 58(1), 7–19.

Dotov, D.G, Nie, L., & Chemero, A. (2010) A demonstration of the transition from ready-to-hand to unready-to-hand. *PLoS ONE* , 5(3), 9433–9442.

Dreyfus, H.L. (2002). Intelligence without representation – Merleau-Ponty's critique of mental representation:The relevance of phenomenology to scientific explanation. *Psychology and the Cognitive Sciences*, 1, 367–383.

Freud, S. (1930). *Civilization and its discontents*. Print.

Kandel, E.R. (2006). *In search of memory: the emergence of a new science of mind*. New York: W.W. Norton.

Ophir, E., Nass, C., & Wagner, A.D. (2009). Cognitive control in media multitaskers. *Psychological and Cognitive Sciences*, 106(37), 15583-15587.

Toffler, A. (1970) *Future Shock*. New York: Random House.

Turing, A.M. (1950). Computing machinery and intelligence. *Mind*, 59(236), 433-460.

Chelsea Biemiller

Odd Girl Out: The Loss of the Fashionable Oddball and Why We Need Her Back

"I dress for myself. Not for the image, not for the public, not for the fashion, not for men."

–Marlene Dietrich

I am mourning the loss of the fashionable oddball. Hopefully, you have been lucky enough to know one of her kind. She is the girl who unabashedly wears whatever she wants on a regular basis, despite the stares and negative comments she will surely receive. The stylish oddball dresses in a way that is decidedly against the grain; she dresses for herself, in the clothing that she finds most representative of who she is as an individual. Often described as "eccentric," "quirky" or "nonconventional," she may come in a vintage lace cocktail dress, a menswear three-piece suit, or a patchwork skirt and dreadlocks; but she never looks like those around her. Though she can be found in many forms, one thing about the fashion oddball is certain: she sends the message—through her chosen style of dress—that she is unlike everyone else. But for various reasons, the stylish oddball is going out of style. Her absence says a great deal about what we value, and what we lack, and I think it's high time she made a comeback.

We owe a great deal to the oddballs who have come before us, for there was a time when change in fashion and style had the power to change cultural mores, particularly concerning women. In the 1920s, a new kind of woman emerged: one who danced freely, smoked cigarettes, and generally behaved in ways deemed distasteful of a "respectable" lady. With her cropped hair and loose, drop-waist dresses, the "flapper" rejected societal norms and caused quite a scene indeed, killing the narrow image of women as "angels of the house," dearly held in the previous century (Soland 24-26). Later, film stars like Marlene Dietrich and Katharine Hepburn shocked the American public when they shamelessly wore pantsuits, crossing the boundaries of clearly defined gender norms of that time (Riva 65, Britton 32). In the 1940s, the iconic image of Rosie the Riveter in rolled-up denim sleeves, ready to enter the workforce to support the war effort, created yet another new image of women, shedding the stereotype of the 1940s housewife (Lazar, Karlan and Salter 289). These fashionable oddballs rejected the cultural uniform of their day and, in doing so, they changed cultural and societal expectations.

The Fashionable Oddball and the Cultural Uniform

Every generation of teenagers and young adults adopts a "uniform." It is a particular look and style typically worn by most young people. Clothing constructing the uniform is readily available and widely accepted. The sock hoppers had their poodle skirts and saddle shoes. The hippie style of the late 1960s went mainstream in the seventies, with everyone in fringe and bellbottoms. The eighties had a particularly unfortunate uniform—one that included shoulder pads, fluorescent daywear and polyester windpants. However it is styled, the cultural uniform unites a generation in appearance and sets it apart from those that came before it.

But the fashionable oddball rejects the uniform of her generation, happily stepping out of clothing that's so widely accepted. She dares to dress in something different, something that makes her stand out and apart from the crowd. She represents a rejection of the status quo, and in doing so, she visually demonstrates to others that she is unlike her peers. By rejecting the uniform, the fashionable oddball rejects the societal constructs that come with it. She presents the opportunity for change, not just for fashion, but also for the many entrenched, long-standing norms of that culture. The oddball represents the breaking down of old traditions, and the potential for creating something new. But this significance and power historically held by the oddball has increasingly lessened. The message she sends has become muffled, for a variety of unfortunate reasons.

Problems of the Current Cultural Uniform

The first problem is one of the current cultural uniform itself, which the oddball must work against. Uniforms of previous generations have reflected something very distinct about those groups. Their uniform said something about the values, the beliefs and the interests of the people wearing it, and thus, it provided the oddball with a statement to respond to. Unfortunately, the aesthetic of the *current* cultural uniform is painfully boring and uninspired. One need only to go to a public place frequented by young adults—the shopping mall, a college campus, or the grocery store, for example—to see the staples of our current uniform repeated again and again: jeans, tee shirts, hooded sweatshirts and other variations of unremarkable basics.

What our uniform says about our generation, as a group, can be interpreted in various ways. I would argue that this style is largely a leftover version of the grunge uniform popular in the 1990s. Though we've scaled back the flannel and holes in our jeans, we have, on the whole, been unable to create anything new to distinguish ourselves. Our generation's disinterest in the use of fashion as a means of expression seems to suggest that we don't have much to say about ourselves, leaving the fashionable oddball with very little to respond to.

This uninspired uniform is likely the result of corporate competition and more pervasive marketing techniques. In an effort to appeal to the largest possible demographic (and, I would argue, keep manufacturing costs to an absolute minimum), stores like The Gap, Abercrombie & Fitch and Hollister Co. (to name just a few) have made the plain tee shirt sexy. These retailers take the same basic item and cover it in different versions of their logo. The glorified tee shirt is then situated in front of massive in-store marketing, displaying hyper-sexualized models (who, ironically, often don't wear much of anything). Even those who don't shop at those *particular* retailers still wear the uniform: the jeans and the tee shirt. Young people have found this easy, basic uniform desirable, and it has become the primarily acceptable style for one hoping to fit in with her peers.

Clothing companies have been branding their items for decades, yet this hasn't, until now, seemed to prevent a generation's youth from developing a unique uniform that represented their ideals. But with million-dollar advertising campaigns, clothing companies have barraged young people through every possible medium—be it in print, television, film, online and the celebrities paid to endorse their brand—with a very narrowly defined conception of the norm and what it means to look attractive. As a group, young people are told by this ever-present advertising that in order to be accepted, we *must* look a certain way (and that way, of course, is in overpriced jeans and tee shirts bearing brand names). It would seem that we're complacent to accept these prescriptions handed down to us for truth, wearing whatever is popularly advertised and easily available, despite what that clothing actually looks like and says (or fails to say) about us and our values.

The development of this disinterested uniform has left the oddball in a difficult position. Unlike her peers, the oddball *does* have something to say about herself, and she does it through personal style. With such a lackluster uniform to rail against, it would *seem* that oddballs today have ample opportunity for making a statement. But in practice, she is met with multiple obstacles, established by our current culture, which make it difficult for her to send that message effectively, if at all. As such, more and more individuals who would be prompted to dress differently have simply given up.

Where Have the Oddballs Gone?

There are multiple reasons for this loss of the fashion outlaw. To begin, we must remember that the oddball is often not *born* an outsider, but is instead *inspired* to dress like one. Upon discovering some strange source of inspiration (be it music, film, or an entirely different culture altogether), she is encouraged to channel this interest in how she dresses. As a former fashion oddball, I'll use myself as an example. My particular fascination concerned vintage clothing, developed over summers spent at my grandmother's home, watching classic films and poring over old photographs. I wore fur and silk headscarves for a month upon seeing *Grey Gardens* for the first time. I humiliated my brother by wearing vintage military coats and 1960s cocktail dresses to our high school. My grandmother pin-curled my hair for the prom to match my flapper dress. Without that exposure to old films and photos, I may never have been inspired to step outside of the boundaries dictated by the current cultural uniform.

Today, sources of inspiration are slowly waning for the would-be oddball. The women we are all encouraged to style ourselves after are no longer dressed in unique, unusual clothing. Instead, we are bombarded with images that endorse the norm, and there is little inspiration to be had by anyone. Instead of conveying our interests or ideals as a generation, our current cultural uniform sends the message that we don't have the effort or the inclination to send a message in the first place. The norm to which the oddball compares herself (and speaks out against) has become stagnant, voiceless and still. Because it says little about *who we are* as a generation, the oddball is left unable to respond with a message about *who she is* in relation. With few current artists, celebrities and fashion designers actively attempting to change this norm, the oddball is easily gripped, with everyone else, by the ennui of our current uniform—one that is uninteresting and apathetic.

But for those girls who *do* find the inspiration to dress differently, there has developed another barrier: stores like Urban Outfitters, and their corporate philosophy that's mainstreaming the strange. These companies have pinpointed the *would-be* style maverick and provided her with a one-stop-shop for all of her eclectic needs by mass-producing items that *look* vintage or unusual. Stores like Urban Outfitters would have us believe that they're doing the oddballs a service. They provide a wealth of unique items, available in many sizes and colors. Sold in malls everywhere, however, the style they've created is certainly not unique. Furthermore, the widely available retro fashion offered by these stores is only the *reinterpretation* of an earlier era. It is painfully obvious that this reinterpretation almost always includes elements that are important to the *current* industry: cheap fabrics, swift manufacturing and skin-tight fits.

Urban Outfitters further supports their brand image (one of "nonconformity") by filling their stores with kitschy items that try so hard to be cool: coffee mugs reading "Slut," the "Birthday Bitch Card Game" and "Buy Me a Shot" tee shirts. But these items only further endorse harmful stereotypes and leave a bad taste in the mouth of those of us who don't find them funny. The fashionable oddball, though rebellious in her appearance, is mindful of how she will be perceived. She understands the power of her argument, and she attempts to make it with class, not shock value.

Instead of providing potential oddballs a wealth of truly inspired pieces, Urban Outfitters has reinforced a view of women as cheeky and irresponsible, churning out girl after girl in tight retro concert tees and skinny headbands. They have taken the stylish oddball and made her look like everyone else.

Why We Need the Fashionable Oddball

There are many who would say that in the grand scheme of things, this concern for the disappearing oddball doesn't really matter—it's only *fashion*, after all. But the *power* of style—as a means of communication, as a rejection of the norm, and as a method for breaking down barriers—deserves a closer look.

Style is, and always has been, a medium for self-expression. It allows us to create a physical representation of who we want to be and how we want to be perceived. Fashionable oddballs take risks with this representation, and they do it boldly, without apology. Eccentrics show the world that they will not be constrained by how the media and the fashion industry tell them they should look. By showing others that we're not constrained by what we wear, we show them that we're not constrained in what we do or how we think.

By dressing exactly as we wish, we tell our up-and-coming oddball sisters that it is acceptable for them to do the same, as well. Young women now, more than ever, are pressured to fit into the mold created by a television culture that idolizes increasingly younger celebrities, generally bad behavior, and a laissez faire attitude in most areas of life (including ambition, respect, sex, equality and education, among many, many others). Girls are left with few role models encouraging them to act, to think, and to *be* different from their peers and reality show celebrities by rejecting the uniform and the constructs that come with it.

The argument we can make about ourselves to other young women, through our use of style, is a strong one. Take, for example, the responses of a group of high school-aged girls interviewed by cultural researcher Emilie Zaslow (2009). Zaslow interviewed seventy young women on their beliefs and understandings of feminism, gender equity and what it means to grow up as a girl today. When asked to describe a character from popular culture that represented a strong, independent woman, a vast majority of interviewees named Phoebe Buffay from the sitcom *Friends*. Phoebe, unlike the show's other female leads, did not have a steady job, displayed little sense of direction or ambition, and was often mocked for her ditzy behavior. When asked why they viewed Phoebe as strong and independent, the interviewees cited her sense of style: quirky, unconventional and very much against the norm (87-89). By not caring about how she looks, Phoebe represented, to Zaslow's participants, a woman who values her own interests above others' perceptions of her and thus, was free to attain what she wants from life.

The results of this study clearly demonstrate the power of style as a means of communication, and suggest the opportunity to use fashion to send a positive message. When women in the "real world" (and not just characters from a television show) are willing to brave the sneers and dress differently, not only are they perceived differently themselves, they also show young women that they can, and should, do the same.

How Do We Bring Her Back?

The oddball has an opportunity to make a statement, on a daily basis, about who she is and what she believes in. In a generation of young people that don't seem to believe in very much at all, the necessity for those willing to stand out is even greater. We need the oddballs to help us break down barriers that have persisted over time, despite the efforts of those eccentrics who came before us. With such a blasé uniform to work against, and the grip of advertising ever upon us, there is no easy answer to how she should do this effectively. But those of us who believe that the world needs more fashion mavericks must start with ourselves. We must look for inspiration, avoid shopping malls and department stores, and never apologize for how we're dressed. Being a fashionable eccentric requires confidence; it is not for the faint of heart. The oddballs must never apologize or explain away our outfits. By remaining steadfast in our eccentric ways, we will speak volumes about ourselves and dismantle the view of our generation as one that has little to say. It's time for the fashionable oddballs to make a comeback. It is time for us—uninspired by the current uniform and brave enough to reject it—to start playing dress up.

Works Cited

Britton, Andrew. *Katherine Hepburn: Star as Feminist*. New York, NY: Columbia University Press, 2006. Print.

Lazar, Allan, Dan Karlan and Jeremy Salter. *One Hundred Most Influential People Who Never Lived: How Characters of Fiction, Myth, Legends, Television and Movies Have Shaped Our Society, Changed Our Behavior, and Set the Course of History*. New York, NY: HarperCollins, 2006. Print.

Riva, David J., ed. *A Woman at War: Marlene Dietrich Remembered*. Detroit, MI: Wayne State University Press, 2006. Print.

Soland, Birgitte. *Becoming Modern: Young Women and the Reconstruction of Womanhood in the 1920s*. Princeton, NJ: Princeton University Press, 2000. Print.

Zaslow, Emilie. *Feminism, Inc.: Coming of Age in Girl Power Media Culture*. New York, NY: Palgrave Macmillan, 2009. Print.

Arhama Rushdi

Death with Dignity

Physician-assisted suicide has been a widely debated topic over the past few decades. These debates have mostly centered around ethics and religion, with the focus on whether the act itself is right or wrong. Like other highly debated topics, it usually ends without any compromise because every individual has the right to his or her own personal view. However, today we are faced with a larger challenge, a bigger problem, which affects society as a whole. Active euthanasia or physician-assisted suicide has been legalized in Oregon, Washington, and Montana. This is a problem because these laws contain holes that can be abused and if spread, such laws can cause more harm than good. Laws that make euthanasia legal and thus make it part of the system are detrimental not only to individuals but also society and therefore, the death with dignity laws such as the ones in Oregon, Washington, and Montana should be repealed or at least modified so that they are not able to be abused.

To assess the problem clearly, we must first look at the laws themselves, which are all pretty much the same. For example, Oregon's Death with Dignity Act basically says that an adult (18 years or older), who is an Oregon resident and is terminally ill (within 6 months of his or her demise), can make a voluntary request for lethal medication. The request must be an oral request, followed by another oral request in no less than 15 days along with a written request. Two witnesses who are not related to the patient must sign the written request form. The statute also requires that both the attending physician and a consulting physician inform the patient about his or her prognosis, risks, and alternatives to taking the lethal medication. The attending physician is also required to submit a detailed report and fill medical record documentation requirements *after* the lethal medication is prescribed (Lunge).

The most common argument against legalizing active euthanasia is that it will lead to very undesirable consequences (the slippery slope). Legalizing euthanasia would cause more difficulties than it would remove. Current death-with-dignity laws in Oregon and Washington make only voluntary euthanasia legal. However this is not that simple. Currently, there is no way of making sure that the act is voluntary or without any coercion. Legalizing euthanasia and making it common practice will only lead to more and more people being influenced by family and society as a result of either financial or caretaking burdens. Reports show that financial burden was the core motive in 7.9% of the cases of physician-assisted suicide in the United States (Emanuel). There are real-life examples of patients being pressured, as in the case of Oregon resident, 85-year-old, Kate Cheney. Her physician, in compliance with the death with dignity statute, refused to prescribe her lethal medication because he felt that her daughter, who was her caregiver, was pressuring her. The family changed their doctor, and the new physician, who was not as familiar with their case, agreed to the request and she is now dead. Changing of doctors, also known as "doctor shopping," because of an initial refusal to write the prescription, even if the case does not follow the guidelines of the statute, has happened on multiple occasions in Oregon (Golden).

Decriminalizing voluntary euthanasia could also lead to involuntary euthanizing of the disabled, incompetent, and others, whose lives society considers not worth living. The Netherlands, where voluntary euthanasia has been socially acceptable for a relatively longer time, is a good example to look at to see the long-term effects. Recent reports estimate the minimum number of Dutch physician assisted suicide cases per year at approximately 5,000. Weighting for population differences, this corresponds to about 80,000 projected PCVAE deaths annually in the United States (CeloCruz). Furthermore, one commentator, Richard Fenigsen, believes that the practice of voluntary active euthanasia in the Netherlands has been "inseparable from, and inherently linked to overtly involuntary forms" of active euthanasia. This has led to major social changes; polls show that 77% of the Dutch public approves of some form of involuntary active euthanasia (CeloCruz). If the Netherlands has been unable to prevent such undesirable consequences, how can we be sure that legalizing euthanasia in America will? There is no foolproof way of preventing involuntary euthanasia if voluntary euthanasia is legalized and becomes common practice.

Current euthanasia statutes or the death with dignity laws in Oregon and Washington only require physicians to comply with certain procedural requirements, but do not impose the requirement that the "physician act from merciful, beneficent, or even human motives" (CeloCruz). Furthermore, the laws contain a good faith clause, which ensures that no physician will be legally liable for any actions if they claim that they acted in "good faith" (Golden). This makes it very easy for doctors and HMOs to abuse the system and use euthanasia for incentives other than those that have the patient's best interests in mind. This can lead to some serious problems, as doctors can be influenced by monetary potential, or even pressure from health insurance companies (it would save health insurance companies a fortune if a cancer patient was euthanized before going through costly treatments like chemotherapy and radiation). A Georgetown University study showed a scary but strong link between cost-cutting pressure on doctors and their willingness to prescribe lethal drugs to patients. The study further warns that "there must be a sobering degree of caution in legalizing [physician-assisted suicide] in a medical care environment that is characterized by increasing pressure on physicians to control the cost of care"(Golden).

Inequalities within the population further the adverse effects of legalizing euthanasia. Polls show that the majority of pressure to legalize euthanasia comes from wealthy, upper-middle class, well educated, young white people. These people are less likely to be coerced into euthanasia because they have less financial burdens and are only looking for the reassurance of knowing the option is available. Such people are also less likely to fall victim to the other negative consequences of legalizing euthanasia and being abused by the system because they tend to have good health insurance; intact, supportive families; and the social skills and know-how to maneuver their way through the bureaucratized health care system (Emanuel 641). Those who disfavor legalizing euthanasia tend to fall on the other side of the socioeconomic spectrum and are thus more vulnerable to the negative consequences of decriminalizing euthanasia. They are financially less well off and many of them don't have health insurance. Thus, they are more likely to opt for euthanasia because of economic hardships. They also usually tend to be less educated, which makes it harder for them to navigate the healthcare system, and are thus more likely to be abused by the system (Emanuel 641). The same socio-demographic disparities that are common among the healthcare system today will be present if euthanasia is legalized. It will only reinforce the current inequalities: the wealthy will benefit and the poor will be harmed (Emanuel 642).

However, physician-assisted suicide is not always wrong. If done under the right circumstances and with the right safeguards, it can relieve a patient's suffering without causing the side effects mentioned before. Therefore, I propose that new laws be made where euthanasia is currently legal that provide such safeguards. The major problem with current laws is that they call for a full report by the physician *after* the medication has been prescribed or taken, when it is too late. Because of this it is more likely that this practice will be abused and will lead to corrupt and unethical practices. The laws should be changed so that a complete and thorough report has to be submitted to a "death-with-dignity board" for approval and only once approved can the doctor prescribe lethal medication. The board should consist of doctors, psychologists, lawyers, and other specialists in the field. This way, the board can take a better look at the big picture and make sure that neither the patient nor the system is being abused. The board can make sure that the physician isn't being pressured to reduce medical costs. This can prevent HMOs, insurance companies, and doctors from using euthanasia to their advantage, to cut their costs and reinforce current inequalities by abusing the underprivileged.

Furthermore, the board can make sure that the attending physician has been the patient's doctor for a reasonable amount of time to prevent "doctor shopping" and discrepancies like the Cheney case. This can prevent incidents of physician-assisted suicide in which the patient is being coerced by family or friends. Finally, such precautions will help control the physician-assisted suicide rate, ensuring that the practice isn't being abused and thus providing a distinct line between voluntary and involuntary euthanasia, something the Netherlands has failed to do.

In conclusion, completely legalizing voluntary euthanasia, without providing the necessary safeguards, would make it a part of the bureaucratic healthcare system, which would not be in the patient's best interest. Euthanasia could become death-through-coercion rather than death-with-dignity. Keeping the patient's, doctor's, and society's best interests in mind, it is best that a fair and non-partisan death-with-dignity board be established wherever physician-assisted suicide is legal. This will help counter the side effects and lessen the negative aspects of euthanasia while respecting the patient's true wishes.

Works Cited

CeloCruz, Maria T. "Aid-in-dying: Should We Decriminalize Physician-assisted Suicide and Physician-committed Euthanasia?" *American Journal of Law and Medicine* 18.4 (1992): 369-94. *Academic OneFile.* Web. 6 Feb. 2011.

Emanuel, Ezekiel J. "What Is the Great Benefit of Legalizing Euthanasia or Physician-Assisted Suicide?" *Chicago Journals: Ethics* 109.3 (1999): 629-42. *JSTOR.* Web. 13 Feb. 2011. <http://www.jstor.org/stable/10.1086/233925>.

"Physician-assisted Suicide Definition — Medical Dictionary Definitions of Popular Medical Terms Easily Defined on MedTerms." *MedicineNet.* Web. 14 Feb. 2011. <http://www.medterms.com/script/main/art.asp?articlekey=32841>.

Golden, Marilyn. "Talking Points Against AB 1592 "Death with Dignity Act"" *Disweb.org.* CDA. Web. 23 Feb. 2011. <http://disweb.org/cda/issues/pas/golden3.html>.

Lunge, Robin. "Oregon's Death with Dignity Law." *Vermont Legislature.* Legislative Council, 2004. Web. 01 Mar. 2011. <http://www.leg.state.vt.us/reports/05death/death_with_dignity_report.htm>.

Andrew Seletsky

Synthetic Biology: Creating Life from Its Most Basic Components

Science has changed drastically over the last decade, so that we are now on the edge of a real revolution. With revolution, comes controversy—and at the forefront of the controversy is the debate over synthetic biology.

Synthetic biology, dubbed "extreme genetic engineering," is the design and construction of new biological parts, devices and systems, or the re-design of existing natural biological systems for useful purposes (Synthetic Biology Project). Put simply, scientists take an organism and re-engineer its DNA so that it produces something beneficial to society. For example, microorganisms such as viruses and bacteria could be altered to produce pharmaceuticals, detect toxic chemicals, break down pollutants, repair defective genes or even destroy cancer cells (Tucker and Zilinskas). The possibilities of synthetic biology are limitless.

Tremendous progress has been made already, fueling the drive for even more research in this dynamic field. One such example is the herb artemisinin (*Artemisia annua*), or as it is commonly known in the West, sweet wormwood. This herb is a critical ingredient in anti-malarials and although Asian and African farmers have begun to plant it in mass quantities, the herb supply remains drastically low. The World Health Organization expects that for the next several years the annual demand of five hundred million units will far exceed the expected supply (Specter 3). Not only will there not be enough to go around, but relying solely on such a small source could prove to be catastrophic if anything were to impact these farmers. "Losing artemisinin would set us back years, if not decades," said Kent Campbell, a former chief of the Malaria Control Program at the Centers for Disease Control and Prevention. "One can envision any number of theoretical public-health disasters in the world. But this is not theoretical. This is real. Without artemisinin, millions of people could die" (Specter 3).

In 2000, this information came to the attention of Jay Keasling, Professor of Biochemical Engineering at UC Berkeley, who had been looking for a compound to use to demonstrate the ability of synthetic biology. Professor Keasling realized that if developed correctly, an entirely new source of artemisinin could be produced through cells that "naturally" manufacture the chemical required for malaria medications. By creating these artificial metabolic pathways inside of a host cell, Keasling would be able to produce the raw elements of an anti-malarial much cheaper than ever before, and by doing so he could eliminate the risk factors that exist with third world farming (Specter 2-3).

Within three years Keasling's team was able to successfully implant this new metabolic pathway into E. coli. Upon publishing the promising results of his work in *Nature Biology*, Keasling was able to obtain a $42.6 million grant from the Bill and Melinda Gates Foundation to further develop the science in order to benefit those who truly needed access to the drugs. Upon receiving the grant, Keasling commented, "Making a few micrograms of artemisinin would have been a neat scientific trick. But it doesn't do anybody in Africa any good if all we can do is a cool experiment in a Berkeley lab" (Specter 4). The BMGF grant allowed Keasling to found Amyris Biotechnologies, which in the last decade has successfully increased the amount of artemisinin produced by a single cell of E. coli to a factor of one million, thus bringing the cost for malaria treatment even lower. Amazing breakthroughs like Keasling's have fueled synthetic biology research and transformed the field from theory to reality.

As revolutionary and beneficial as these ideas are, they have come under increasing amounts of pressure from the scientific community and from the media and general public. The question often posed is, "Do the benefits of synthetic biology outweigh the possible consequences?" There are many concerns, some more rational than others, but the major ones tend to revolve around three central themes: the ethics of 'playing God,' possible environmental impacts, and the consequences of this beneficial research being used with malicious intent.

The ethical ramifications of synthetic biology have proven to be a significant stumbling block for the science. By altering the DNA of living organisms, scientists are controlling life, which many consider akin to 'playing God.' In fact, technology has already progressed to the point that scientists now have successfully created a 'synthetic' living organism from standardized pieces of DNA. By using these "BioBricks," as Jay Keasling has termed them, it becomes possible to build entire organisms out of bio-engineered chemical compounds (Specter 1).

In the mid-nineties, Craig Venter of the Institute for Genomic Research, along with his colleagues Clyde Hutchison and Hamilton Smith, wondered if living organisms could be created from the most basic components of genomes. To test their theory, they inspected the genome of a small bacterium called *Mycoplasma genitalium*. By removing genes one by one from the bacterium, they slowly discovered the minimal set of genes necessary to sustain life. This experiment became known as the Minimal Genome Project, and by 2008 a new version of the experimental organism was successfully created using chemically synthesized fragments of DNA. This important breakthrough resulted in the very first truly artificial organism.

Venter, who is now widely considered the father of modern synthetic biology, hopes the creation, which he named "Synthia," will be able to serve as a vessel that can be modified to carry different packages of genes (Caplan). Specifically, the results of the Minimal Genome Project has proven that a bio-engineered organism can produce a drug, or digest carbon in the atmosphere, or any number of other uses that can tremendously benefit society (Specter 7).

While the experimentation done by Venter, Hutchison, and Smith clearly has its benefits, many people believe that by creating/altering life (i.e., 'playing God'), we are interfering with the natural order of life as it is meant to occur. But is altering the natural progression of life always such a bad thing? Many who complain that genetic engineering is 'playing God' have not taken into account that as a society we have been 'naturally' altering plants and animals through selective breeding for thousands of years. Scientists believe genetic engineering is simply a more efficient method of achieving the ends of selective breeding (La Bossiere).

Professor Jay Keasling has been quoted as saying, "We have got to the point in human history where we simply do not have to accept what nature has given us" (Specter 3). However, in the case of synthetic biology, it becomes a foggier issue since scientists are creating life from artificially engineered genes. "Many a technology has at some time or another been deemed an affront to God, but perhaps none invites the accusations as directly as synthetic biology," the editors of *Nature* wrote in 2007 (Specter 8). Thus the controversial debate can be summarized as, "Are synthetic biologists playing God, and if so is that wrong?"

According to an article published by the Associated Press in February 2011, a Massachusetts based biotechnology company is now able to produce diesel fuel by using only sunlight, water, and carbon dioxide. The 'trick' is using synthetic biology. "Joule Unlimited has invented a genetically engineered organism that it says simply secretes diesel fuel or ethanol wherever it finds sunlight, water and carbon dioxide" (Lindsay). This means that if this technology is properly executed, within a matter of years, it is hypothetically possible for the United States to shed its reliance on foreign fuels. Obviously much skepticism has arisen since this announcement, to which Joule chief executive Bill Sims has replied, "We make some lofty claims, all of which we believe, all which we've validated, all of which we've shown to investors." Sims continued, "If we're half right, this revolutionizes the world's largest industry, which is the oil and gas industry, and if we're right, there's no reason why this technology can't change the world."

Using synthetic biology, Joule was able to take an existing organism, cyanobacteria, and alter its genome so that it "naturally" produces something very useful to society. Incredibly, Joule Unlimited has claimed that its artificially engineered cyanobacteria are capable of producing 15,000 gallons of diesel fuel per acre, per year, at a cost of only $30 a barrel, and could be fully operational within two years (Lindsay).

This discovery somewhat validates the second and quite possibly the more plausible concern shared by the general public: what would be the environmental consequences if artificial life created in a lab was released, either accidentally or purposefully? Using the previous example, what would happen if even one cyanobacterium found its way into the environment? Imagine the devastation that could be caused by an organism that can go anywhere with sunlight, water, and CO_2, and begin to produce diesel fuel. The recent Gulf of Mexico oil spill would pale by comparison to the damage that could be caused by an uncontrolled, self-replicating and self-sustaining living organism producing such a potentially harmful product to the environment. So while it is imperative for research in synthetic biology to continue, it must be conducted with extreme caution, as it could have disastrous results if mishandled.

Furthering the concept of uncontrolled destruction, the third popular societal concern that has arisen in the last couple of decades is the threat of bioterrorism or "Bio-Terror." What would the consequences be of this technology falling into the control of terrorists or other criminals with malicious intent? If utilized incorrectly or inappropriately, synthetic biology has as much capability to cause destruction as it does to provide solutions. With access to the proper research, one could hypothetically design a bacterium or super virus that could potentially kill millions, wreaking havoc upon society.

Rob Carlson, a research fellow at the Molecular Sciences Institute, has said, "This is open-source biology, where intellectual property is shared. What's available to idealistic students, of course, would also be available to terrorists. Any number of blogs offer advice about everything from how to preserve proteins to the best methods for desalting DNA" (Specter 14). Several years ago, in order to "see what could be accomplished using mail order and synthesis," Carlson opened his own experimental biotechnology company, Biodesic, in his Seattle basement (Spencer 14). He was able to develop a molecule on his laptop and then send the sequence to a company that synthesizes DNA. However, Carlson later stated, "most of the instruments needed [to create the synthetic organism] could be purchased on eBay. All you need is an internet connection" (Specter 14).

As an example, consider Methamphetamine, or as it is commonly known, "Crystal Meth." Initially used during World War II, Methamphetamine was beneficial in treating a variety of symptoms; now Crystal Meth is a severely addicting and very popular street drug that has been illegal since the early 1980s. How is it still in existence if pharmaceutical companies have halted manufacturing it? Simply, anyone with an internet connection can find out in seconds exactly how to make Crystal Meth. In fact, as the street value of Crystal Meth increased, Methamphetamine production has grown from homemade labs to more professional and centralized manufacturing facilities (Specter 14). Carlson has noted that "[t]he black market is getting blacker. Crystal Meth use is still rising, and all this despite restriction. Strict control would not necessarily insure the same fate for synthetic biology, but it might" (Specter 14).

As research and development pushes forward, concerns related to the field of synthetic biology are not likely to go away. In fact, these issues are going to come to a head within the next decade as scientists begin to unlock the full potential of synthetic biology. In December, the Presidential Commission for the Study of Bioethical Issues gave synthetic biology a temporary green light after President Obama asked them to review this emerging field and establish ethical boundaries. After considering research and testimonials on both sides of the argument, believing the benefits outweigh the possible consequences, the Commission ruled that research should "proceed with appropriate attention to social, environmental, and ethical risks" (Laboratory Equipment). But did the Commission draw the correct conclusion? Does the possibility of curing cancer or being fuel independent really outweigh the threat of environmental ruin or a bio-terror attack?

Works Cited

Caplan, Arthur. "The Wide Angle: Do Synthetic Biologists Play God?." Discovery
    Channel. *Discovery Channel*, n.d. Web. 3 Mar 2011. <http://dsc.discovery.com/
    technology/my-take/synthetic-biology-caplan.html>.

Ferber, Dan. "Microbes Made To Order." *Science*. 9 January 2004: 158-161. Web. 3 Mar
    2011. <http://www.sciencemag.org/content/303/5655/158.full.pdf>.

LaBossiere, Michael. "The "Playing God" Argument."*A Philosopher's Blog*. 4 January
    2008. Web. 3 Mar 2011. <http://aphilosopher.wordpress.com/2008/01/04/the-
    %E2%80%9Cplaying-god%E2%80%9D-argument/>.

Lindsay, Jay. "Mass. company making diesel with sun, water, CO2." *Associated Press* 27
   February 2011: n. pag. Web. 3 Mar 2011. <http://news.yahoo.com/s/ap/20110227/
   ap_on_bi_ge/us_growing_fuel>.

Specter, Michael. "A Life Of Its Own." *New Yorker* 28 September 2009: n. pag 1-16.
   Web. 7 Feb 2011. <http://www.newyorker.com/reporting/2009/09/28/090928fa_
   fact_specter?currentPage=all>.

Synthetic Biology Project. Woodrow Wilson International Center for Scholars, 2011. Web.
   27 Jan 2011. <http://www.synbioproject.org/>.

"The Ethics of Synthetic Biology and Emerging Technologies." *Laboratory Equipment*
   17 Dec. 2010: n. pag. Web. 15 Feb 2011. <http://www.laboratoryequipment.com/
   news-the-ethics-of-synthetic-biology-and-emerging-technologies-121710.
   aspx?xmlmenuid=51>

Tucker, Jonathan B., and Raymond A. Zilinskas. "The Promise and Perils of Synthetic
   Biology." *New Atlantis* 12.Spring (2006): n. pag. Web. 27 Jan 2011. <http://www.
   thenewatlantis.com/publications/the-promise-and-perils-of-synthetic-biology>.

Giby George

The Ethics of Medical Involvement in Lethal Injection Executions: Discussing the Role of the Anesthesia Provider

Introduction

Assuming that capital punishment is legal in more than half of the states that comprise the U.S. and that the most frequently employed mode of execution in each of these states is death by lethal injection, the medical community, specifically physicians and nurses, should be permitted to participate in lethal injection executions, as to moderate the physical pain of the condemned.

Currently, in most cases, physicians and IV-certified and -experienced medical professionals are either prohibited from or strongly advised against partaking in lethal injection executions by governing medical associations (Waisel 2007). Medical societies, Board associations, and overseeing healthcare professionals and authorities regard the involvement of medical personnel in lethal injection executions to be a direct violation of the ancient Hippocratic Oath and therefore of medical ethics (Waisel 2007).

In instances in which physicians are either prohibited from participating or reluctant to become involved in executions, non-medical personnel, commonly referred to as "lethal injection technicians," may be requested to provide medical assistance (Johnson 2008). Such medical assistance may entail establishing intravenous (IV) access for the subsequent administration of the drug(s), administering the drug(s) via IV infusion, maintaining IV access, monitoring the sentenced individual's cardiac rhythm and/or electroencephalography (EEG) activity, or pronouncing death (Gawande 2006).

The involvement of non-medical personnel, who are not educated, experienced, or certified in medical practices, in lethal injection execution poses a risk to the physical welfare of the condemned. This endangerment may then be termed "cruel and unusual punishment," thereby violating the eighth amendment to the U.S. Constitution (Johnson 2008).

Execution by lethal injection thus remains an impasse between the U.S. government and the medical community, as participation by medical professionals is commonly regarded as a violation of the *Code of Medical*

Ethics set forth by the American Medical Association (AMA) (Lanier and Berge 2007). The non-participation of medical personnel, however, in lethal injection executions, may violate the Constitutional prohibition against "cruel and unusual punishment."

It is important to note that the issue here is not whether capital punishment itself constitutes "cruel and unusual punishment," and is therefore permissible under the U.S. Constitution. Putting that controversy aside, in considering capital punishment, specifically execution by lethal injection, the issue becomes whether or not allowing medical personnel to participate in lethal injection executions would conflict with modern medical ethics.

In considering the *Code of Medical Ethics* maintained by the AMA, which has since been incorporated by a number of additional medical organizations, it may be argued that the participation of trained and experienced medical personnel, specifically of physicians and nurses, is in accordance with the AMA's opinion. To continue to prohibit the medical community from assisting during lethal injection executions would, in addition to possibly violating the U.S. Constitution, be contradictory to the public role of the physician, which remains "to [heal] the sick and [alleviate] suffering" (Black and Slade 2007). In fact, as a result of the current prohibition against physician involvement in lethal injection executions, lethal injections have been, in many instances, performed by inexperienced, untrained, and uneducated "lethal injection technicians," often leading to a number of unnecessary complications.

Complications Reported with Lethal Injection Executions Performed by Non-Medical Personnel

A number of lethal injection executions have been reported over the years, in which the execution was either performed incorrectly or the condemned was inadequately anesthetized or both, with either presumably leading to the sensation of pain. In fact, it has been reported that of the 1,054 lethal injection executions performed to date in the U.S., at least 40 of the executions entailed unexpected complications (Johnson 2008).

Dr. Mark Heath, an anesthesiologist, cites a lethal injection execution case in which the condemned individual, Mr. Diaz, was subjected to unnecessary physical pain as a result of an incorrectly performed execution (2008). Dr. Heath states:

> During Mr. Diaz's execution, both catheters were
> improperly positioned in extravascular locations in the
> soft tissues of his arms, and none of the administered
> drugs were delivered into the circulation. After failing

to deliver thiopental in Diaz's first arm, the executioners
administered a massive overdose of pancuronium into
his other arm. If the second intravenous catheter had
been functioning properly, Diaz's execution would have
appeared serene and humane... However, Diaz slowly
died of the gradual absorption of infiltrated thiopental,
pancuronium, and potassium. During a 34-minute interval,
he gasped "like a fish out of water" and gradually became still.

Dr. Heath concludes by noting that the pain and suffering endured by Mr. Diaz were, in fact, a direct result of the lack of experience and knowledge of the non-medical personnel that had performed the execution.

Similarly, Kevin Johnson, a Certified Registered Nurse Anesthetist (CRNA), describes an instance in which the condemned had experienced a number of unanticipated, adverse effects as a result of participation by inexperienced and untrained technicians (2008). Johnson recounts the execution of Mr. Clark, who was punctured repeatedly with a needle—reportedly, 22 attempts—in order to establish IV access. Following the administration of the three drugs, it was observed that Mr. Clark's arm was swelling noticeably. Mr. Clark, meanwhile, was fully conscious, stating repeatedly that the drugs were not working. Technicians then decided to re-establish IV access, requiring another 30 or so minutes. Mr. Clark was subsequently pronounced dead, following the total duration of 90 minutes, as opposed to the expected 10-15 minute time period (Kellaway 2003).

As suggested by the each of the discussed examples, had professional medical participation in the lethal injections executions been permitted, then perhaps the reported complications might not have arisen, thereby moderating or altogether eliminating the physical pain of the condemned.

Inadequate administration of one of the drugs in the three-drug regimen may also be classified as a lethal injection complication in which the condemned is inadequately anesthetized. For instance, in considering the effects of the neuromuscular blocking agent, the second of the three sequentially delivered drugs, which is meant to induce paralysis of the muscles, the resulting paralysis of the sentenced individual's limbs may mask inadequate initial anesthesia (Curfman, Morrissey, and Drazen 2008). Essentially, the condemned individual, ultimately in pain by the last step of the three-drug regimen, will be unable to convey his or her internal pain to the external world.

For this reason, then, in permitting physicians and IV-certified and -experienced healthcare providers to partake in lethal injection executions, priority must be given to anesthesiologists and CRNAs, the majority of whom possess both the knowledge and experience "to ensure [that] lethal injection is humane" (Johnson 2008). As execution by means of lethal injection requires the use of three—or, in some cases only one—anesthetic agent(s), lethal injection execution indirectly falls under the jurisdiction of anesthesiology (Johnson 2008).

Anesthesiologists, however, are specifically forbidden by the American Board of Anesthesiology (ABA), a division of the American Board of Medical Specialties, from partaking in any form of capital punishment, with the consequence being loss of board certification by the ABA (the American Board of Anesthesiology (ABA), Inc., 2010). Both nurses (including CRNAs) and remaining physicians are only strongly advised against participating in lethal injection executions by the American Nurses Association (ANA) and the AMA, respectively (Gawande 2006). If deemed necessary, however, either the ANA or the AMA may involve state licensing boards, in which case either the nurse's or physician's license, respectively, to practice in a given state may be revoked.

In the case of many physicians and nurses, however, though all are certainly IV-certified, most are not, in fact, IV-experienced, with the exception of most anesthesiologists and CRNAs (Johnson 2008). In addition to IV experience, anesthesia providers, both physicians and CRNAs, are well aware of both the pharmacodynamic and pharmacokinetic principles and the properties of the various drugs. For instance, non-anesthesia providers may not, as often is the case, be aware that, due to a precipitation reaction, sodium thiopental and pancuronium cannot be administered either simultaneously in a single syringe or directly sequentially through the IV without having flushed the IV (Johnson 2008).

The participation of IV-certified and -experienced medical professionals, specifically of anesthesiologists and CRNAs, may thus moderate, if not altogether eliminate, the pain entailed with lethal injection execution, thereby alleviating the suffering of the sentenced individual. Additionally, this participation by anesthesia providers may rectify any reported unconstitutionality claims associated with lethal injection executions.

Prior to elaborating on this argument and addressing the counter-arguments that may be posed, a brief history of execution by lethal injection, namely its development and the current drug regimen(s), may aid in understanding the basis behind lethal injection execution.

History of Execution by Lethal Injection and Current Drug Regimen(s)

Originally, lethal injection was proposed as a humane alternative to existing methods of execution, including electrocution, hanging, the gas chamber, and the firing squad (Kellaway 2003). Following a Supreme Court ruling in 1971 in *Furman v Georgia*, the aforementioned modes of execution were established to be unconstitutional, as they constituted "cruel and unusual punishment" (Lanier and Berge 2007). The existing modes of execution were found to be either too time-consuming or dangerous, in terms of the possible risks posed to the condemned (Johnson 2008). The death penalty was therefore revoked for a period of approximately five years, during which suitable, alternative modes of execution were being investigated.

Following this brief hiatus, the death penalty was reinstated by the Supreme Court in 1976 in *Gregg v Georgia*, prior to the development of the lethal injection (History of the Death Penalty 2010). Subsequently, execution by a three-drug regimen lethal injection was first developed by Jay Chapman, MD, later approved by Stanley Deutch, MD in 1977, and then first performed in Texas in 1982 (Denno 2007; Kellaway 2003).

After the introduction of lethal injection, Oklahoma became the first state to adopt it as its primary means of execution (Methods of Execution 2010). Since the first lethal injection execution in 1982, presently, of all 35 states that permit capital punishment, all list lethal injection as their primary mode of execution (Methods of Execution 2010). Of these states, 17 states require either direct or indirect physician participation (Zimmers and Lubarsky 2007). In comparison, few states still provide the condemned with the previous alternative modes of execution (Methods of Execution 2010).

According to the three-drug lethal injection regimen, three drugs are delivered sequentially via IV infusion. First, sodium thiopental, a short-acting barbiturate, is administered and is intended to sedate the sentenced individual (Koniaris et al. 2005). Administered next is a dose of pancuronium bromide, a neuromuscular blocker, intended to induce paralysis of the individual's bodily muscles, including those that are responsible for respiration (Koniaris et al. 2005). And, finally, a dose of potassium chloride is given, which is aimed to cease the cardiac function of the condemned (Koniaris et al. 2005).

Essentially in this regimen, it is the final dose of potassium that acts as the "executioner," while the administration of the former two drugs is intended to lead to, respectively, first insensitivity to pain and next paralysis of the muscles (Heath 2008). If solely potassium chloride were administered via IV, this dose alone would be excruciatingly painful, leading to uncontrollable chest pain and severe vascular irritation (Heath 2008). As such, this single dose would, in addition to violating the U.S. Constitution, fail to adhere to the goals of the Department of Corrections. Briefly, these goals include "death," "noncruelty," "avoiding unpleasant visual experiences for observers and staff," "rapidity," "preservation of staff anonymity," and "minimized psychological stress on staff" (Heath 2008). In returning to the purpose of each of the drugs in the three-drug regimen, the administration of sodium thiopental is absolutely crucial, as it prevents the sensation of pain entailed with subsequent potassium chloride administration (Heath 2008). Therefore, in this three-drug protocol, sodium thiopental serves the role of the anesthetic (Heath 2008).

Due to the reported complications associated with this three-drug regimen, a newer single-drug protocol was introduced, in which solely sodium thiopental is administered in excess (Methods of Execution 2010). In this method, sodium thiopental no longer serves the role as the anesthetic agent, as it produces death as a result of apnea (Heath 2008). In 2009, Ohio was the first state to legally adopt this single-drug lethal injection protocol in place of its original three-drug regimen (Methods of Execution 2010). The state of Washington, as of March, 2010, also approved this single-drug regimen; however, the condemned are still offered the option of the original three-drug protocol (Methods of Execution 2010).

In considering the discussed drug regimen(s), it must be delineated which drug(s) are applicable under the jurisdiction of a medical procedure. As Dr. Heath states regarding the initial dose of sodium thiopental, "Administration of general anesthesia, including the induction, maintenance, and continued assessment of anesthetic depth, is done to prevent severe pain; it is a therapeutic procedure and a medical procedure" (2008). The latter two drugs, however, intended to induce paralysis and cease cardiac function, respectively, are not administered "with therapeutic intent" and therefore are not technically medical procedures (Heath 2008). Execution by lethal injection is thus essentially an amalgamation of both medical and non-medical procedures.

Medical Involvement in Lethal Injection Executions

With lethal injection execution being classified as both a medical and non-medical procedure, the paradox thus remains as to why the medical community refuses to participate.

Proponents of the ancient Hippocratic Oath and leaders of medical associations such as the AMA and the ANA, among others, and select Board associations (namely, the ABA) believe the participation of physicians and medical personnel in lethal injection execution to be contrary to medical ethics. In reciting the ancient Hippocratic Oath, the physician vows "not to give a to give a lethal drug to anyone if [he] [is] asked, nor will [he] advise such a plan" (Greek medicine: the Hippocratic Oath 2002). Accordingly, the AMA incorporates this philosophy into its *Code of Medical Ethics*, specifically into Opinion 2.06 regarding capital punishment. It denotes the role of the physician by stating: "A physician, as a member of a profession dedicated to preserving life when there is hope of doing so, should not be a participant in a legally authorized execution" (AMA 2010). The AMA further defines physician participation, specifically in the case of lethal injection execution, by stating that any sort of physician involvement in lethal injection execution may be regarded as physician participation, excluding the ultimate certification of death of the condemned (AMA 2010). To date, this statement has only been incorporated by one Board association thus far: the ABA, which has announced that anesthesiologist participation in capital punishment may be punished with board certification suspension (ABA, Inc. 2010).

With regard to the original Hippocratic Oath, it may be important to note that the Oath has since been repeatedly rewritten and rephrased, as to accommodate changes in recent legislation. For instance, the modern Oath states that while the overall goal of the physician may be to save a life, the physician may also be required to take a life (Lasagna 1964). Presumably, it may be this version of the Oath that is applied to explain the controversy of abortion. As such, the AMA does note in its Code of Ethics that physicians are permitted to perform abortions. Again, however, a paradox emerges, as both lethal injection and abortion constitute the taking of a life. With regard to the anesthetic component of both procedures, in both instances, the anesthesia provider's ultimate goal would be to alleviate, or altogether eliminate, the physical pain of the individual.

Medical authorities continue to assert, however, that the role of the physician is to heal and not to harm. In speaking of lethal injection execution, however, the physician's role would be neither to heal nor to harm. Essentially, in this context, the physician's, or more specifically, the anesthesiologist's or CRNA's, role would be to alleviate the suffering of the individual. The anesthesiologist or CRNA would be preventing any unnecessary physical harm by participating in the procedure. When countered with the aforementioned point, opponents tend to argue that medical participation in capital punishment would equate medicine with death and execution, thereby tarnishing its reputation. However, if the ancient Hippocratic Oath could be amended and the Code of Ethics can be revised to accommodate legislation such as *Roe v Wade*, then it should likewise be applicable in the case of execution by lethal injection.

Similar to abortions, lethal injection executions are capable of being performed without direct physician or nurse involvement; however, the results, as discussed prior, would undoubtedly be calamitous, with the individual's health and safety at dire risk. True, in the instance of lethal injection executions, the condemned have been sentenced to death and therefore will undoubtedly die with or without medical assistance. However, as emphasized by Black and Sade (2007), "healing the sick and alleviating suffering is the primary role of physicians in U.S. society." Thus, it is not up to the physician to judge and discriminate which individuals deserve medical assistance and which might not. Furthermore, there are undoubtedly those that will argue that, in the instance of lethal injection executions, considering that the condemned might have committed some sort of heinous crime, he or she deserves to suffer. Again, however, physicians and healthcare professionals are not in a position to discriminate, as to do as such would be contrary to medical ethics.

In returning to the AMA's *Code of Medical Ethics*, specifically Opinion 2.06 regarding physical involvement in lethal injection execution, the AMA distinguishes that the role of the physician is to preserve life "when there is hope of doing so" (AMA 2010). In this specific instance, however, the fate of the condemned has already been determined by a separate governing body and therefore, the preservation of life by the medical community is not exactly feasible. At this point, the role of the anesthesia provider should be to alleviate the suffering of the condemned during the remaining moments prior to their execution. In this interpretation of the *Code*, physician and nurse participation would not therefore be in violation of modern medical ethics.

Conclusion

Medical involvement in lethal injection executions, specifically by anesthesiologists and CRNAs, should be permitted by governing medical authorities, including the ABA and the AMA, as to moderate, if not altogether eliminate, any physical pain that the condemned may otherwise suffer. Such participation by medical personnel would not be in direct conflict with the ABA's policy, as there is no hope of preserving life in this instance, in which the fate of the condemned has already been determined by the government.

In response to this assertion, the argument might then become that should the medical community "concede" to government mandates such as this, the physician will essentially be acting as a "tool of the government" (Waisel 2007). However, as differentiated by Dr. Waisel, "In this case, a physician is not acting as a tool of the government; he is acting as a physician whose goals temporarily align with the goals of the government" (2007). Even further, he delineates, "Although the outcome may be death, the act of the physician may be solely to provide comfort" (2007).

The current impasse between the U.S. Government and the medical community may thus be resolved by allowing physicians and nurses, specifically anesthesiologists and CRNAs, to participate in lethal injection executions, as to ensure the respectful and physically humane treatment of the condemned. Should such an agreement be unattainable, then it may perhaps be required that policymakers, and not physicians, devise a suitable alternative to the current mode of lethal injection execution that would not be said to conflict with the ethos of the medical profession.

Works Cited

American Board of Anesthesiology, Inc., The (2010). "Anesthesiology and Capital Punishment: Commentary." Raleigh, NC: ABA.

American Medical Association. (2010). *Code of Medical Ethics: Current Opinions with Annotations, 2010-2011.* Chicago: AMA.

Black, L. & Sade, R. M. (2007). "Lethal injection and physicians: state law vs. medical ethics." *JAMA,* 298(23), 2779-2701.

Curfman, G. D., Morrissey, S., & Drazen, J. M. (2008). "Physicians and execution." *NEJM,* 358(4), 403-4.

Denno, D. W. (2007). "The lethal injection quandary: how medicine has dismantled the death penalty." *Fordham Law Review,* 76(1), 49-128.

Gawande, A. (2006). "Perspective. When law and ethics collide – why physicians participate in executions. *NEJM,* 342(12), 1221-29.

Greek medicine: the Hippocratic Oath. (2002). U.S. National Library of Medicine. National Institutes of Health. Retrieved 8 October, 2010, from http://www.nlm.nih.gov/hmd/greek/greek_oath.html.

Heath, M. J. (2008). "Commentary. Revisiting physician involvement in capital punishment: medical and nonmedical aspects of lethal injection." *Mayo Clinical Proceedings,* 83(1), 113-23.

History of the Death Penalty. (2010). "Death Penalty Info." Death Penalty Information Center. Retrieved 8 October, 2010 from http://www.deathpenaltyinfo.org/part-i-history-death-penalty#const.

Johnson, K. W. (2008). "The medical-legal quandary of healthcare in capital punishment: an ethical dilemma for the anesthesia provider." *AANA,* 76(6), 417–19.

Kellaway, J. (2003). *The History of Torture and Execution.* Guilford, CT: Lyons Press.

Koniaris, L. G., Zimmers, T. A., Lubarksy, D. A., & Sheldon, J. P. (2005). "Inadequate anesthesia in lethal injection for execution." *The Lancet*, 365, 1412-14.

Lanier, W. L., & Berge, K. H. (2007). "Physician involvement in capital punishment: simplifying a complex calculus." *Mayo Clinical Proceedings*, 82(9), 1043-46.

Lasagna, L. (1964). The Hippocratic Oath: modern version. NOVA. Retrieved 8 October, 2010 from http://www.pbs.org/wgbh/nova/doctors/oath_modern.html.

Methods of Execution. (2010). "Death Penalty Info." Death Penalty Information Center. Retrieved 8 October, 2010 from http://www.deathpenaltyinfo.org/methods-execution.

Waisel, D. (2007). "Commentary. Physician participation in capital punishment." *Mayo Clinical Proceedings*, 82(9), 1073-80.

Zimmers, T. A. & Lubarsky, D. A. (2007). "Physician participation in lethal injection executions." *Current Opinion in Anesthesiology*, 20(2), 147–51.

Brian Zilberman

Niels Bohr: The Past, the Present and the Future of the Atomic Bomb

Before the invention of the atomic bomb at the end of WWII, never before had mankind achieved the potential for destruction as was possible with the advent of the bomb. The explosions above Hiroshima and later Nagasaki were the results of years of endless work from the brightest minds of the Allied Forces. The tremors that these explosions sent through Japan were mimicked by the shockwaves that reverberated throughout the scientific community; the twisted roads of a ravaged land represented the turns that human history had undergone. Only one man was central to every part of the existence and pre-existence of this weapon. From its theoretical conception, to its deployment in war and peace, Niels Bohr remained attached to this project spanning years and continents. Some of this connection had to do with his disposition to scientific thought; a large portion of it was pure fate, as in the case of his complex relationship with Werner Heisenberg and his escape from Nazi-occupied Denmark; and yet it seems so proper for Niels Bohr to be the force pushing for the bomb's use not for war, but peace after its invention. Having been involved in every step of this atomic revolution, Niels Bohr was one of few individuals who looked upon nuclear power as a new start for Western civilization as well as the probable cause of its destruction. Yet considering Bohr's upbringing as a curious, Danish boy, he seemed like the least likely candidate to take on the daunting task of becoming the international emissary for the nuclear revolution.

On October 7, 1885, Niels Henrik David Bohr was born into a rare, intellectual situation in Copenhagen. His father Christian Bohr was soon to become a renowned physiological professor, yet in Niels's life, his encouragement of curiosity within his children would serve a greater purpose. From the beginning Niels showed an immense talent for problem solving and technical work. His intelligence was only matched by his naïve kindness. An anecdote from Niels's childhood tells of a time when Niels was implored to tease his beloved brother Harold: the best he could do was conjure a remark about a stain on Harold's coat. Another story recounts the instance when Niels was prohibited from building a puppet theatre for his brother in his school woodworking class, so his father merely gave him a workbench and tools with which Niels was able to complete the gift for his brother and dearest friend. This workbench would also be the site of Niels's first work with metal, an interest that would persist throughout his life. The Bohr brothers, as they would come to be known in Denmark for their academic and athletic achievements, would often listen to the discussions held between their father, other professors at his institution and on occasion, artists and writers that came to stay at the Bohr residence during their time in Copenhagen. Niels's parents carefully cultivated an intellectual environment in which he could grow and at the time Copenhagen was a major center for progressive thought in all areas, ranging from physics to art. From his start at the Gammelholm School and into his tenure at the University of Copenhagen, Niels Bohr showed his unbelievable abilities in physics and mathematics. Though from his future contributions it is easy to infer the quality of intellect that Bohr possessed, in some ways it is more important to comprehend the kind nature, which he also possessed, that affected his later opinion on atomic weaponry, as well as understand his ability to bridge the gap between scientific findings of different national sources because "Denmark with its proximity to Germany and its ties with England was in an advantageous position to appreciate the work in both countries" (Moore 18). This balance would be essential for Bohr's future success in determining atomic structure, especially during his time in Cambridge (Moore 6-19).

Bohr's chance to jump into a larger scientific pond as the proclaimed "big fish" of Copenhagen came in 1911 when he came to Cambridge to work with Joseph John Thomson and Rutherford. Thomson did little more than ignore Bohr's original work on atomic structure, not getting around to reading it, yet submitted it to a scientific publication which in the end never published the article due to its verbosity. Rutherford, on the other hand, was just the mind that Bohr needed to pick in order to nail down the loose ends of his theories. Years earlier, Rutherford had conducted experiments in which he shot alpha particles at atoms. The prevailing notion was that if atoms were composed of free space, the alpha particles would pass through unhindered and reach a zinc sulfide screen. Yet when Rutherford closely examined the screen, he noticed many particles that deflected from the straight-line path and some that had been reflected back altogether. Rutherford was thoroughly perplexed as to what could cause high speed particles to be reflected backwards. He came to the conclusion that in the center of atoms exists a solid nucleus which constitutes most of the mass of the atom. This model proposed that electrons existed outside of this nucleus. Upon meeting, Bohr and Rutherford took a liking to one another and it was not long before Bohr had joined Rutherford's research team in Manchester. Bohr flourished under Rutherford's watch and even helped his superior arrive at an explanation for chemical properties that Bohr had developed previously. Bohr watched as others were praised for theories he had independently worked out, yet this did not discourage the Dane from his work. Bohr's breakthrough came in a far-reaching revelation. He proceeded to explain to Rutherford that his theoretical model for the atom involved electrons inhabiting discrete energy levels like perfect circles around the nucleus and that each of these energy levels could contain a maximum of seven electrons. As an electron was added to an atom, it became a different element and as each energy level was filled, a new energy level was formed around the previously filled level. In his excitement, Bohr stated that the electron systems of each atom accounted for its various properties and that molecules and compounds were only formed between elements with compatible electron systems or configurations. Overall he sought, "...a possible explanation of the periodic law of the chemical properties of the elements by help of the atom-model in question" (Bohr in Moore 45). This work set the way for quantum mechanics and the theoretical existence of nuclear fission. In a lecture 20 years later, Bohr described this as "inducing transmutations of elements by bombardment with high-speed heavy particles which, in colliding with the nuclei, may cause their disintegration" (*Atomic Physics and Human Knowledge* 16-17). The process by which fission would be carried out across the Atlantic also happened to be the centerpiece for the experiment that led to Bohr's rationalization of atomic structure. In this way, Bohr's main body of work, for which he won a Nobel Prize and is remembered to this day, is inextricably tied to the nuclear fission that powered the explosions in Japan some 30 years later in the final blows of WWII (Moore 31-45).

Leading up to the onset of WWII, Bohr spent a majority of his time at his institute in Copenhagen. His work included furthering the scientific inquiries of his past as well as pursuing new and more theoretical ideas in physics, such as his respected theory of complementarity. During this time, Copenhagen and Bohr's institute in specific welcomed many foreign physicists such as Werner Heisenberg, the architect of the uncertainty principle, with whom Bohr made a very strong connection. Copenhagen rightfully seemed to be a major source of innovation in the field of physics. As always, Bohr remained loyal to his birthplace. Though Niels Bohr had expounded on the applications of the atomic structure for energy utilization, he remained wholly outside the loop of the select few who pursued such an end. When war in Europe broke out, Bohr and his institute served as a refuge for fleeing scientists. Though a Jew himself, Bohr resolved to stay in Copenhagen, always aware of the presence of a possible German invasion. In 1941, Bohr's one-time pupil and friend Heisenberg returned to Copenhagen for a controversial visit. Bohr was a staunch opponent of the Nazis and since the start of the war Heisenberg had been put in charge of the German atomic effort. These one-time friends were now on opposite sides of the largest struggle in human history. Though the exact exchange that occurred in this meeting is unknown, Bohr's account is very clear in a set of letters addressed to Heisenberg. In a book by Robert Jungk, Heisenberg sought to explain that he was not a supporter of the Nazi regime and did his best to sabotage Hitler's efforts of obtaining atomic weapons; Bohr seems to have a vividly different memory of their meeting. In one of many letters to Heisenberg Bohr says to his one-time friend, "I am greatly amazed to see how much your memory has deceived you... you and Weizsacker expressed your definite conviction that Germany would win and that it was therefore quite foolish for us to maintain the hope of a different outcome... under your leadership, everything was being done in Germany to develop atomic weapons" (*Niels Bohr Archive* Document 1). Heisenberg also claimed that he had stunned Bohr with the revelation that atomic weaponry was a realistic possibility, to which Bohr wrote to him saying, "From the day three years earlier when I realized slow neutrons could only cause fission in Uranium 235 and not 238, it was of course obvious to me that a bomb with certain effect could be produced... In June 1939 I had even given a public lecture in Birmingham... where I talked about the effects of such a bomb" (*Niels Bohr Archive* Document 1). It seems that in the postwar years, Heisenberg's sole objective was to clear himself of any association with the Nazis and have his legacy remain untarnished. This meeting resulted in a fracture in their relationship that would never truly be fixed and though Bohr later sent Heisenberg a kind birthday message on the latter's 60th birthday, it still mentioned that he had not forgotten all that had passed between them. For no other reason than their previous connection did Heisenberg share Germany's atomic plans with Bohr, and it was Bohr's first realization that countries engaged in combat were now utilizing his theories to create the world's first atomic bomb.

Finally in 1943 when it came to Bohr's attention that his arrest was inevitable, Bohr decided to flee to Sweden and ultimately England to aid in the development of atomic weaponry for the Allied Forces. He brought with him the information shared by Heisenberg as well as his years of experience and discovery concerning atoms, the sole reason he was so closely watched after by the British government. His previous work on atoms secured his and his family's freedom. His family, except for his son Aage, was to remain in Sweden for the duration of the war. While being dramatically flown to London in the bomb-bay of a Mosquito, Bohr passed out and only survived the flight because the pilot had inferred from the lack of response that Bohr was suffering from oxygen deprivation and lowered the plane. The reason for his near-death experience: the intercom headset was too small for Bohr, so he did not hear instructions to don his oxygen mask; in a way, Bohr's enormous mind almost killed him. Bohr became fully involved in the British atomic project named "Tube Alloys" and later was part of the team transferred to continue work at Los Alamos in the U.S. Throughout the building process, Bohr was referenced whenever the team hit a roadblock due to his vast theoretical knowledge of atoms as well as his technical knowledge of metals due to his metal-working days. He served as an encyclopedia and work manual for some of the greatest minds struggling to end a bloody war. Upon its completion, the atomic bomb came to represent a tangible product of the theoretical work Bohr had been carrying out since his days at the University of Copenhagen almost 35 years before that day (Rozental 191-197).

It took the genius of Bohr to help complete the bomb for the Allies, but even more importantly it took his genuine kindness to look upon it as more than a killing machine, as the impetus for peace between the United States and the Soviet Union. Bohr believed sharing the atomic bomb and its technology with the Soviet Union would create a pact between the two superpowers. In good faith, the nations would prevent nuclear proliferation and usher in an era of postwar peace. He wanted more than anything to avoid, in his words long before the term became popular, a nuclear "arms race" (Rozental 198). His involvement in every step of the bomb's existence up until its detonation, gave Bohr an almost prophetic insight. Using his contacts, much like in the way Einstein was used to reach the President, Bohr obtained a meeting with Roosevelt. The president was open to the idea of sharing the atom bomb with the Soviet Union and Bohr was once again sent to England to discuss this with Winston Churchill. Unfortunately, Churchill was so opposed to Bohr's idea of openness with the communist nation, that he not only disregarded his proposal, but also made sure Bohr was kept under watch. This effectively ended Bohr's effort to establish an international nuclear pact. Though he remained involved with many international organizations and wrote an open letter to the United Nations, Bohr could not accomplish his hopes of averting a future clouded by the threat of nuclear war. It was his strongest desire that the materialization of his life's work not merely become the play toy of warring nations (Rozental 198-214).

It seems only fitting that the man whose theories made the creation of the atomic bomb possible was one of the few in his time to see the potential it contained. Far beyond the Joules of energy released and the miles of destruction caused, Niels Bohr's unique position as the companion of the atomic bomb from its conception to detonation allowed him to see the world its existence would go on to create. Bohr was always the purveyor of this scientific revolution which still shapes our world.

Works Cited

Bohr, Niels, and Margrethe Bohr. "Document Release. Title Page." *Niels Bohr Archive*. Trans. Felicity Pors and Finn Aaserud. 6 Feb. 2002. Web. 12 Nov. 2010. <http://www. nba.nbi.dk.html>.

Bohr, Niels. *Atomic Physics and Human Knowledge*. New York: Wiley, 1958. Print.

Moore, Ruth E. *Niels Bohr, the Man, His Science & the World They Changed*. Cambridge, MA: MIT, 1985. Print.

Rozental, S., ed. *Niels Bohr: His Life and Work as Seen by His Friends and Colleagues*. Amsterdam: Sole Distributors for the U.S.A. and Canada, Elsevier Science Pub., 1985. Print.

First Place – Graduate

Kate Sherlock

No Such Thing as a Free Lunch: Why the 2010 Healthy, Hunger-Free Kids Act Fails to Make the Grade

Introduction

For the first time in over 200 years, children in the United States have a shorter predicted life expectancy than their parents.[1] Since the late 1970s, obesity rates for adults and children have risen steadily; currently, over one-third of American children are overweight or obese.[2] Obesity increases a child's risk of developing a chronic disease, such as type 2 diabetes, heart disease, high blood pressure, cancer, and asthma.[3] In addition, obese children have a 70% chance of being overweight or obese as adults.[4] While many Americans do not consider obesity a fatal disease, the first, second, and third leading causes of death in US adults–heart disease, cancer, and stroke–are all obesity-associated diseases.[4] Not surprisingly, obesity-related healthcare spending totals $147 billion annually, a 350% increase in spending since 1998.[6]

---

[1] Pam Belluck, *Children's Life Expectancy Being Cut Short by Obesity*, N.Y. TIMES, Mar. 17, 2005, http://www.nytimes.com/2005/03/17/health/17obese.html; *see also* TASK FORCE ON CHILDHOOD OBESITY, SOLVING THE PROBLEM OF CHILDHOOD OBESITY WITHIN A GENERATION 3 (2010) [hereinafter TASK FORCE OBESITY REPORT], available at http://www.letsmove.gov/pdf/ TaskForce_on_Childhood_Obesity_May2010_FullReport.pdf.

[2] Belluck, *supra* note 1; *see also* TASK FORCE OBESITY REPORT, *supra* note 1, at 4.

[3] Belluck, *supra* note 1; *see also* TASK FORCE OBESITY REPORT, *supra* note 1, at 4 (indicating that one third of all children born in the year 2000 are expected to develop diabetes during their lifetime).

[4] TASK FORCE OBESITY REPORT, *supra* note 1, at 3.

[5] *Id.*

[6] *Childhood Obesity- 2009 Update of Legislative Policy Options*, NATIONAL CONFERENCE OF STATE LEGISLATURES (Jan. 2010), http://www.ncsl.org/default.aspx?TabId=19776; *see also* TASK FORCE OBESITY REPORT, *supra* note 1, at 3.

Scientists point to numerous behavioral and environmental factors for the recent spike in childhood obesity rates, including increased "screen time," decreased physical activity, junk food advertisements, and the abundance of cheap, processed foods and snacks available at school and at home.[7] As a result, "the diets of most American children do not come close to meeting nutritional recommendations."[8]

Recognizing the serious consequences of childhood obesity, Congress recently passed the 2010 Healthy, Hunger-Free Kids Act,[9] which attempts to combat childhood obesity by improving nutrition standards for all foods sold in schools, strengthening nutrition education, and increasing the federal meal reimbursement rate for the National School Lunch Program (NSLP).[10] While the Healthy, Hunger-Free Kids Act represents a significant improvement in the NSLP, it fails to provide adequate support for implementing the changes necessary to "solve the problem of childhood obesity within a generation."[11]

This essay evaluates the strengths and weaknesses of the Healthy, Hunger-Free Kids Act and provides recommendations for improving the NSLP. Part I provides a brief history of the NSLP and its relationship with U.S. agricultural policy. Part II discusses the role of the U.S. Department of Agriculture (USDA) in shaping the American diet, focusing on the impact of corn subsidies and the conflict of interest present in permitting the USDA to oversee both agricultural and nutrition policy. Part III analyzes the Healthy, Hunger-Free Kids Act and concludes that in order to properly effectuate

---

[7] TASK FORCE OBESITY REPORT, *supra* note 1, at 6-7 (defining screen time as time spent watching television, playing computer games, or video games); *see also* MARION NESTLE, FOOD POLITICS, 175-76 (Darra Goldstein ed., University of California Press 2007) ("Children eat one out of every three meals outside of the home where foods are demonstrably higher in calories, fat, saturated fat, and salt, as well as lower in more desirable nutrients.")

[8] NESTLE, *supra* note 7 at 175.

[9] Pub. L. No. 111–296, 124 Stat. 3183 (2010).

[10] U.S. DEP'T OF AGRIC., NATIONAL SCHOOL LUNCH PROGRAM (2011), http://www.fns.usda.gov/cnd/lunch/AboutLunch/NSLPFactSheet.pdf (providing nutritious, free or low-cost meals to school children throughout the United States).

[11] *See America's Move to Raise a Healthier Generation of Kids*, LET'S MOVE!, http://www.letsmove.gov/about.php (last visited Mar. 8, 2011).

the goals of the Act, Congress must stop undermining nutrition policy by subsidizing processed food.

Part I: History of the National School Lunch Program

In 1966, Congress passed the Child Nutrition Act to combat malnourishment and hunger by providing school districts with cash subsidies, commodity foods for each meal served, and bonus commodities from agricultural surplus.[12] The Act constituted an important step in combating domestic hunger and establishing national nutrition standards for public and parochial schools.[13] The USDA established nutrition guidelines, food equivalency charts, and healthy menus, but it was up to local school administrators to manage day-to-day operations.[14] Determining which children were "needy" under the Act was left to the states, resulting in varied income qualifications across the country.[15] In some states, children on welfare qualified for free lunch, whereas other states disqualified such children because school officials believed that "parents who received welfare could afford to pay for lunch."[16] The NSLP soon came under attack by nutrition professionals and child health advocates—many blamed the USDA for the program's deficiencies, claiming "a department which has as its main aim the improvement of agriculture and the lot of the farmer suffers a conflict of interests when its second duty is to feed the poor."[17]

When President Nixon took office in 1969, he promised to improve the NSLP by increasing spending for food and nutrition expansion programs.[18]

---

[12] SUSAN LEVINE, SCHOOL LUNCH POLITICS 113 (2008); see also Clint G. Salisbury, Make an Investment in Our School Children: Increase the Nutritional Value of School Lunch Programs, 2004 BYU EDUC.. & L.J. 331, 334 (2004).

[13] LEVINE, supra note 12, at 113.

[14] Id. at 116.

[15] Id.

[16] Id. at 118 (citing Hearings to Amend the District of Columbia Public School Food Service Act, 90th Cong., 8 (1968)).

[17] Id. at 111 (quoting nutritionist Michael Latham).

[18] Id. at 153. (From 1969 to 1975, nutrition assistance program budgets, including the NSLP, increased from less than $500 million to over $8 billion.)

Unfortunately, Nixon's plan backfired after Gerald Ford cut funding in 1975, which forced schools to raise prices for paying students to compensate for lost funds, resulting in decreased overall participation.[19] Unable to effectively provide meals to all school children at a low-cost without additional federal funding, many schools turned to the commercial food-service industry.[20]

Once private industry entered the lunchroom, the USDA was forced to relax nutrition standards.[21] An amendment to the school lunch reauthorization bill lifted the restriction on competitive foods, permitting schools to sell competitive candy bars, soda and chips during lunch.[22] The Amendment was widely criticized for increasing private profits "at the expense of children's eating habits."[23] Despite nutritionist warnings, schools embraced convenience foods and the additional revenue they provided.[24]

Part II: How the USDA Shaped the American Diet

Corn Country

Following WWII, farm production shot up after farmers began using chemical fertilizer.[25] The federal government capitalized on this overproduction by selling surplus crops to foreign countries for a profit.[26] Unfortunately, increased foreign demand combined with a poor domestic harvest resulted

---

[19] *Id.* at 154.

[20] *Id.* at 158.

[21] *See id.*

[22] *Id.* at 162.

[23] *Id.* (quoting Jack Anderson, *New York Times* columnist.)

[24] *Id.* at 163 ("[W]ithin a few years, at least one-quarter of all middle schools and 42 percent of all high schools regularly sold soda and candy, and by the end of the century 43 percent of elementary, 74 percent of middle schools, and 98 percent of senior high schools had contracts with vending machine companies and soft drink distributors.").

[25] Jodi Soyars Windham, *Putting Your Money Where Your Mouth Is: Peverse Food Subsidies, Social Responsibility & America's 2007 Farm Bill,* 31 ENVIRONS: ENVTL. L. & POL'Y J. 1, 7 (2007) (noting that farmers used ammonium nitrate as chemical fertilizer, an ingredient used to make explosives during the war).

[26] In 1972, Richard Nixon arranged a sale of 30 million tons of American grain to Russia. *Id.* at 9.

in skyrocketing food prices.[27] Facing a consumer revolt, President Nixon and Secretary of Agriculture Earl Butz re-engineered the American farm system "to drive down prices and encourage farmers to vastly increase their output. The goal was to provide plenty of cheap food for Americans to eat at home while permitting America to capitalize on the food surpluses by selling abroad."[28] Under the 1973 Farm Bill, the New Deal's non-recourse loans were replaced with direct deficiency payments.[29] In promising to pay farmers a target price for a bushel of corn when prices are weak, the government "removed the floor under the new price of grain. Instead of keeping corn out, the new subsidies encouraged farmers to sell their corn at any price, since the government would make up the difference."[30] Butz advised farmers to "plant their fields 'fencerow to fencerow' and advised them to 'get big or get out.'"[31]

While Butz's plan successfully maintained commodity prices in the 1970s due to foreign market demand, prices plummeted in the 1980s due to a world recession and high interest rates.[32] The entire world could not absorb the American corn surplus and the U.S. government was forced to bail out American farmers yet again.[33]

In the 1990s, Republicans advocated to eliminate crop subsidies and switch to a free-market system.[34] In an effort to wean farmers off crop subsidies, Congress passed the Freedom to Farm Act, which provided farmers with fixed

---

[27] Id. See also MICHAEL POLLAN, OMNIVORE'S DILEMMA 51 (2006) (discussing how the inflation rate for food had reached an "all-time high").

[28] Windham, supra note 25, at 9.

[29] Id. at 10.

[30] POLLAN, supra note 27, at 52; see also Windham, supra note 25, at 10 ("The payment amount farmers received was directly linked to the farmer's yield so the more the farmer produced the more subsidies he received.").

[31] POLLAN, supra note 27, at 52. Butz also encouraged farmers to refer to themselves as "agribusinessmen." Id.

[32] Windham, supra note 25, at 11.

[33] Id. ("Direct payments to farmers went from an average of $3 billion a year in the 1970s to $26 billion a year by 1986.").

[34] Id. at 11.

income support payments that phased out over the course of seven years.[35] Shortly after passing the Act, commodity prices fell, "farmers panicked and Congress abandoned its plans to deregulate the agricultural economy."[36] In 1998, Congress returned to traditional farming policies and increased subsidy payments by 50%.[37]

The 2002 Farm Bill allocated $89.7 billion in commodity subsidies, "reposition[ing] U.S. Agribusiness as America's largest corporate welfare recipient . . . ."[38] While payment-based subsidies for commodity crops have drawn recent criticism for rising obesity rates, Congress avoided overhauling agricultural policies and passed the Food, Conservation, and Energy Act of 2008, "which kept many of the provisions of the 2002 Act unchanged."[39]

Convenience at a Cost

Commodity subsidies have dramatically changed the way Americans eat by encouraging farmers to shift from biologically diverse crops to commodities: "[a] century ago the typical Iowa farm raised more than a dozen different plant and animal species: cattle, chickens, corn, hogs, apples, hay, oats, potatoes, cherries, wheat, plums, grapes, and pears. Now it raises only two: corn and soybeans."[40] Michael Pollan, bestselling author of *Omnivore's Dilemma* and

---

[35] *Id.* at 12. The Act was designed to save a projected 56.6 billion dollars over seven years. *Id.*

[36] *Id.* at 12 (citing David Hosansky, *Farm Subsidies: Do They Favor Large Farming Operations?*, 12 CQ RES., May 17, 2002, at 435.

[37] *Id.* at 12. Following Congress' return to traditional farming policy, "the "Freedom to Farm Act" became known as the "Freedom to Fail" Act. *Id.*

[38] *Id.* at 12.

[39] Charlene C. Kwan, *Fixing The Farm Bill: Using the "Permanent Provisions" in Agricultural Law to Achieve WTO Compliance*, 36 B.C. ENVTL. AFF. L. REV. 571, 586-87 (2009).

[40] MICHAEL POLLAN, IN DEFENSE OF FOOD 116 (2008); *see also* Windham, *supra* note 25, at 14 (noting that corn farmers received the most support under the Bill, 46% of total commodity subsidies from 2002-2005. Under the 2002 Farm Bill, however, subsidies are unavailable for fruits, vegetables, and most organic crops).

In Defense of Food, claims obesity is a product of the industrialized western diet, "a food system organized around the objective of selling large quantities of calories as cheaply as possible."[41] Industrial agriculture, combined with government-subsidized commodities, has resulted in cheaper food, bigger portions, and increased calorie consumption.[42] On average, Americans are consuming 300 additional empty calories per day than they consumed in 1985.[43] This "quantity-over-quality" diet has created the ultimate nutritional paradox: overfed, yet undernourished people.[44]

Simplifying the American agricultural landscape to two main crops has created a diet that mainly consists of processed foods made from reassembled corn and soy.[45] As Pollan points out, "the big money has always been in processing foods, not selling them whole,"[46] which makes corn and soy every food manufacturer's dream—they're "storable, portable, fungible" and (most importantly) cheap.[47] Farmers sell corn to food manufacturers for a price below cost; food manufacturers then "add value" by breaking down the

---

[41] POLLAN, *supra* note 40, at 161 (2008). Pollan has been labeled the "designated repository for the nation's food conscience" by Frank Bruni, *The New York Times*, and "one of the most respectable voices in the modern debate about food," by Tristram Stuart, *Financial Times*.

[42] *Id.* at 122. ("Since 1980, American farmers have produced an average of 600 more calories per person per day . . .").

[43] *Id.* ("The overwhelming majority of the calories Americans have added to their diets since 1985—the 93 percent of them in the form of sugars, fats, and mostly refined grains—supply lots of energy but very little of anything else.").

[44] *Id.* at 122-23 (finding that historic deficiency diseases, such as rickets, affect obese children who "subsist on fast food rather than fresh fruits and vegetables and drink more soda than milk . . . ."); *see also* TASK FORCE OBESITY REPORT, *supra* note 1, at 61.

[45] POLLAN, *supra* note 40, at 117.

[46] *Id.* at 111; *see also* NESTLE, *supra* note 7, at 17 (noting that producers of raw foods receive only a fraction of the price that consumers pay at the supermarket, approximately 20% of the retail cost. The remaining 80% of the food dollar goes for labor, packaging, advertising, or other such value-enhancing activities).

[47] Windham, *supra* note 25, at 10; *see also* POLLAN, *supra* note 40, at 117-18.

grain, removing the fiber and micronutrients, adding sugar, fat, and flavoring, packaging the new product and advertising it as "food."[48]

While the modern American supermarket carries over 47,000 different products, the majority of them are simply processed corn products.[49] By subsidizing corn and soy, the government has effectively lowered the cost of junk food, which explains why a Big Mac costs less than a salad.[50] Unfortunately, many Americans cannot afford to purchase "nutrient-dense" foods (fresh produce, lean meats, and whole grains), and instead rely on "energy-dense" foods (high-calorie, cheap processed foods).[51] Energy-dense foods provide cheaper calories; "[a]s long as the healthier lean meats, fish, and fresh produce are more expensive, obesity will continue to be a problem for the working poor."[52]

Part III: The Healthy, Hunger-Free Kids Act

Taking Action

In February 2009, Michelle Obama launched the "Let's Move!" campaign, an initiative geared toward tackling obesity by improving food in schools,

---

[48] *See* POLLAN, *supra* note 40, at 117-19; NESTLE, *supra* note 7, at 17-19.

[49] FOOD, INC. (Magnolia Pictures 2008) ("Corn products include ketchup, cheese, Twinkies, batteries, peanut butter, Cheez-Its, salad dressings, Coke, jelly, Sweet & Low, syrup, juice, Kool-Aid, charcoal, diapers, Motrin, meat and fast food.").

[50] David Leonhardt, *What's Wrong With This Chart?*, N.Y. TIMES (MAY 20, 2009), http://economix.blogs.nytimes.com/2009/05/20/whats-wrong-with-this-chart/ ("Relative to the price of everything else in the economy, sodas are 33 percent cheaper than they were in 1978. Butter is 29 percent cheaper. Beer is 15 percent cheaper. Fish is 2 percent more expensive. Vegetables are 41 percent more expensive. Fruits are 46 percent more expensive.").

[51] Tom Philpott, *How the Feds Make Bad-For-You Food Cheaper than Healthful Fare*, GRIST (Feb. 26, 2006), http:www.grist.org/article/phipott7/ ("For energy-dense, think of a package of Ding Dongs -- 360 calories, 19 grams of fat, and a liberal dose of high-fructose corn syrup. For nutrient-dense, think of a three-ounce chunk of wild salmon, delivering high-quality protein and essential fatty acids, among other nutrients, in a 185-calorie package.").

[52] *Id.* (quoting Adam Drewnowski, professor of epidemiology at the University of Washington).

providing nutrition education to children and food service operators, and increasing physical activity.[53] The goal? To reduce the rate of childhood obesity from 31% to 5% by the year 2030.[54] In support of "Let's Move," President Obama created the first Task Force on Childhood Obesity, to review existing national child nutrition programs and develop an action plan in support of the First Lady's initiative.[55] In May 2010, the Task Force issued their recommendation report for improving the school nutrition environment, including "updat[ing] federal nutritional standards for school meals, improv[ing] the nutritional quality of USDA commodities provided to schools, and increas[ing] resources for school meals."[56]

Seven months after receiving the Task Force report, President Obama signed into law the Healthy, Hunger-Free Kids Act. The purpose of the Act is to combat childhood obesity and hunger by increasing federal funding for qualifying students and increasing the number of students eligible for the NSLP. With over 31 million children receiving meals through the federal lunch program, "schools often are on the front lines of our national challenge to combat childhood obesity and improve children's overall health."[57]

---

[53] *America's Move to Raise a Healthier Generation of Kids*, LET'S MOVE!, http://www.letsmove.gov/about.php (last visited Mar. 8, 2011) (defining the initiative's purpose as "solving the problem of obesity within a generation, so that children born today will grow up healthier and able to pursue their dreams.").

[54] *Id.* at 9.

[55] *White House Task Force on Childhood Obesity Report to the President*, LET'S MOVE!, http://www.letsmove.gov/obesitytaskforce.php (last visited Mar. 8, 2011) ("The goal of the action plan is to reduce the childhood obesity rate to just five percent by 2030 – the same rate before childhood obesity first began to rise in the late 1970s.").

[56] TASK FORCE OBESITY REPORT, *supra* note 1, at 39-42.

[57] *Child Nutrition Reauthorization: Healthy, Hunger-Free Kids Act of 2010*, Let's Move! (2010), http://www.whitehouse.gov/sites/default/files/Child_Nutrition_Fact_Sheet_12_10_10.pdf

The Good

The Healthy, Hunger-Free Kids Act reauthorizes child nutrition programs and provides $4.5 billion dollars in new funding over the next ten years, the first increase in federal reimbursement for school lunches in over 30 years.[58] The Act authorizes the USDA to issue new nutrition guidelines for meals served in the school cafeteria, including snacks found in vending machines and a la carte items.[59] In addition, the Act establishes a monitoring and reporting system to improve school compliance with nutrition guidelines.[60]

Under the existing school nutrition standards, schools must comply with federal nutrition requirements set forth in the 1995 Nutrition Standards and Meal Requirements to receive federal reimbursements.[61] In 2009, the Institute of Medicine released recommendations updating the meal patterns for the NSLP to make them consistent with the 2005 Dietary Guidelines for Americans. The USDA is expected to implement IOM's recommendations over the next eighteen months. Updated nutritional guidelines will significantly increase the quality of school meals by requiring increased portions of fruits, vegetables, and whole grains, while limiting sodium and calories in the meal.[62] IOM's recommendations include, but are not limited to, serving only skim or 1% plain milk, requiring green vegetables and whole grains, limiting starchy vegetables, and capping calories and sodium.[63]

---

[58] *Id.*

[59] *Id.* at 2.

[60] *Id.*

[61] *Id.* See also *The Healthy, Hunger-Free Kids Act of 2010 Fact Sheet*, NEW ENGLAND ALLIANCE FOR CHILDREN'S HEALTH (2010), http://www.childrenshealthne.org/assets/pdfs/CNRFactSheet.pdf (indicating that the federal government reimburses schools $2.68 per lunch per student for students who qualify for a free lunch).

[62] *See generally School Meals: Building Blocks for Healthy Children*, INSTITUTE OF MEDICINE (Oct. 2009), http://www.iom.edu/Reports/2009/School-Meals-Building-Blocks-for-Healthy-Children.aspx.

[63] *Id.*

The Bad

While proponents of the Act claim it increases child nutrition spending without increasing the deficit, Congress funded the Healthy, Hunger-Free Kids Act with Supplemental Nutrition Assistance Program (SNAP) funds. Unfortunately, many children who receive free lunches under the NSLP also receive assistance under SNAP. Nancy Rice, School Nutrition Association President, has criticized the source of funding, stating, "[I]n the effort to raise 'Healthy, Hunger-Free Kids' we don't want to risk compromising their dinner to improve their lunch."[64] Shifting funds from one federal nutrition-assistance program to another is not a permanent solution and is, in essence, robbing Peter to pay Paul.

The Act also requires schools to annually raise meal prices for students who do not qualify for the federal school lunch program.[65] Historically, raising school lunch prices has had a negative effect on the NSLP.[66] Two-thirds of the meals served under the NSLP are free or reduced-price meals, which means that raising meal prices indefinitely is unsustainable "because the burden is disproportionally borne by the pupils who buy the one-third of meals sold at full price."[67] Significant price increases could lead to decreased participation, resulting in insufficient funding for the program.

---

[64] Diane Pratt-Heavner, *SNA Commends Senate Passage of Child Nutrition Reauthorization; But Calls on House to Make Critical Changes to the Bill*, SCHOOL NUTRITION ASS'N, (Aug. 5, 2010), http://www.schoolnutrition.org/Blog. aspx?id=14263&blogid=564.

[65] Pub. L. No. 111–296, § 205, 124 Stat. 3183, 3218-19 (2010). Effective July 1, 2011, school nutrition programs will be required to charge students an increased price that is on average equal to the difference between free meal reimbursement and paid meal reimbursement.

[66] In the mid 70's, school lunch prices soared after President Food cut the School Lunch Program Budget. As a result, approximately 1 million paying children dropped out of the program. See LEVINE, supra note 12, at 154.

[67] Alex Johnson, *Some schools cut lunch options for kids who struggle to pay*, MSNBC, http://www.msnbc.msn.com/id/41631002/ns/health-diet_and_nutrition (last visited Mar. 8, 2011).

Schools that comply with the new federal nutrition guidelines will receive a 6-cent reimbursement increase per student/per meal; however, adhering to the new guidelines, which requires increasing whole grains, lean meats, and fresh fruits and vegetables, could cost schools an additional 11 to 25 cents per student/per meal.[68] The government continues to undermine its own federal nutrition policies by subsidizing the corn and soy industries.[69] As Pollan explains:

> We write checks to farmers for every bushel of corn and soy they can grow, and partly as a result they grow vast quantities of the stuff, driving down the cost of the processed foods we make from those commodities. In effect, we're subsidizing high-fructose corn syrup. And we're not subsidizing the growing of carrots and broccoli. Put another way, our tax dollars are the reason that the cheapest calories in the market are the least healthy ones.[70]

Until the government eliminates surplus commodity subsidies, unhealthy processed foods will continue to be the most affordable option for the majority of school lunch programs working with a limited budget.

Rather than shifting funds from SNAP, or requiring paying students to subsidize the program, Congress should eliminate commodity crop subsidies and devote a portion of such funds to support the Healthy, Hunger-Free Kids Act. This would provide adequate funding to increase the federal reimbursement rate to 18 cents per meal, in addition to correcting the cost imbalance between healthy calories and unhealthy calories—"so that it becomes rational for someone with little to spend on food to buy the carrots instead of the cookies, the orange juice instead of the Sprite."[71]

---

[68] Peter Eisler, *Sweeping school lunch bill clears Senate panel*, USA TODAY, Mar. 25, 2010, http://www.usatoday.com/news/education/2010-03-24-school-lunch-safety_N.htm

[69] According to the *American Journal of Clinical Nutrition*, a dollar can buy 1,200 calories of potato chips or 875 calories of soda, but just 250 calories of vegetables or 170 calories of fresh fruit. Andrew Drewnowski & SE Spector, *Poverty and Obesity: The Role of Energy Density and Energy Costs, in* 79 AM. J. CLIN. NUTR. 1, at 9.

[70] Micahel Pollan, *Why Eating Well is Elitist*, ON THE TABLE, (May 11, 2006), http://michaelpollan.com/articles-archive/why-eating-well-is-elitist/

[71] *Id.*

The Ugly

While the Healthy, Hunger-Free Kids Act requires the USDA to evaluate and update federal nutrition guidelines, the Act fails to remedy the underlying conflict of interest present in having one department responsible for administering agricultural programs, protecting the interests of farmers and food manufactures, in addition to "overseeing all government-sponsored nutrition programs and . . . ensuring that the public-health interests attendant to such programs are served."[72] The USDA, which chooses to subsidize the foods we are supposed to eat less of, is also responsible for establishing federal nutrition guidelines and implementing food assistance programs such as the NSLP. The USDA may have been able to effectively manage agricultural policy and public nutrition programs in the early 1900s, but the interests of farmers and consumers are no longer aligned.[73]

While the USDA recommends a diet based on whole grains, fruits, and vegetables, it provides billions of dollars in subsidies for "feed crops"—"[b]y funding these crops, the government supports the production of meat and dairy products—the same products that contribute to our growing rates of obesity and chronic disease.[74] Fruit and vegetable farmers, on the other hand, receive less than 1 percent of government subsidies."[75]

---

[72] Emily J. Schaffer, *Is the Fox Guarding the Henhouse? Who Makes the Rules in American Nutrition Policy?*, 57 FOOD & DRUG L.J. 371, 376 (2002).

[73] *Id.* at 377; *see also* Mark Bittman, *A Food Manifesto for the Future*, N.Y. TIMES, Feb. 1. 2011, http://opinionator.blogs.nytimes.com/2011/02/01/a-food-manifestor-for-the-futuure/ (explaining the USDA's conflict of interest in "expanding markets for agricultural products (like corn and soy!) and providing nutrition education. These goals are at odds with each other; you can't sell garbage while telling people not to eat it.").

[74] *See generally Health vs. Pork: Congress Debates the Farm Bill*, GOOD MED. MAG., Autumn 2007, at 11.

[75] *Id. See* also POLLAN, *supra* note 71 at 39. (noting that the flood of cheap corn made it profitable to fatten cattle on feedlots instead of on grass, and to raise chickens in giant factories rather than in farmyards, even though both cattle and chickens are grass-eaters.)

Nutrition science indicates that Americans need to eat less to improve their overall health—a recommendation that clearly conflicts with food industry interests.[76] The USDA is caught in the middle: "to serve the interests of the food industry, which currently produces a surplus of fat- and energy-rich foodstuffs, [the] USDA must promote many foods whose consumption even at current levels flies in the face of the public's interest in sound nutrition."[77] This conflict of interest carries over to USDA-administered commodity programs. For example, the USDA recommends a diet high in fruits and vegetables and low in saturated fat, but in 2002, the USDA purchased $338 million dollars worth of surplus beef and cheese for schools, but purchased only $159 million dollars worth of canned and frozen fruits and vegetables.[78] In Jean Mayer's article, USDA's Built-In Conflicts, he describes this conflict of interest in the context of USDA nutrition programs, stating, "[b]ecause the donated commodity program is used to help resorb the farm surplus, it often largely consists of inappropriate foods."[79] Many nutritionists argue that the interests of farmers, food manufacturers, and consumers will never align.[80] In order to resolve this conflict of interest, Congress must empower the FDA to develop, implement, and administer government-sponsored nutrition programs.[81]

Part IV: Conclusion

Unfortunately, there is no simple cure for obesity. While the Healthy, Hunger-Free Kids Act represents an important step toward improving the health of American children, it fails to provide a permanent and self-sustaining solution for reversing the obesity epidemic.

---

[76] *See* Schaffer, *supra* note 72, at 375.

[77] *Id.* at 376.

[78] Salisbury, *supra* note 12, at 342.

[79] Schaffer, *supra* note 72, at 376-77 ("[For example] ...school programs ... have to use whole milk ... even in urban areas where 20 percent of the children and adolescents may be obese, when skim milk ...would clearly be more appropriate") (quoting Jean Mayer, *Built in Conflicts, in* U.S. NUTRITION POLICIES IN THE SEVENTIES 207 (Jean Mayer, ed., 1973).

[80] Schaffer, *supra* note 72 at 377; *see also* Marion Nestle, *Food Lobbies, the Food Pyramid, and U.S. Nutrition Policy*, 23 INT'L J. HEALTH SERVICE 483, 494 (1993); Bittman, supra note 73 at 1.

[81] Schaffer, *supra* note 72 at 377; *see also* Nestle, *supra* note 80, at 494.

The awkward marriage between U.S. agricultural policy and U.S. nutrition policy has often resulted in policy favoring the food industry, at the expense of our children's health. In order to properly effectuate the goals of the Healthy, Hunger-Free Kids Act, Congress must stop undermining U.S. nutrition policies by subsidizing commodity crops and the processed food industry. In order to correct the cost imbalance between unhealthy processed foods and healthy fresh foods, legislators must immediately begin phasing out, or reducing, corn subsidies supporting the processed food industry. Eliminating agricultural subsidies totaling over $8 billion per year would allow legislators to fully fund the Healthy, Hunger-Free Kids Act, replenish SNAP funds, increase the federal reimbursement rate, and maintain fair lunch prices for paying students. Finally, in order to remedy the longstanding conflict of interest present in permitting the USDA to regulate both U.S. agricultural and nutrition policy, Congress must empower the FDA to oversee all federal nutrition policy. Once Congress takes these necessary steps, we can begin working toward solving the problem of childhood obesity within a generation.

Stephanie Sendualat

Diary of a 20-Something: A Decade of Selling My Life Online

I first heard the word seven years ago during a staff luncheon at a mediocre restaurant in the Manhattan neighborhood of Chelsea. My boss was telling everyone *everything* about her new kittens and, not surprisingly among dog owners, few people were paying attention. When I asked her how she found them, her one-word answer—Craigslist—changed my life forever.

Until 2004, I was unaware of the cultural phenomenon that is Craigslist. It didn't take long before I used the site to find an apartment, a side job as an usher at an off-Broadway theater, and a roommate who spoke so little English that we communicated in a botched form of sign language. My coworkers and I browsed the "Best of Craigslist" during our lunch hour, laughing until our cheeks and sides hurt. Around this time, I discovered the ever-popular "for sale" section. It would be the beginning of the end of my hoarder tendencies.

I was raised in a family of hoarders. The trunk and backseat of the family car were filled with so many tchotchkes that only two people could sit in the car at one time, including the driver. (This hasn't changed.) The car was out of commission for road trips because there wasn't enough room for a handbag, let alone a suitcase. (This hasn't changed either.) The inside of our house wasn't much better. I was the child who always slept over everyone else's house.

As a result of my parents' hoarder tendencies, I became the extreme opposite. I would sort, purge, and shred whenever possible. Once I moved away for college in 2001, I joined Amazon and eBay and began selling my unwanted items on a regular basis. Throughout college, I sold CDs and DVDs on Amazon—I have always had fickle taste in both—while selling anything that didn't fit within Amazon's rigid categories on eBay. This usually included jewelry, perfume, and clothes. However, I grew increasingly frustrated as the entire eBay process involved *a lot* of waiting. I waited seven or ten days for my auction to end. I waited for people to mail a check or for PayPal to process an eCheck. I waited for a post office employee to process my PS3700 form, which allowed me to ship to Germany or Australia. Of course, I could have refused to accept checks or ship outside the United States, but that would have significantly decreased sales and I was a perpetually broke college student. I *needed* sales.

Also, there were all of those pesky fees including the notorious insertion fee, which is a fee to list an item even if it doesn't sell. (I've always believed this fee is one of the reasons many artists and crafters flocked to Etsy. Like Amazon, Etsy only charges commission if an item sells.) Toward the end of my eBay heyday, I was hand-coding my listings because eBay had experienced such a surge in traffic that it was now charging for everything from bolding a headline to uploading more than one photo. To work around this, I uploaded multiple photos to flickr and coded the HTML in the posting.

Craigslist, on the other hand, was simple. There were no listing fees, no commission, and no registration required. (The registration aspect has since changed.) Plus, sellers could upload up to four photos for free. I was instantly hooked. The joy of selling on Craigslist, especially in large cities such as Philadelphia and New York City, is that everyone saw everything *immediately*. I quickly learned the nuances of the site, such as posting early in the morning if I wanted something gone by the end of the day and including my first name and phone number in each listing. My friends urged me not to do this for safety reasons, but it helped me weed out flakes, which Craigslist is known for besides prostitutes and serial killers. How often do you actually call someone? Exactly. If someone calls you, it's because they *seriously* want something.

In the past seven years, I have sold a bookcase, an armchair, a floor fan, an air-conditioner, at least two DVD players, a memo board, stuffed animals, a broken lamp, a TV stand, full and fitted sheets, a fax machine, an armoire, several *The Baby-sitters Club* books, and used pair of Kenneth Cole heels. I've sold so many items that I have trouble remembering them all. Sometimes I wonder how people are enjoying their items, like the couple who moved from Washington D.C. to New York on the hottest day of the summer and used mobile.craigslist.org to find someone who was selling an air-conditioner *as soon as possible* so they could install it in their third-floor walk-up before they began the long and tiring process of dragging boxes up and down the stairs. I wonder if they are enjoying the fancy remote that came with the unit and if they had to buy another air-conditioner for their bedroom because sometimes having only one isn't enough.

Anyway, here are my letters to other people I met from Craigslist, whose stories are just as interesting:

Dear Penn Frat Boys,

I am still unsure of why you wanted bright pink teddy bears, but I'd rather not know. Did you know I won them at Great Adventure when I was in high school? I get frustrated when people call it Six Flags. No, it's just Great

Adventure. My first job was at Great Adventure, selling candy at one of the many retail stores. I quit after a day.

Anyway, I suspected that was your car idling outside my apartment, but I didn't pay much attention because there was *always* someone double parking in front of my apartment. I hope you didn't get blinded by Temple's campus lighting system during your first, and probably last, trip to North Philly. The lights are so bright, they hurt my eyes sometimes. Do you know the first time I ever went to West Philly? Yes, it was when I left the teddy bears on the porch of your frat house, as instructed. I always complained about Temple students never leaving the overly-lit, police-laden confines of campus. At that moment, I realized I was one of those people I've always complained about.

It's been a while now so I doubt that any of you still have those stuffed animals, but I hope you enjoyed them while they lasted. I really hope you didn't give them to a girlfriend(s) because teddy bears are as cliché as chocolate and flowers.

—Stephanie

Dear Real Estate Agent:

When you asked me if I wanted to go bowling with you, I was thoroughly creeped out. Who asks someone they just met on Craigslist to go to a bowling networking event with them? Also, I didn't even know bowling networking events existed. However, I'm glad I went with you because I met a lot of other people who work in my field. Sometimes it's hard to meet people after you graduate from college, you know? And I recently moved to New York from Philadelphia so I didn't know many people in the city.

I'm sorry you weren't interested in my apartment. It really was a beautiful brownstone before bedbugs took over. My entire floor was infested and both my roommate and I moved out within a few weeks of each other. I moved five blocks away and my roommate moved to the Upper West Side. I'm not entirely sure about the girls on the 3rd floor. The last I heard, they moved back to Omaha. I hope they weren't traumatized for life. I know I am, but it does make for a good story to tell my future grandchildren. The family on the 1st floor refuses to leave, despite the infestation, but I understand their attachment to the brownstone since they have lived there for years and have memories and whatnot.

I'm sure you found another brownstone in the neighborhood. There are plenty of them that don't have bedbugs, as far as I know. And although we lost touch a few months after bowling, thanks for inviting me. It was more fun than I expected.

—Stephanie

Dear New Daddy,

I was skeptical that anyone would want my broken turquoise lamp, mainly because it was broken and also turquoise. The lamp never matched any of my furniture, but I kept it for years because I loved the color. It was propped against a wall so no one could tell that it was broken. You should probably do that too, if you don't get around to fixing it.

Did you know I bought the lamp at a Housing Works all-you-can-bag sale? It's not far from your apartment. You fill a shopping bag with as many items as possible. No matter how many items are in the bag, the cost is always $20. As you can imagine, it is complete chaos, but you should stop by if you are still in the process of decorating your daughter's bedroom.

For some reason, it was exciting to meet someone who only lives a block away from me because I'm one of those people who never knows any of their neighbors, even though I see them every day. I just always tell myself that I will make an effort to get to know my neighbors, but then I never get around to it mainly because I don't want them to see how boring my life is.

By the way, I left the neighborhood late last year. You probably heard about the woman who committed suicide by jumping from the 4th floor of the building on 41st Street. Gossip spreads fast. As you know, I lived on the 3rd floor. It became hard not to think about it each time I went outside. It still makes me sad because I loved that neighborhood and I know your daughter will enjoy growing up there. I just knew it was time for me to move on.

—Stephanie

Week of
Writing

Introduction

Drexel University's sixth annual Week of Writing (WoW) was held in May of 2011. WoW is a weeklong celebration of writing with an emphasis on creative writing, sponsored by the Department of English and Philosophy, the College of Arts and Sciences, and Magnificent Minds. This past year's events included panel discussions and workshops about the graphic novel, travel writing, sketch comedy writing, and the young adult novel, as well as both a raucous story slam and open-mic extravaganza. WoW also featured multiple drop-in creative writing workshops and the *Painted Bride Quarterly* Book Fair for Literacy. And, once again, at the reading marathon, faculty and students read their own original creative writing back-to-back, a new reader every few minutes, as the audience came and went throughout the days.

Each year, the lead-up to the marathon is the WoW Writing Contest, used to determine which students will be invited to read at the event. The faculty judging panels determined the best fiction, poetry, creative nonfiction, humor, and opinion/editorial writing submitted by Drexel students in 2011. Those winning students not only read at the WoW marathon and earned prizes, but also now have their writing published in the fourth volume of *The 33rd*.

Creative writing is among the most challenging fields. Even experienced authors who have been writing for years often struggle to find just the right word. As author Gene Fowler famously said, "Writing is easy. All you do is stare at a blank sheet of paper until drops of blood form on your forehead." The writers whose work appears in this section have stared at that blank sheet of paper, or that computer screen. Whether or not blood formed on their foreheads, they have struggled for the right words to touch their readers and bring their vision to life. The Week of Writing will continue to celebrate and reward their efforts.

Chelsea Biemiller

On the Men I Have Loved

Stevie, before he killed my grasshopper.
Jason, before he told me I couldn't play.
Roald Dahl, before they turned his world into a movie.
Daddy, before I realized not every father drank like he did.
Josh, before he kicked me off the team.
Father Lahey, before he told me not to tell.
Joel, before he slid his hand down my pants on the school bus.
Granddad, before I saw him sick.
Jesus, before I realized I was talking to myself.
Uncle Hank, before we learned of the affair.
Brian, before he convinced me if I loved him, I would do it.
Shakespeare, before he killed off both Romeo *and* Juliet.
Mr. Samuels, before he refused to let me write my paper on *Lolita*.
Jack, before he told me to never speak to him again if I left for school.
Professor Myers, before my term abroad ended.
Walt Whitman, before I found that not everyone contains multitudes.
Leon, before he cried into my lap and begged me not to leave him.
Eddie, before he said *The Bell Jar* wasn't worth the read.
Pablo Naruda, before I realized that not every man can love as he does.
Mr. Lexington, before he gave the promotion to Roger instead.
Roger, before he got the promotion.
Dr. Malone, before the pills stopped working.
Gary, before he taught me how to mix martinis.
Alex, before the bruises.
Matthew, before he found me naked and puking on the floor.
Peter, before he stood me up on my first date in months.
Ryan, before he showed me how I wrong the ones I love.

Laurel Hostak

Summersick

When I think about the summers I spent
chasing a white van
(like a white rabbit)
with the pictures on the side, you know the ones,
I always get a little sick.
Sick from the memory of artificial flavors
stinging my tongue so sweet
and sticking to my face and fingers, leaving stains
of cherry, lemon, blue raspberry, and grape.
Sick with the bellyaches I put up with—
worth it for a taste.
And homesick, too.
For the house on Hollywood (Avenue, not Boulevard).
For the streets and playgrounds
of the old neighborhood
between the highway and the train tracks
where trains no longer run.
Homesick for the body I once inhabited,
that could run long distances
and roll down hills
and jump all the way to the third monkey bar
(Beat that, boys).
For those magnificent bursts of energy
and the heavy slumbers that came after.
I sometimes feel like a hermit crab,
scuttling from body to body
home to home
summer to summer.
The twinkling tune of the ice cream van
is the only connective thread.
What else is there
than the bellyaches
and the sick sick sweetness
and the stains on my hands
to prove that that was me
flying down those streets—

dollar in hand waving
shrieking with the anticipation
of catching that rabbit
and devouring those saccharine treasures?
All other evidence vanished long ago.

Zach Blackwood

What Gives When You Give Up?

The lights are down,
and the refrigerator is leaking black,
and the beak droops on the weathervane outside.
What did he miss out on?

The cracked tile droops in the center,
and the man keeps the jar of
leftover adolescent promises under the sink.
He leaves an imprint in the sofa.

The glow from your big tv
stains your face light blue.
Jeopardy reflected in glazed
still eyes.

Bring yourself back
to the playground too tall,
and too heavy for the swings.

The way your father dragged his
hand through your hair,
and looked you in the eyes
when he smiled.

The garbage slides across the carpet,
closer to your feet every day,
but you can't take out the
cans.

This social anxiety claws deeper
every time you turn the lights off.
The solitaire game on your desktop.
The pervading sense of unimportance.

Which outlet do you plug the hoover into?
Which straw broke your back?

Nicole McCourt

The Witness

I'm watching from above. Floating amidst the dwindling smoke and waiting. Inside a small beige sudan, an unkempt and older model, but I am un-cramped, un-restrained, in a transcendent state. The girl below feels the tension as well.

So like me floating above, but different in make-up and chemistry. I am alone. But she's not. Physically, she is me. Same blue eyes, tattoos, same moles, even the constellation of marks on her thigh that she adamantly claims looks like the ladle of the big dipper. In essence, she is me. But realer than me. With mannerisms and defects reserved for humans. For beings who really exist. Created by the blood she was born into. She quivers, and a low moan, barely a whine, escapes her lips. I know why but I can do nothing. I am merely here to watch.

The car has been moving the whole time. Erratic and at high speeds. I remained undisturbed, floating above but not subjected to the same inertia as the rag doll girl being thrust against her seat belt below. The car comes to a stop, parked diagonally, with the front bumper up against a curb, next to another parked car. After pulling up the emergency break, he climbs up on top, scraping his way into my immediate vision. Before he was just a ghost, a shadow next to the curtain, not a player of immediate importance. We switch roles. I am merely a ghost now, if not less so.

He climbs atop of her, straddling her body. She bucks him, which I take as a good sign. Degraded most definitely, but her spirit, not entirely broken just yet. Even with the greatest pull, she is still fastened, locked, buckled in. And so her hips stay put. But she kicks and scrapes regardless. He has no time for such antics, or no patience at least. One hand reaches her throat and already both she and I know this will end like last time. The other hand directed at his own pants. I cringe. I stop myself, once again composed. I am safe here. She doesn't have the same resolution as I do. And her own cringing face contorts itself into a pained grimace as she kicks her legs more fervently. Pushing her head from side to side with little consequence.

I watch indifferent from above. But I am not the only witness.

Two boys on the sidewalk, young and ignorant, laugh, pointing in the parked car's direction. They're hollering now with glee, delighted to be the ones to catch two adults in a weak moment of passion. The girl below notices too, and she screams, She begins banging the window with the side of a fist. The man on top grabs her arm and pushes a free fist into her mouth to quiet her, but she doesn't relent, His knuckles, bulging from her mouth, stretch the skin taught white around her lips and keep her from biting down. He rolls into the driver's seat, cursing with his pants still down. Once again she slaps her barreling hands against the window, pulling at the door handle. He throws a sudden punch to the side of her face, connecting with force. Quiet again, for the moment.

Her eyes are my eyes in this moment. The window is almost opaque from salt and grime. The light shows through from street lamps orange. With both palms pressed up against it, she screams of some pain I couldn't feel. The boys are still pointing and laughing as the car peels out. She lets go and slumps back into the vinyl. They will not help her. Neither will I.

Chelsea Biemiller
Like Moths to the Flame

I don't belong here. I scan the faces of each girl that sits in the circle we are forced to form every morning; our way of creating a false sense of unity. Only four of us remain. I cannot avoid the nervous energy of the other girls in such close proximity.

Maya arrived two weeks ago, withered to nothing more than bone and hairy skin, barely able to carry her own bags in those emaciated arms. She has already gained four pounds. She nervously taps both bony legs in a constant, calculated rhythm.

Paige, in the spirit of Sylvia Plath, had crawled beneath the garage of her mother's home after downing her stockpiled Valium. It had taken the fire department six hours to drag her out after the police dog picked up her scent. She cries all the time.

Emily sits cross-legged in the chair next to mine. She set fire to her freshman dormitory, nearly killing three of her classmates who slept on the top floor as the smoke curled in under their doorways. Her parents, though willing to pay for the lawyer who had the case dismissed due to their daughter's "emotional disturbance," are not yet ready to welcome her back into the family home. She is my only friend here.

Dr. Reese has arrived. She fills the fifth seat in our stifling circle, her blonde ponytail bouncing like a cheerleader's. As usual, she is far too chipper to discuss what ails us at nine in the morning. "Helena," she says with a toothy smile, "would you like to start off Group today?"

I climbed into my father's truck after drinking a bottle of whiskey. I had only wanted to go to the beach. I just needed the fresh air.

No, I would not like to start off Group today. I am planning my escape.

***

We don't have much down time at the Rose Hill Recovery House for Women. Our days are kept highly structured so that we might "benefit from the security of a well-planned schedule." After Morning Group, we spend an hour doing chores.

Then every day at noon, Emily and I lounge across the wicker furniture of the smoke porch. Rose Hill is a voluntary treatment center, so they don't stop us from smoking. The nurses and Dr. Reese encourage us to journal or meditate during the hour-long break before Lunch, but spending it on the smoke porch with Emily proves more therapeutic than any journal entry ever could.

Emily has been here longer than any of the other girls. She and I have become allies, brought together by nicotine and our refusal to concede that we are somehow damaged. I don't let her past affect my impression of her; she is all I have here. We spend this time every day gossiping about the other patients. It's become harder, now that so many are gone.

The last batch graduated on Saturday. The families had come, faces stained with mascara tears, bearing flowers and gifts to welcome their daughters home. The six graduating girls had stood smiling in sundresses in the yard behind the center, proud of their "recovery." Liars, all of them.

"Lisa will be back," Emily says matter-of-factly as Carl, an orderly, hands her another lit cigarette and hurries back into the building to catch the end of a baseball game. He is supposed to monitor us through the window, but instead he watches television, occasionally glancing at us and running out to spark a match for Emily. They won't let her keep her own lighter.

"She was kissing ass from the moment she walked in. She'll be back."

Lisa had arrived the month before with finger-shaped bruises circling her throat like a necklace. Her parents, horrified by her drug-addicted boyfriend and their daughter's inability to laugh anymore, had dropped her here to re-find her self esteem. Lisa had volunteered to start every Morning Group. She would constantly show off her "pieces" in Art Therapy. She read aloud bad poem after bad poem, her tales of strength and self determination. She had only wanted to get out faster, back into the track-marked arms of the boy who had gotten her here.

"Maybe she had the right idea," I shrug, raking my fingers through Emily's snarled brown hair. We sit like this every day. Me, with my back straight against the floral-patterned cushions; and Emily, her legs slung over the opposite arm of the wicker sofa, her head resting in my lap; both of us blowing smoke toward the ceiling fan whirling overheard.

"She was full of shit," Emily says before exhaling. She has been here so long because she refuses to play along. She doesn't listen to the rules because she doesn't believe they work. She doesn't think she will get better because there isn't anything wrong. I don't know how long she'll be here, but she refuses to budge. I like that about her. But I also want to leave.

***

Emily and I sit together, at a table for six, every day at Lunch. The other girls sit at their own table beside us. Maya spends the meal sobbing into her food, holding her breath, pretending to choke. Paige usually starts crying at some point, too, when Dr. Reese rushes over and coaxes them through the impossible process of finishing their lunch.

After Lunch comes Art Therapy, where I doodle intersecting rectangles for an hour before dramatically crumpling the page and tossing it into the trash on my way out the door to Recreation. This usually involves some sort of light physical activity like yoga or swimming in the center's small indoor pool.

Today, in the sweltering August heat, Dr. Reese tries to coordinate a game of badminton. She's made Carl string up a sagging net in the yard, and is disappointed to find that most of us aren't interested in physical activity. Maya is the exception, who must repeatedly be reminded to stop doing jumping jacks and lunges.

None of us listens as Dr. Reese explains the rules. Instead, I stare out across the yard, noticing for the first time that no fence surrounds the perimeter. Perhaps the staff thinks that the dense forest lying beyond the fifty feet of our landscaped lawn will deter those girls who would consider making a break for it. Not knowing how far the forest spans or where it leads, I realize that the staff might be right.

Without anything else to do outside on the lawn (where smoking isn't permitted) Emily and I join the game, half-heartedly tossing the birdy back and forth over the net to Dr. Reese and Gail, the day nurse. Paige stands awkwardly off to the side, holding her racquet in a limp arm. Maya, who's offered to join Dr. Reese's team, crouches behind her and does leg lifts.

After Recreation, we're forced through an hour of Individual Counseling every other day. Today is Monday—my off day—so I wait in the den while Emily, behind the closed door of Dr. Reese's office, talks her way out of accepting any responsibility for herself. An hour later she emerges, unaffected by Dr. Reese's endless questioning.

Together we head to Dinner (which is very much like Lunch). After another round of chores, Peggy, the night nurse, gathers us in Rose Hill's own small movie theater, where we watch an "inspirational film," which cannot contain any reference to drugs, alcohol, self-injury, promiscuity or defiance of any kind. Our options have been whittled down to made-for-TV specials and Disney movies, so tonight, we watch Finding Nemo. Paige laughs at the talking fish as if they're the funniest characters she's ever seen, while Emily and I count how many times she looks to Peggy for approval. By the end of the film, the count is ninety-seven.

***

At last, we reach my favorite part of the day—Quiet Time. Emily and I spend the entire hour before Lights Out on the smoke porch, sitting exactly as we had in the afternoon. Dr. Reese goes home at nine, and Peggy spends the hour in the back office, catching up on filing she's put off until her boss has gone. Now that there are only four of us, the general level of security at Rose Hill has decreased. Paige and Maya aren't a threat to anyone but themselves, I haven't spoken much at all in the last two months, and Emily's been here long enough to have made friends with nearly every staff member.

Arriving to the porch before Emily, I curl up on the couch and wait for her. I can't imagine being here without her, and wonder what she'll do when I'm gone. Surely, I must get out of here before she does.

Five minutes later, she arrives as usual, but something is strange tonight. With wide eyes, she moves quickly. She curls up against me on the couch, and I instantly smell alcohol.

"Em, where the hell did you—" I realize it isn't alcohol. It's familiar, but it's not liquor.

"Shh!" she hisses, laughing quietly. "Don't say anything, for fuck's sake!"

I lean close to her and inhale deeply through the nose. It's nail polish remover, but I can't figure out where it's coming from. She covers her stomach with a pillow, hiding the pouch on the front of her hooded sweatshirt.

Just as the heavy chemical smell, masked beneath the pillow, starts to fade, Carl comes out to light our cigarettes. I'm surprised when he hands me the pack of matches.

"Playoffs," he says, as if that means anything to me. "This game is a big one." He gestures his head toward the door, meaning he wants to get back to the television as quickly as possible. "If I leave these here, will you promise not to let you know who use them?" With a slight grin, he peers at Emily, whose history has become a small running joke between herself and the non-medical staff. I'm pleased that Carl has trusted me, so I nod and slip the matches into the back pocket of my jeans.

Emily turns to me as soon as he's gone. "This couldn't have been more perfect," she says, sitting up. Her wide eyes focused into mine, her face more serious than I've ever seen before, she wraps her hands firmly around my shoulders. "Do you want to get out of here?"

Perhaps Emily knows what I know; that I will not last much longer here. I can't. As the other girls come, and cry, and leave; return and cry again, we are being crushed by the endless days, me and Emily. Crushed by the days spent pretending we aren't capable of help, the days of refusing to accept that this is where we belong, the days after days of meaningless motion.

"Do you want to get out of here, Helena?" she asks again, shaking me gently by the shoulders, waiting for me to agree. I don't know what she's planned, but she will do it with me or not at all. I try not to think of how it will happen. Try not to think about the worried parents who have left me here, the doctor who has been trying for months to help us, the girls down the hall crying themselves to sleep, the night nurse filing away in the back office. I try not to think about where we will go or what will happen to us. I've become good at trying not to think. Instead, I force myself to believe that Emily's plan, whatever it is, is my only option. I have wanted for so long to leave this place, and now I've been given the chance, by the one person here who understands me.

Her hands still tight on my shoulders, her eyes still connected to mine, I nod. "Let's go."

We immediately spring into motion. Emily reaches into my back pocket, where she knows I've just placed the matches. Reaching into the pouch of her sweatshirt, she withdraws a clear plastic bag. Inside is a pink, clumped cloth, which I realize is a tee shirt, soaked through with the nail polish remover. She flips the shirt out of the bag and into the small trashcan we use to empty the ashtrays.

"Carl couldn't have picked a better night," she speaks quickly, but is calm. "I thought we'd have to waste a perfectly good cig, trying to light this thing."

She takes the book of matches and with one hand, rips all of them out at once. In a single motion, she lights them all, striking them together only once. She promptly tosses the tiny ball of flame in with the soaked, stinking shirt. Instantly, the whole can whooshes aflame.

"Let's go," Emily says, excited. "Carl will be flipping his shit in a minute."

We rush away from the fire toward the opposite end of the porch. The only door leads back into the center's den, so with one heave, we break through the screen that encloses the porch. We take off running for the woods beyond the limp badminton net, away from the smoke already flooding the porch and spilling out into the yard. The grass is wet, seeping through my socks. I hadn't thought to grab my shoes. Surely, they were on fire by now, left beneath the wicker sofa. As we near the trees, the soles of my feet begin to sting, torn and punctured by the branches and briars left uncleared by the landscaping staff.

We reach the woods and don't stop running until we've passed the trees, which aren't as dense as I had imagined. Just beyond them is the hill after which the center is named. With heaving chests we stand at its peak, looking down on the Rose Hill Recovery House for Women, faint now, through the black smoke. I think about taking Emily's hand, then think better of it. Like moths to the flame, we stare, unmoving.

Flames begin to lick at the sides and roof of the building, faster than I would have imagined. Smoke pours from where, just moments ago, we had been, and rises toward the empty sky. I imagine the hundreds of girls who have passed through Rose Hill, told from the start they were damaged. Their inches of progress, their poems of hope, the secrets their doctors will never learn; all crinkle into ash and rise up to the sky in smoke. Perhaps, so too, will the memory that they—that we—were ever here.

"Now *that's* a smoke porch," Emily says with smile, proud of the blaze.

I am reminded of another fire, this one in the early summer, and coming from a car spun off on the side of the expressway. Beneath the crumpled hood, smoke had curled out like steam rising from blacktop. I had stood off to the side, trying to keep out of the way. A trickle of blood from the throbbing lump on my head had crept toward the corner of my eye, the taste of Jack Daniels on my tongue making me sick.

They had told me the car carried a family of five. A mother, a father, and three blonde little boys. I hadn't believed them at first. I thought they were lying so that I would tell them what had happened.

There was nothing to tell. I had only wanted to go to the beach.

I didn't believe them until I watched as the mangled ends of the car were pried apart from one another like a ribcage, and the reporters and onlookers were told to get away.

"You think Carl will make it out okay?" Emily's calm question snaps me out of my memory.

I turn to her without answering.

"I lied," she says nonchalantly, without looking at me. "I slept with him so he'd leave you the matches. He thought it was so we could smoke in our rooms after Peggy locks up the porch."

Something surges in my stomach and immediately, I feel more tired than I have ever felt. I stare at Emily's profile, the slight grin in the corner of her lips. Alone with her on the hill, far away from what we've done, it's as if I'm seeing her for the very first time.

Abby Davis

Canary Song

December 20, 2009

Grandpa once told me that if you could iron out West Virginia it would be even bigger than Texas. He would joke that people around here actually sleep standing up in their beds even though they thought they were lying down.

The town of Comfort sat nice and snug on the very edge of the lee side of the mountain. When I was in elementary school I could walk down Coal River Road and teeter my toes between the lush green side of the hills behind me and the long, brown rocky slide in front of me. You could sit there and lean forward into a wall of wavering wind that licked up the slope.

Comfort was just a little bump of a town with one main street. We had one doctor's office and three restaurants, but for just about anything else you wanted you had to make the drive down to Charleston. All we really had were the spindly edges of the Blue Mountain Ridge.

There was one thing those mountains were good for though: and that was coal. My Daddy says that people don't use coal like they used to-a lot more people use gas now. Not enough to stop the mine but enough to slow it down a little. I asked him why, and he would shrug and tell me that maybe it was cheaper and maybe it was safer. But coal was special. You could never find diamonds in a pit of gasoline.

When I was little I asked him if he would ever bring me a diamond and he said he would. One as big as my fist so we could sell it and move down to Palm Beach. Of course he was joking, no one ever found diamonds in that dirty old mine. More than once though, Daddy would bring me home hunks of coal with ancient sea creatures embedded on them. Underwater ferns that stretched like fans and weaved across the hard black stone, or primitive clam shells that had been hollowed out in the dust. I loved whatever little treasures he could give me-I knew he would never find a diamond down there. There was nothing down there but coal dust-and methane.

Grandpa once told me that people used to take canaries down in mines to find methane. If that bird stops singing then all the miners found it best to high-tail it out of there. But today there aren't any more canaries. There are gas readers that light up and inspectors in white plastic helmets to check on them and make sure they are working.

Nobody likes going down in that mine, but our mine is our benefactor and she has a quicksilver temper. You could go on digging for months or years without any problems, and then one day it can swallow people's families up with hardly a hiccup of a warning. You just had to listen for the canaries.

No one liked it, but that mine was Comfort's meal ticket. We ate our bread with butter and coal dust.

December 21, 2009

Jim Matheson is in my English class. His older brother is a digger, as was his daddy before him, and his daddy, and so on. I watch him sometimes concentrating really hard on in-class essay questions. Jim was no good at school, as was his brother before him. But he *tried*. I asked him once to be careful not to concentrate too hard or his eyes might pop out of his head.

"Terra Lee," he told me, as usual, with my middle name, "leave me alone so I can do this right." He said it with a glazed look of fear behind his eyes.

"What are you so afraid of, Jim? It's just an essay, it's not like it matters."

"I'm turning fourteen next month."

He didn't need to say any more for me to understand what he meant. Fourteen was working age. Almost everyone in Comfort started working around that age. Sure, they may not be old enough to do mine work, but it was a start of something. This was the start of when people began to figure out who was going to stay in town and who the few people who were going to leave and go to college were. The people of Comfort were like rice in a strainer, Jim was the grain, and I was a lost stone passing through.

He concentrated so hard that the graphite in his pencil snapped.

January 3, 2010

Daddy came home last night with his hand bandaged. The white gauze looked so out of place on a man stained so black. When Daddy came home from the mine he looked as black as the fossils he brought home for me. His hair was stiff with coal dust, his eyes were rimmed and red. When he smiled, his teeth looked pearly and alien-like the bandage on his hand that was slowly collecting grime.

I asked him what had happened and he told me that the conveyor belt that carried the coal had been making a strange grinding noise, and when he had reached down to check it the darn thing had nicked him. After he showered and looked peachy and sandy-colored again, I rubbed ointment into the palm of his hand and wrapped clean gauze around it, like my mother used to do when he would come home banged up. I wasn't peachy and sandy-colored like him. I was dark, long-legged and mousy-haired like her. As I bandaged him up he smiled at me, his strange, awkward smile that said, "I know, I know."

January 7, 2010

I was just waking up for school as the dawn broke over the mountains when I saw my Daddy carrying two heavy bags of rock dust out the door with him on his way to work. It was the rock dust we usually used when we gardened in the spring. It was winter, a cold and bitter one at that. I asked Daddy what on God's green earth he was thinking about using rock dust in the dead of this chill for. He grumbled at me and said he was hoping he could fill his foreman's fat mouth with it.

I didn't think there was anything wrong with the foreman, but Daddy got mad at him because he never helped fix any of the things Daddy asked him to help fix. Grandpa said having a bad foreman is like having a bad landlord-nothing gets better. At the same time I think Daddy knew it wasn't the foreman's fault-he can't help it if he requests stuff from the company and the company never responds.

I looked at Grandpa, who was hardly awake enough to absorb any of the conversation, but was slowly stirring sugar into his morning coffee.

"What did he mean by that?" I asked him.

Grandpa was a veteran of the mines. When he wrinkled his brow I sometimes thought I could see lines of dust hidden in the folds of his skin. He coughed his old, powdery cough and told me, "You can mix rock dust with coal dust so it's less combustible," he shrugged his shoulders, like this was as much of Daddy's morning routine as brushing his teeth. "Guess the boss man asked him to bring it in."

January 11, 2010

A kid at school today told me his daddy saw the conveyor belt smoking. He said that his dad felt it and it was warm to the touch.

January 12, 2010

Daddy came home with a bit more bounce in his step today than he had in the previous couple of weeks. When I asked him what he was so happy about he told me that they were shutting down the mine.

I felt all the blood drain out of my face. This was by no means good news to anyone in Comfort.

After seeing my face turn the color of talcum Daddy held up his hands as if to proclaim his innocence and said, "Not permanently, just to get things fixed up around there. I've been giving the foreman hell for the conditions down there and an inspector came by yesterday and saw that conveyor belt. After the inspector threatened the company with a fine, the foreman said we should try to 'encourage people to do things right the first time'" he said making quotes in the air with his fingers.

"You're not out of work then?"

"Naw, just gotta fix some things up, that's all. It's about time, too."

He also said that he got to go in late to work the next day. So he said that, if I wanted, I could go in late to school too. After he was clean, me, Grandpa, and Daddy stayed up late and popped popcorn and watched Stargate on the SyFy channel. I watched Daddy's bone white knuckles rifle through the popcorn bowl. He had spent so much time underground that his skin was papery white. I wondered if he had ever seen more light than a sunset and a sunrise in any of his working days.

January 20, 2010

Daddy came home today and his smile was gone. His boots tracked in more dust than usual. I asked him what was wrong and he said, "Nothing baby, just tired is all. Fixin' is takin' a lot longer than I thought, but the foreman says he's getting it done."

I asked him why he bothered to work there anyway, why not find something else to do? He just shrugged his broad workman's shoulders and smiled with just the corners of his mouth, "I'll apply to Subway tomorrow," he said, sarcasm dripping from his words. I don't know who I was kidding. There was no other money coming out of this town.

February 20, 2010

The fourth marking period is starting soon, and that means placement exams for high school. Jim is still not doing well, and I can tell he's worried. I told him I was a little worried too.

"Terra Lee," he told me, "how could you possibly be worried? You have the best grades in our class."

I smiled and told him I guess so, and I told him I would help him study. I never told him that I meant I was worried for him.

March 2, 2010

I heard Grandpa and Daddy arguing last night. Grandpa was telling Daddy something about going back to school for awhile. Getting a degree, getting a job someplace away from Comfort.

"It's too late for that." Daddy had said.

"It's never too late."

Then they started talking about me.

"Terra's gonna start high school in the fall. She's a smart kid, Dad, real smart. She deserves to have enough money to go to college and not have to work so hard only to drop out and get stuck here like I did. How can I burn off everything I saved for her on myself? She's the one with a future, not me."

"We can keep saving. She can get a scholarship-"

"Scholarship isn't gonna pay for it all and you know it. A scholarship will let us maybe get her enough money for food and clothes and books-"

"How can you talk about being so selfless when you're puttin' your life on the line like this, Jack? You know somethin's been cookin' down in that mine for ages. You know if it goes up like Sago and somethin' happens to you that girl has nothin'. *Nothing.*"

"Things like Sago aren't supposed to happen anymore! They took 'em to court. The mine inspectors are supposed to be cracking down on this. Things won't end up like Sago, I know they won't. They'll get to it..."

Sago. I knew Sago. It was the worst mine blast in West Virginia, in my lifetime, anyway. Twelve men died, and one had been stuck under the earth for almost two whole days before he was rescued. I imagined my father there with his moonlight-white hands, grasping at sunbeams coming through the cracks of the rocks. I scuttled back to bed and buried my face in my pillow so no one could hear me howling like the child I sometimes felt I was.

April 13, 2010

I was at school when I heard the canaries stop singing. I was back in English class with Jim Matheson, hearing his pencil snap again and again whenever he got frustrated with a new essay question. He had no idea that they had stopped singing. My father had stopped hearing them three weeks before when a ventilation intake duct started sucking in air the wrong way. He told the foreman, of course, who then told the men in suits who owned the energy company that owned the mine. In return, the men in suits told the foreman it wasn't a problem. They stuffed rock dust down his throat.

I never saw the blast. But I heard it cracking. Like thunder. A tangible echo licking up and down the mountain. People who had been sleeping standing up in their beds now slept lying down in the earth. Twenty-nine of them.

Twenty-nine of them were not the foreman who ignored
The air sucking out of the mine the wrong way
The rock dust spread about on the floor like a garden path
The warm, smoking conveyor belt
And the fine coal dust that hung in the air
Like so many words
That went unsaid.
Twenty-eight of those men were not my father.

I did not want to think about it. I didn't want to think about the unsealed electrical cords the news reporters found mentioned in the unattended-to reports from the men in the white plastic hats. Cords which had laid on wet ground, six inches deep in coal dust. I didn't want to think about the look on Grandpa's face when he came home the hours after the sirens died away.

I wanted to think that Daddy found a diamond down in that mine. One big enough to take us to Palm Beach. But I knew there were no diamonds in that mine. Everyone knew that.

It was nine months ago that the canaries had really stopped singing. Even though everyone pretended not to hear that foreboding silence. It was only two days ago that we buried my father.

April 20, 2010

I stay with my Grandpa now. He knows his pension checks won't be enough to keep us on our feet so he applied to a Wal-Mart down in Charleston. He's too old to mine anymore. He says he doesn't want me to work, he wants me to focus on school. He tells me not to worry, he tells me the company will pay for my college and our health care costs. But I forge his name on my work permit anyway. He doesn't look at me when I bring home milk and bread, but he doesn't ask me where I got the money for it either.

Jim came up to me in school and told me he was sorry. His father and brother had survived the explosion—it wasn't their shift when it went off. But I was the one who was sorry. I could still breathe the fear that came off of him. A fear that grew stronger after the blast. We both knew that there was coal under the mountains, and one day the mine would be fixed and opened up again. All the companies could do was apologize and promise that next time the conditions would be better, and pay the families who had lost loved ones. Unlike Jim's. They would fire the management and start again anew, build a safer mine, keep Comfort running. Like his father, and his father before him, and so on.

I don't know what my father looked like before we lowered him into the earth. My Grandpa had taken care of all of the arrangements, and said a closed-casket funeral was best. I didn't know what my father looked like after the blast and he wasn't about to tell me.

But I know what he must have looked like. He looked like how he always did when he came home from the mines, painted black with dust.

Kerri Sullivan

How I Learned My Lesson Or: Will Roommate Number Three Have Better Candy?

I am the roommate who is offered excess candy and unwanted condoms.

On Valentine's Day, Maggie knocked on my door tentatively. "Hey, uh, are you busy?"

"Nah, not anymore," I mumbled. "Come in!"

"I got this candy gram thing, do you want it?"

Stupid question. She has lived with me for four months now. She knows I never say no to candy. "Sure, thanks."

She tossed the bag to me. "I only wanted the chocolate bar. There's some good stuff left, though. There's a condom at the bottom of the bag, too." She rolls her eyes. "We all know I've got no use for those!"

"I know, right?" I say, my mouth already full of conversation hearts. "Sex is, like, eight *million* times better without them."

Maggie politely disguises her disgust. I don't know which is more offensive: what I said or the pastel-colored spit dripping onto my blouse.

"Kidding," I say, wiping the spot with my free hand.

She smiles slightly. "Enjoy the candy."

I don't know what I did to be known as the gluttonous, slutty roommate. Okay, *fine*, I guess I have some ideas. It probably has a lot to do with the fact that I ate an entire large bag of candy corn when I was unpacking my things. Or that the first time Maggie saw me eat breakfast on a Monday morning, it happened to be one of those huge swirly, rainbow lollipops. And I suppose the fact that I had very loud (but not because it was good) shower sex with our neighbor didn't exactly make me look like a purity club member.

***

I had another roommate at the beginning of the year. Annie. I wanted her to be like a sister, so I shared very intimate details with her. I would coerce things out of her, mostly about her back-home boyfriend, Ben. He was a cute, gawky, uncultured sort of guy. Annie was a naïve, skittish, wholesome girl. I thought it was a great match and I constantly told her how excited I was to meet him. Finally, the day before his first visit, Annie said, "Can I ask something of you? Could you maybe stay somewhere else while Ben is here?"

I had never been more excited to be sexiled. I told her so and offered her six condoms. She pursed her lovely red lips and said, "Actually, it's not that at all. We aren't going to consummate anything. It's just that," she drew in a breath and huffed it out.

"What, girl, just tell me." Annie and I were a week and a half into living together, practically sisters. I walked from the shower to my closet naked, I told her in graphic detail about the guy down the hall and his small dick, and I shared my popcorn with her. So what if she never once changed in front of me, told me nothing about Ben's penis besides the fact that she felt it occasionally through his jeans and it seemed "sufficient," or rarely ever even wanted popcorn at eight in the morning?

"It's just that I don't really want Ben to meet you, is the thing."

What did that even mean?

She sat on the edge of her bed and twisted her fingers around. "I don't really want Ben to find out that girls like you actually exist."

"What the hell does that mean?" I wasn't mad. You don't get mad at your sisters. You love them unconditionally, always. I was just confused.

"Ben has never been to a city. He's never met girls who aren't from the country. He thinks girls are either trashy hicks or wholesome, Midwest wife material." She started crying a little. "And you're just so...*sexy*. You're like the girls on TV and in movies and that rock songs are written about. You should be a complete fallacy, but here you are. I'm afraid if Ben knows you're real, he'll know there are more ladies like you and he'll suddenly know that there's more out there besides me and my very unsexy cotton shirtdresses."

"Oh honey," I got out of my desk chair and sat next to her. "I don't even know Ben, but from everything you tell me, I know one thing: that boy *loves* you. He wouldn't be with you for so long without having sex if he didn't."

She agreed to let me meet him. He was just as boring as I thought he would be. I stayed in the room with them for less than an hour, then I headed out to a party.

Early in the morning, I stumbled into our room and found Annie sitting in the dark, staring at the wall. "Oh my God, are you on acid?" She didn't laugh. "Ben knows he doesn't need to wake up at four to milk any cows, right? Where is he?"

Less than seven hours after meeting me, Ben broke up with Annie. And less than seven hours after that, I had drunkenly packed all of my belongings. I knew one thing for sure: Annie and I would never be sisters. We wouldn't, soon after, even be roommates. I was approved immediately for a housing switch, and so I moved out, taking one of Annie's shirtdresses with me.

***

So it's perfectly cool with me that Maggie sees me as purely a caricature. It's probably less complicated that way. She can laugh with her friends about her roommate—who is whorish and ridiculous and fun for only fleeting moments, but isn't anything like a *real* person. She can continue to think that I'm not a person who is worth talking to about anything besides which brand of chocolate is best. I won't bother to correct her. She'll never know the truth about me: that although it looks like the worst thing about me is how I live my life, the really bad thing is how I possess the ability to ruin people.

I won't get involved in Maggie's affairs or tell her I'd like to meet people who matter to her. Part of me is terrified that if her best guy friend sees me for more than half a second (when they are watching a movie in the living room and I sprint past them to get to my room without saying hi), he won't come around anymore. And that would be a shame. The kid's pretty fine.

Joshua Stolle
The Morning Shakes

"Happiness in intelligent people is the rarest thing I know." –Hemingway

The red lights were always on at night. They were much harder to see from a distance and didn't give away position like fluorescents. The ship was moored since the previous afternoon, but the red lights were used so that the crew could work and sleep. People were always rising and sleeping in the berthing and it made things very difficult for Bragg. He needed total blackness and total quiet and there was very little of either anywhere on the boat. Bragg spent most nights staring at the overhead of his coffin locker, smelling the sweat and the shoe polish and listening to the sleeping sounds of all the men.

The rover came down from the top to wake his relief. The relief was 18 years old from Bolingbrook, Illinois. He was very good looking and friendly but had scored exactly four points below the cutoff on his aptitude tests. They needed extra bodies during wartime, so it was alright to relax the minimum requirements. The rover made an awful racket as he searched for his relief, kicking boots and shining his flashlight into each rack.

Bragg lay on his back. The inside of the coffin locker didn't quite give enough room to turn over, so he lay looking at a torn-out part of a letter from his grandfather that was taped to the overhead. It read, "Every great man serves his country." His grandfather was sent home from the Navy after a nasty pneumonia almost killed him. The coffin did have a tiny shelf and Bragg's two books were on it. One was *Confederacy of Dunces*. The other, *Johnny Got His Gun*, about a faceless horror kept prisoner within his own body, had a laminated obituary of his grandmother, Audrey, sticking out of the pages. Also, there was a small journal that Bragg sometimes wrote in when he was especially drunk. There was a little light for reading and an outlet. The outlet didn't work.

Bragg didn't like being in the berthing too long when he couldn't sleep. The snores from all the men sleeping on their backs and not having enough room to turn over were unnerving. The fireman who slept above him had some sort of apnea that caused him to wear a mask when he slept. If he didn't wear it, he would forget to breathe. He was obese and had failed his last six physical fitness assessments. The limit was three before they sent you home. His skin was gray and barely masked the blue veins that crawled across his bulging frame. The red lights and that terrible mask and the mechanical breaths that the fireman took were no way to try and fall asleep. Bragg dressed in his utilities and moved aft through the ship.

At this time in the morning, few people were awake. It was watch-standers, mostly. They were always either roaming the ship with a Beretta .9mm stuck to their hip or they carried a clipboard and arbitrarily turned knobs and valves. The red lights were on in all the passageways and there was always the hum of the machinery. Underway, there were engineers playing spades into the morning. The decks were deserted now. Everyone who could leave the day before had wasted no time.

At the very aft of the ship was a space that only Bragg and the other members of his work station had a key to. There were six dog handles on the hatch and Bragg undid them all and locked the hatch behind him. He laid down on the deck for a few minutes with his eyes closed, then used some tools from a cabinet on the far side of the space to open a control panel behind a conduit line. Inside, there was a bottle of Aberlour and a bottle of Laphroaig 30 yr. One of the former techs, Gibson, had picked them up when the boat was in Australia.

He set the bottles down by a small hatch and opened it to reveal the first bluish bits of the morning. The water from the harbor was right outside the hatch. It smelled slightly of sulfur. Bragg sat and poured a nice bit of the Laphroaig into a coffee mug. The room began to smell like peat from the Laphroaig. It was a fine scotch and Bragg took another long pour before putting the bottle away. He didn't want to be too drunk this early in the morning. He also didn't want to be too sober this late at night. But it was a fine scotch. Gibson had excellent taste in fine whiskeys. It was surprising since his family was very poor. He had married his girlfriend two years after they graduated high school and joined up when she announced that she was pregnant.

Bragg really wanted to smoke and used the tools again to hide the bottles. Only officers could bring back liquor, even whiskeys as fine as these. He could hear car alarms through the small window hatch as he closed up to leave the space. When Bragg got topside, there was a general commotion from the handful of people who were awake this early. There had been a small earthquake, and those who felt it were anxious to talk about it, excitedly, and at great length. Bragg hadn't felt anything at all. It was a minor earthquake, but they all huddled around to talk about it.

Bragg moved past the men and produced his ID card to the watchman, Jeffries. Jeffries had been a chief, but lost his anchor when he followed a deck seaman into a men's room at a bar in Guam and tried to perform oral sex on him. The deck seaman was picked up on the side of the road, crying, by the shore patrol. Jeffries' wife divorced him and took his two daughters to San Jose. He had three wives since and got to go back to sea duty after three years at a reserve center in Chicago. He married his most recent wife in a grand ceremony on the same flight deck where Jeffries was standing watch. The whole ship was in attendance. Crewman didn't have to work if they attended. Bragg saluted Jeffries and then turned to salute the flag and walked off of the ship.

Leftovers from the return festivities littered the pier. Paper plates and white hats and grass skirts from the hula dancers were all over the ground. Those leftover grass skirts marked any major event on Oahu. Waves slapped against the pier with great enthusiasm and the car alarms were still going off. Bragg wondered to himself how he didn't see those earthquake waves when he was drinking that fine scotch and looking out the hatch. The water in Pearl Harbor had really been shaken up. Nighttime was on its way out. The day was now ashy and blue, like gunmetal. It got even bluer by the time Bragg got all the way down the pier to the smoke deck. Nobody in America liked a smoker anymore, not even sailors. Bragg had to go all the way down the pier and sit under a dumpster. Sometimes the bottom of the dumpster would be rusted out in spots and maggots would pour out. They would be all crunched and crushed by the smokers. It was no way to try and smoke a cigarette. Bragg sat on the metal bar and rolled a smoke from the pouch in his pocket.

A junior officer jogged by. Officers were allowed to leave the boat, even on duty, if they wanted to exercise. When she wasn't working, the junior officer was always working out. She had thick ankles and worked out so much to avoid the weight as long as possible. She was a terrible drunk. She was always getting way too drunk during the port visits and sleeping with everyone. She tried to drink with the men, but she always ended up sleeping with them. Officers and enlisted men, both, it didn't matter to her. She piloted the SH-60 and felt a lot of pressure to compete with the men, but couldn't handle her liquor. Sometimes, she would forget to take off her wedding ring if she was too drunk. Sometimes she would cry during. Sometimes she wouldn't.

A worker on the pier was picking up some tools he had been using. He was local, and Bragg called him over to use his matches.

"You feel that quake?" the worker asked Bragg.

"No."

"Nuttin', huh? I felt it big-time. Where you stay?" Bragg flipped his thumb at the boat.

"Oh, you din't feel nuttin' on dare, huh?"

"No, nothing," Bragg tossed him back his book of matches, "Mahalo." The worker stuck out his thumb and pinky.

Bragg smoked and watched the morning. Hawaii air is cool at first and pleasant and the fish in the harbor jumped for food. In the first light, the water was deep blue, except around the ship where the red lights from the deck shone down on all the cigarette butts and trash and yellow film. Bragg used to smoke early in the morning with two other guys, Betts and Gibson. They couldn't sleep either with the lights and all the bathroom smells that were in the berthing. The three of them smoked together and watched the morning. All of them loved to fish and they would sometimes talk about the fish jumping or times they had fished off of the back of the boat when there was no land on any side. Sometimes they wouldn't talk at all. They would just smoke. Betts finished his contract and was at a university in Philadelphia. Then Gibson and Bragg would sit and talk about scotches and sometimes the fish. He was taken off the boat in Singapore, though. They flew him back to Pearl Harbor to be processed out. In Australia, Gibson had smoked some grass from a cab driver at a concert. The next day they tested everyone on the ship for drugs. They did that after all the best port stops, so that the men would be too scared to try to take any. Gibson failed and went off with a dishonorable discharge. He had a baby and another on the way. His division officer was arrested that same day for hitting a woman in the mouth with a bottle of vodka. He was restricted to the ship for thirty days.

It was pretty light out, and Bragg stubbed out his butt and started to make his way back to the ship. Some of the car alarms were still going off, but the waves in the harbor had gone back to normal. People were starting to move around the ship. Behind the harbor with all the ships jutting out were the mountains. The first sun beams were lighting up the green cliffs that were not yet old enough to be just rock. Behind them were the rain clouds. Bragg turned back to the boat.

Chelsea Biemiller

The Faults of My Father

My father has been writing to me from rehab. Each letter is carefully penned on lined notebook paper, heavily creased as if he has folded and unfolded the page many times, coming back to it again and again before deciding it is finished. He writes of the nursing staff, his progress, his weight loss. He writes of the steps he is slowly beginning to accept. He writes that he is sorry.

I read each letter carefully, saving them all in the small lacquered box my father brought back for me after a trip to Canada. I haven't found the energy to write back. Instead, I have come to an Alcoholics Anonymous meeting.

Finding the meeting had been easy. Listed among hundreds of others in the classifieds at the back of the local paper, I had easily spotted one close to where I work: *A.A. Open Meeting, Holy Trinity Church, 1904 Walnut Street, 7:00pm.* Now that I'm here I realize that the easy portion of my task is behind me. Summoning the courage to actually walk into the church and go to the meeting—this is the hard part.

I'm not sure what good my coming here will do, but I want to know that there are others out there like my father. I am comforted by the thought of meeting those who have done just as much damage. I want to know that other families have been where mine is now, that other children have seen what I have seen. I'm not looking for answers or searching for some shred of hope. I'm not interested in their stories of success. I'm just tired of feeling alone.

We are all, undoubtedly, hurt by the human failings of our parents. Perhaps it's after they've inadvertently forgotten to pick us up from a friend's house, or after seeing them cry for the first time, but there comes a moment for every child when the image of her parents as the invincible, immortal champion is tarnished, and the realization that they are imperfect, just like everyone else, is forced upon her. But the children of addicts—we're a special breed. We learn, very early on, that promises are often broken and the ones we love most can lie. We're taught to escape, to keep quiet, and when the going really gets tough, to just stay away. Perhaps we're damned from the start.

After one long, last drag on my cigarette, I toss the butt toward a nearby shrub, take a deep breath, and go in through the heavy doors. It has been years since I've been in a church. I've never been to this one, but the dark, cool interior and the comforting smell of old books are instantly familiar. I make my way down a small staircase to the basement, where a bearded man in a plaid shirt is setting out coffee and paper cups.

I've come early to explain why I'm here. It's true that I am four times more likely to become an addict than the child of a non-alcoholic parent.[1] But I am not one, not yet; and I want this man, whoever he is, to know that.

He greets me with a smile before I have a chance to speak. *Fool*, I think to myself.

"Hi there, I'm Dave," he says with an extended hand. I expect him to finish with "and I'm an alcoholic," but much to my disappointment, he doesn't.

I fake a smile and shake his hand. With feigned confidence, I introduce myself. "I hope you don't mind, but would it be alright if I just sat in on tonight's meeting? I have a family member who..."

I hadn't thought of how I would explain my being here before beginning to speak. As my voice trails off, Dave's expression changes from one of polite welcome to one of understanding.

"Not a problem," he replies before I can come up with a lie. "You can sit wherever you like. We'll be getting started in about ten minutes, so feel free to grab some coffee."

I take a seat at one of the four shabby folding tables that are set up around the basement. Small, black books with *Twelve Steps and Twelve Traditions* embossed on the covers have been left at each table. Dave returns to his duties, and I try to keep my head down as people begin shuffling in.

Over two million people consider themselves members of Alcoholics Anonymous at any given time.[2] I'm not sure why I thought the members at *this* meeting would be some strung-out group of drug-addicted psychopaths, but as they begin to take their seats around the tables, I am proven wrong.

Many of them are middle-aged men like my father, casually dressed in jeans and sweatshirts, smiling as they greet one another like old friends. Some are young, not much older than me. I am stunned by the woman,

---

[1] "Effects of Parental Substance Abuse: Behavioral Consequences." *The Center on Addiction and Family*. Coaf.org. n.d. Web.

[2] "A.A. Fact File." Prepared by the *General Service Office of Alcoholics Anonymous*. Print. 2010. New York: A.A. World Services, Inc.

dressed impeccably in a hand-tailored suit, who sits down across from me and anxiously drums her manicured nails on the table. She looks so much like the strong, smart women attorneys at the law firm where I intern. She looks like the kind of woman I have always wanted to become.

At exactly seven o'clock, Dave promptly starts the meeting. It is not until he welcomes the newcomers that I realize I am probably not the only person here for the first time. Then together, as if they have done this many times before, the members recite the familiar, uninspired words of the Serenity Prayer:

"God, grant me the serenity to accept the things I cannot change, the courage to change the things I can, and the wisdom to know the difference."

What a crock of shit, I think to myself. These people may all look very friendly, but alcoholics are not accepting of change. They are not courageous. They are selfish and weak-willed. They know not of the pain they bring to others; or perhaps they do, and just don't care enough to stop.

After the prayer, Dave opens the floor for a brief discussion. Members are encouraged to share anything they like: their struggles, their successes, their plans for moving forward in their "recovery." An older man in a Phillies baseball cap offers to start.

"Hi there," he says from his seat at the table neighboring mine. "I'm Chuck, and I'm an alcoholic."

Yes, I find myself thinking, *I've heard it at least once.*

"I just wanted to say that this was a tough week," Chuck continues. "Tuesday was the third anniversary of my wife's death, and I've gotta be honest, it was hard." He looks down at his hands and taps his fingertips together, as if looking for the right words before proceeding. He looks up in Dave's direction and smiles with tired eyes. "I just wanted to take a sec to recognize Dave and thank him for helping me get through all this. I've been sober a year now, but without Dave's sponsorship, I really don't know where I'd be."

Dave smiles and thanks Chuck for sharing before moving on to the next member.

I did not come here for this. I don't want to hear sob stories and tales of success. I want to hear about pain, about damage. I want to hear of the destruction these people have brought upon those who love them. I want stories of honesty.

I have plenty of my own. There was the time my father threw my new, white vanity table down the stairs. It lay there in a heap for two days, its legs snapped in half like broken bones, until my mother and I gathered up the pieces and carried them to the curb to be taken away with the garbage. There was the time I watched my father struggle to complete the field sobriety tests being explained by an officer on the side of the road. I had waited patiently in the cab of his truck, pom-poms in my lap, worried that he would once again make me late for cheerleading practice. There was the time he showed up wasted to an awards reception at my college. He had tried to grab the microphone from the dean before the ceremony started, and then fell asleep, sitting up in his seat, once it had. The list goes on: the time he vomited all over the floor at the family Christmas dinner; the time he threw my mother's keys into the woods so that she couldn't leave him; the time I had to call the police station to ask when I could come pick him up.

No one was sharing such stories. No one wanted to talk about the bad, the *real*. That was what I had come for, and I was being let down.

After a retired mechanic finishes sharing, Dave stands again. "Tonight, we have a special guest speaker," he announces to the group, his hands clasped together with delight. "She's here to talk about her disease, her recovery, and how the meetings have been working for her. Everyone, please welcome Stephanie."

The well-dressed woman sitting across from me rises from her seat. She gives me a weak smile before she goes; perhaps hoping I'll return the favor to boost her confidence. I don't, and instead just stare in disbelief as she approaches the front of the room and clears her throat.

"Hi everyone," she says cheerfully. "I'm Stephanie. I am a grateful, recovering alcoholic."

In unison, the group replies, "Hi, Stephanie." Surprisingly, the tone is much more optimistic than is typically portrayed in the movies.

Stephanie begins to tell her story. At first her voice is strong, like an experienced litigator beginning her opening statement. She starts by telling us that she is an attorney (*I knew it*), but that her road to recovery and success has been a long one. Her voice cracks and weakens as she describes the years of abuse at the calloused hands of her father (also an alcoholic), the molestation from the pastor while away at Christian summer camp, the bad boyfriend after bad boyfriend. She has to pause for several moments before she continues. Her voice isn't much more than a wavering whisper as she tells us of the black eyes, the miscarriage, and the realization that she was powerless at the age of twenty-two, the very age that I am now. As the tears she has been choking back begin to fall from the corner of her eyes, I realize I should not have come here.

As quietly as I can, I gather my coat and bag and make my way out of the basement, up the dark stairs to the church's doors, and out into the cold. On the street, I stuff my shaking hands into my pockets, fumbling for a much-needed cigarette. I struggle to light it, my heart racing and my head throbbing. With a long exhale, I feel incredibly disappointed in myself.

I realize that upon reaching the moment I had been waiting for—a story of honesty—I couldn't stand to listen to the details. Stephanie was willing to tell a room full of strangers her sad tale of destruction. In a hushed voice, she had bared her scars one at a time, honest and ugly as they were. And I, pissed off and selfish, had been too unnerved to stick it out with everyone else. The walk home suddenly feels too long for me to manage, and I sit down on the curb outside of the church and try to make sense of why I am so overwhelmed.

I had acted like a child. We have *all* been damaged by the failings, whatever they were, of our fathers, our mothers. Hearing sad stories of ruin in other families will not mean mine had never happened. Each alcoholic's path to the bottom is destructive in its own way, but I suppose it's the willingness of those who have fallen to get back up that matters. Those people, whatever they had done, were trying to get better. Brought together on Thursdays in the basement of a church, they were somehow brave enough to ask for help.

So too is my father, finally. I may have been one of the many children raised in the home of an addict, but I am not a child anymore. Perhaps it's finally time, for my father and for me, to start growing up.

Nisha Koya

Married to Religion

In many ways, I am already part of an arranged marriage of sorts. Just as my parents were presented to each other by the forces of Indian tradition, I too was betrothed. But my engagement was not with a boy, it was with my religion, with Hinduism.

It all started shortly after I was born. When I came home from the hospital, my grandmother mixed the red powder and water and placed a tiny vermillion dot on my forehead. This was for good luck, for protection from the evil eye and lastly, more subtly, to announce my marriage with Hinduism, and my acceptance of it. The dot was merely a symbol for something that my family and society had already accepted and expected of me, even before I was born. I was betrothed to Hinduism even when I was a fetus inside my mother. I was married even before my parents conceived me. I was one of the millions of Hindu egg cells in my mother's ovaries when she was born. So naturally, when I was born, it was waiting for me. From then on, we were destined to be together forever.

Of course, I didn't mind this so much when I was a child. One hardly thinks of the religious influence on his or her life when one is just learning how to walk and eating mushy baby food. But as I grew older, I began to notice the pictures and statues around my house. I was told they were *Bhagvan*, Gods. They were everywhere and in everything. They were watching over me, watching my every move. They would reward me when I behaved well and punish me for my mischief and insolence. They were my other set of parents. Back then I didn't know any better. I accepted what my parents told me without understanding the consequences of my marriage with Hinduism and how our relationship would pan out later in my life. As far as I was concerned, I was a part of this union, I had to play my part.

I became even more aware of my religion when I learned about other religions in school. Every year I was happy to color in Christmas trees and big-bellied Santas during our holiday parties in class. I embraced the Christian holiday and resented my own family for not celebrating with presents and decorations. I so looked forward to going to class and seeing a red stocking on the wall with my name on it. I imagined myself in the shoes of my peers who were lucky enough to celebrate the twelve days of Christmas. I was whole-heartedly, yet unknowingly, flirting with another religion. My parents soon caught on to this envy I held of my friends and soon Christmas trees became a tradition in my own home. I was appeased and my marriage remained intact.

As I grew older, our relationship had its ups and downs. We began to dance around each other's presence without ever really acknowledging the other. While on the outside, we were a happy couple, there were many moments of silence between us, a lack of communication and at other times, pure disinterest on my part. I played the part of a Hindu, but never really knew what it meant to be one. I felt as if I were betraying my other half when I would learn about Greek mythology in high school and analyze references to the Bible in my English classes. I was more familiar with Zeus, Athena, Apollo and Aphrodite, but could hardly name more than three Hindu deities. Whenever I sensed our relationship was falling apart, I tried desperately to hold on. I would try and learn *shlokhs*, or couplets of Sanskrit poetry that carry their own religious meaning and life lessons. But the harder I tried to force an interest in Hinduism, the more I failed and the more my marriage suffered. Recently, our relationship has been struggling more than usual. No, it's not religion, it's me. In any relationship, communication has to be a two-way street, and to be perfectly honest, I need to be a better listener. A mutual understanding couldn't be forced. I now realize that only a genuine curiosity to understand would have given me the motivation to learn about my religion, my other half. Only then can we understand and accept each other for who we really are, on the inside.

The struggle with my spouse had recently come to its breaking point. On the day of my MCAT, I woke up in the morning intending to pray before I left for my exam. But as I stood before the mini statuettes in my room, I was at a loss for words. What does one say after so much time has passed to someone who you've neglected for so long? There was an awkward tension between us as I tried to remember what my mother always used to say when she prayed. In the end I gave up trying and simply mouthed the names of the deities and then, in English, asked for good luck on the exam. As I left my room, I felt the presence of a giant hole inside me, a hole that had grown as the years went by and my dedication to my spouse had dwindled. That was the day I realized that in order for us to live in harmony I would need to look at Hinduism straight in the eye and come to terms with the fact that I have been neglectful and that I would henceforth make an honest effort to gain more knowledge.

This desire stoked my recent interest in the *Bhagavat Gita*, a Hindu scripture that contains many of the fundamental philosophies of the Hindu religion. I always told myself that I would one day read the entire text, from front to back. But as time went by, I never got the chance. About a month ago, I finally picked up my roommate's copy and began to read the first few pages. The *Bhagavat Gita* is primarily a colloquy given by the deity Krishna to Arjuna, a fearless warrior and peerless archer. As Arjuna leads his army into war, into the battle of Kurukshetra, he is overcome with conflicting feelings. His enemies on the other side are his own family, his own cousins. He is distraught by the idea that he would essentially be killing his own family, his own kin. He gives up his bow and arrow and merely sits in his chariot in the middle of the battlefield. At this time, Lord Krishna who serves as his charioteer explains to him that he must not let fear conquer him and instead be brave in order to fulfill his dharma, his duty to his people, to protect from evil and to fight injustice. Arjuna does not comprehend this command from Lord Krishna and inquires as to how he can promote violence. Lord Krishna explains that there is no such thing as living or dead, and that our bodies are merely fleshy coverings for the soul within. Once we die, our spirits take up another body and thus our superficial bodies should not limit us, they should not prevent us from fulfilling our dharma. Lord Krishna explains to him that one cannot gain wisdom by avoiding action, but rather by ignoring one's ego and ensuring that his or her actions are primarily a service to the divine. Most importantly, Lord Krishna explains that in order to achieve success, one must have control over the mind, a clear conscience and insight into his or her purpose in life.

While reading through the text, I found myself constantly searching for more concrete lessons, more specific duties of a Hindu. I wanted to know if in my day-to-day routine I was fulfilling my role as a Hindu. I wanted to know if it was acceptable to kill a spider on the wall or to curse when I was frustrated. I wanted to know if my actions were distancing me from the relationship I have with this religion. But in all of Lord Krishna's teachings that I read through, I couldn't find these rules. I was confused. I had thought that by reading the *Bhagavat Gita*, I would have found answers to the many questions that I had. Over the next few days I continued to wonder about what the *Bhagavat Gita* was trying to tell me, if anything at all. But as I continued to read through the pages of the text, I began to notice a pattern. I realized that the teachings of Hinduism I found in the *Bhagavat Gita* were never going to tell me what I wanted to hear. Instead, the text simply offers the overarching teachings of Hinduism; because Hinduism is an open religion, the text can be interpreted and applied in many different ways.

In essence, I was searching for something that wasn't there. I was expecting my religion to be overbearing, overprotective, limiting, and envious. I had doomed our marriage to failure by not understanding that rather than impose its own beliefs on me, Hinduism provided me with a mirror in which to notice and realize myself and my duties, my responsibilities to God. Rather than criticize my every move, Hinduism allowed me to find my own way, by guiding me from afar. Hinduism was lenient and it was accepting of my mistakes. My relationship with my religion was not set in stone, but rather could be defined in many ways. In the end, I came to appreciate this fact and have found a sense of stability in my relationship. My journey with my religion has just begun and my faith in my relationship will help me overcome the many obstacles in life. I may not be the perfect Hindu, but I've come to learn that there's really no such thing.

Giby George

Organ Harvest

The set is readied. Blue drapes swathe the metal tables, trays, and basins. Instruments range from assorted bowls, forceps, retractors, scissors, saws, and scalpels. Arranged in an alcove of the theater is the anesthesia equipment: gas machines, medicine drawers, and heart monitors. In place of the usual bouquet of color-coordinated syringes rest two vials, the one morphine and the other pancuronium.

Life enters, tearfully cradling Her child, the donor. She is breathtakingly beautiful, too young to be ripe for the harvest. Accompanying her are members of the cast. Among the troupe are the nurse anesthetist and the anesthesiologist, who possess dual roles as mediators between Life and Death.

Monitors are connected and disconnected, electrodes and wires hurriedly attached, the breathing tube readjusted and realigned. Anesthetic gas—Sevoflurane—is continuously administered. An array of translucent drips—epinephrine, vasopressin, bicarbonate, dobutamine, and saline—is transposed from one pole to the other.

The scrub nurses—once the set builders—convene around the table, awaiting the imminent reception of the donor. Life prepares to renounce Her child, tenderly peeling away her swaddling bed sheets and gown. On the count of three, transference occurs. No longer needed, the bed is extradited. The mortuary gurney idles outside the room.

In walks the surgeon—the maestro—motioning for his costume. Garbed in his blue gown, hat, mask, and gloves, he signals for the drape. The curtain is raised, partitioning the main act from the orchestra. He begins to prep the donor, the betadine paint trickling down the side of the drape, speckling the floor.

Hidden behind the drape are the intermediaries, poised by the monitors displaying numbers and undulating waves. Doses are withdrawn from each vial and dispensed sequentially through the IV line, enabling sedation and then paralysis. The overture commences, punctuated by breaths made audible by the ventilator.

The lighting is adjusted to spotlight the main act. The lead roles—the surgeon and the scrub nurses—encircle the table, erecting a sterile cloister. Off to the side of the symphony stands the transplant coordinator.

The coordinator—the director—rehearses the cast's lines. "Only the lungs. Two hours tops. Maintain the heart rate in the sixties, the MAP at eighty, and the PEEP at five." She uses her clapperboard to signal the start of the performance.

Once the prepping is complete, the maestro positions his baton—the scalpel—and makes his incision. Life winces from behind the drape. She knows that She cannot reclaim her progeny, and yet She clings unyieldingly to Her child. Her foe, Death has not yet arrived. He is scheduled to appear during the final act.

A cluster of tantalizing rubies gleams mockingly, aligned along the lacerative pencil marks. White sponges are used to efface temptation, now tainted by Life's plea. Aroused, the surgeon—now a spelunker—descends deeper and deeper into the wreck.

The scrub nurses use retractors to manually widen the slit of the chest, while the surgeon continues to dissect. Rivers of blood diverge into tributaries, as Life continues to flood the wound with Her tears. Suction is used to swallow Life's breast milk. The surgeon continues resolutely and determinedly.

Gear-equipped retractors are required to enable further access to the thoracic cavity. The retractor handle is wound repeatedly, exposing the wealth of the treasure trove.

The surgeon mimes for the sternal saw. "Hold the respiration." The ventilator is shut off, the balloon fully inflated, the lungs entirely deflated. Using his power saw, he partially bifurcates the median of the sternum. "Resume respiration," he commands. The ventilator is turned back on, and the balloon deflates, while the lungs inflate.

Meanwhile, Death has arrived at the scene prematurely, grinning deviously at the sight. Discontented with His role and overcome by a sudden surge of lust, He looms overhead, threatening to disrupt the ritual. Life quivers in response, and the heart rate plummets to the forties.

Prepared for such an unscripted development, the nurse anesthetist promptly improvises. "Heart rate in the forties. Atropine." She glances in the direction of the coordinator and the surgeon, awaiting nods of approval. The duo nods, sanctioning the remedy. Life regains Her grip, as the heart rate ascends toward the sixties. Death cackles malevolently at His own guile, as He retreats, hovering in a recess of the room.

Unfazed by the momentary setback, the surgeon continues. "Hold the respiration." The previous sequence of events is repeated until the rib cage has been completely, symmetrically dichotomized down the midline. "Resume respiration," he authorizes. Breathing is recommenced, as the balloon deflates and the lungs inflate.

He deposits the saw and signals for the bovie. Scepter in hand, he traverses the foliage of tissue, obstructing his view of the target. In the clearing, he glimpses providence, Life's ploy to cheat Death. He caresses the pleura, and tarries for a second or two, synchronizing his breath with the cadence of the hidden heart. Death yawns both audibly and impatiently. Life glimmers with hope, reassured that She might be able to reclaim at least a piece of Her child.

The surgeon delves deeper, seeking to penetrate the fortress of the pericardium. He unearths the acropolis, the chateau, and gapes at the spectacle, both humbled and awed by its visceral grandeur.

He threads a thin catheter into the left main coronary artery, and then clamps the aortic arch. A rush of potassium is delivered into the coronary artery, and the myogenic pace of the heart ceases within seconds. Life wails, mourning the loss of Her child. Death is stunned, angered that He is forced to scavenge. He prefers to hunt, to chase His prey.

The heart is carefully excised from the abyss, beginning with the severing of the vena cavae, the pulmonary veins and arteries, and lastly the aorta. Setting it aside in a nearby basin, the surgeon then focuses his attention on his objective: the lungs. Life approaches the pensieve, reaching in to coddle the melodic remnant of Her child. Watching Her draw nearer, Death swiftly glides over to the vessel, and greedily snatches His meal from within Her grasp.

The surgeon motions for a cup of chilled saline, and pours it into the chasm, steeping the thorax in the Arctic sea. "Fifty-percent oxygen, fifty-percent air." The lungs inflate, appearing somewhat balloon-like. He cleaves and clamps the pulmonary veins and arteries, and then severs and staples the trachea.

Unfettered, the lungs are now able to be salvaged. They emerge, fluttering like an angel's wings. Life and Death lunge for the freed hostage. They both attempt to snag the loot, as it is being secured in a series of sterile bags, containing chilled saline, and then immersed in a container holding crushed ice.

Figuring that the rest of the feast will be His, Death relinquishes His claim over the pillage. The duel between Life and Death has concluded. They have reached an armistice. With Her allotment, Life hopes to imbue breath into another one of Her children, while Death intends to use His share as payment to sail home along the River Styx.

An unfamiliar player—presumably the recipient's transplant surgeon—enters from outside the odeum, reaching for the cooler. "Half-an-hour max to transport the lungs to New York," relays the coordinator. He exits inconspicuously, with Life floating wistfully behind him.

The performance is nearly completed. The monitors have been shut off, the machines reset, the drips and lines discharged. Quiescence displaces harmony and melody. Their roles completed, the nurse anesthetist and the anesthesiologist depart from the stage.

The donor, once sanguine and rubicund, now appears pallid and wan. The heart is returned to its labyrinth, while Death observes keenly, vigilantly, ensuring that his spoils are not plundered. The chest is sutured, and the body is cleaned. Sapphires are observed in place of the once enticing rubies. The gurney is ushered in, and the body is enclosed inside the pouch. Death seals the sack, and skips off the stage with the stretcher.

The maestro disrobes himself, ripping off his guise. He too departs, along with the director. The set builders linger, now responsible for disassembling the stage and turning off the lights. Left behind following their adieu is an empty amphitheatre, embellished with imported jewels—both red and blue—where Life and Death once sparred, where humanity reconciled itself with mortality.

Chris McGuire

A Tuesday

"Please umm... can I have a medium caramel maki err... uhh... macchiato please?" I stumbled to the cute barista with a pixie haircut.

"Real suave there," I thought to myself sarcastically as she turned to make my drink, "maybe if I drool a little bit she'll give me her number out of sheer pity."

"Thanks, have a nice day," she said with a smile as she handed me my midday caffeine fix.

"Thank you?" I responded. Which I instantly regretted because the "you" had somehow come out in a higher pitch than the "thank," which made the whole statement sound like a question. I broke eye contact and walked away quickly.

"Great job there bud, another potential friend lost."

I've always envied people who can handle social situations gracefully, or even satisfactorily. It seems that in exchange for my good vision, handsome forearms, and ability to remember pointless trivia, I have been cursed with a complete inability to talk to strangers, or even casual acquaintances. And when it comes to women, I take my awkwardness to a whole 'nother level. I lack what some might call charisma, charm, or "game." The worst part is that I am painfully aware of how bad I am in social situations. Some people are lucky enough to be blissfully ignorant of their incredible awkwardness. I, on the other hand, am completely and wholly aware of the dumb, awkward things I say and do, yet somehow have no way of stopping them.

I walked over to a big comfy chair by a window and sat down to do some math homework.

"Question 1.) Show that the limit, as variable u approaches a girl = 'extremely awkward'."

"Nope, I'm in no state of mind to do homework," I thought as I looked up from my math book. Whenever I ruin a conversation, I tend to get flustered and jittery and lose the ability to think coherently for a good half an hour. I sighed and took a sip of my caramel macchiato as I let myself sink into the comfy upholstered chair and looked around the room: a small trendy cafe near my apartment. It was the type of place filled with people who wear fedoras and cardigans, who drive hybrid cars and fixed gear bikes, and who want to move to Brooklyn so they can write their blog about '90s post-new-wave cubist literature. Normally I tend to avoid places like that; they tend to smell like record wax and pretentiousness, but I needed a quiet place to work. I had been temporarily evicted from my apartment building because a church was falling on it. As a result, during the day, while construction workers were trying to prevent a steeple from crashing through my bedroom, this cafe was the best place I could find.

I sat there procrastinating, looking around the room and letting my mind wander. Some guy wearing a flannel shirt, capri pants, and what looked like Benjamin Franklin's glasses was writing something on a macbook. There was a skinny guy with a beard eating a bagel with a fork and knife talking to a young Asian girl eating what looked like white Play-Doh with a spoon. At the front, there was a brown haired girl ordering something from the barista, and dear God, she was beautiful.

I could only see her from the side, but she looked as if Liz Taylor and Natalie Portman had a baby, and then that baby had a child with Princess Leia, then that baby had a baby with Natalie Portman again. She had beautiful brown eyes and a cute round nose. She was gorgeous. Just looking at her made my heart melt. At that moment, I experienced the awful, painful, horrible sensation known as a "crush."

This isn't the first time something like this has happened. As an evil twist to my curse of asociability, I somehow seem to develop crushes insanely easily. So easily, I can walk down the street and fall in love at least fourteen times before I make it to the end of the block. I can develop crushes on girls who are up to 300 yards away and I even once had a crush on a girl I don't think ever even existed. I've been doomed to fall head over heels daily, and yet I lack the capacity to actually talk to girls. You would think by now I would have resigned myself to just buying a latex doll and getting over it, but no. I think I do it to torture myself.

I whipped my head away from her as she turned around and started to walk towards me.

"Holy shit. Holy shit. Holy shit,'" I chanted to myself, panicking because I thought she was walking over to me. I was infinitely relieved when she stopped short and sat at the table adjacent to mine. For a second, I had thought she was going to talk to me, which would have been very, very, bad.

I don't do well with spontaneous conversation. Once, I was walking down the street and a homeless guy asked me for some spare change and I told him, "Sorry, I don't have any poor people." When I talk to someone, I need a game plan. I need topics of conversation, quick transitions, witty one-liners, and yo-mamma comebacks in case things get hostile. Without a game plan, my conversations end up being strange jumbles of verbs and prepositions.

I looked down at my math homework to try to distract myself.

"Question 2.) Show that $\propto$ is part of group G where $\propto$ = 'the girl in front of you' and G is the set of the most beautiful faces you have ever seen."

Nope, no amount of abstract mathematics was going to be able to distract me. I glanced up at her for a quarter of a fraction of an instant. She was reading a book. I took another glance. It looked like a science fiction book. A third slightly longer glance. Holy hell, it was *Dune*, one of my absolute favorite science fiction novels involving giant sand worms. Damn it. Why couldn't she have been reading Sarah Palin's autobiography[3] so I could have gotten over her and gone on with my day? I cursed the fates for giving me a ray of romantic hope. Now, because we shared a similar interest which might form the basis of our future relationship, I had to try to talk to her.

In middle school English, they teach you to always open with a "zinger": something to grab their attention. That's what I needed. Something like, "Did you know that the barnacle has the biggest penis to body size ratio of any animal?" I ran a few ice-breakers through my head:

"Hello, how are you?" —Too forward. Plus she might think that we had met before and she'd be all weirded out and distracted trying to remember where we'd met.

"Excuse me ma'am," —Ma'am!? That might work if she were sixty, not so much on a twenty-year-old.

"Hello, I just noticed you were reading one of my favorite novels," — Seemed good at first, what if she hated the book? What if she was reading it ironically so she could laugh at it? Then I'd look like a huge dork.

Disappointed that my zingers were all missing a certain zing, I reverted to my normal pessimistic ways. I pictured myself saying hello and her laughing

---

[3] My least favorite science fiction novel involving giant sand worms.

in my face and insulting my penis size[4]. I imagined myself writing my number on a piece of paper and her tearing it up and throwing it away. I pictured her gossiping with all of the girls in the city about the nerdy loser who tried to talk to her and how they should all secretly laugh at him whenever he walked by.

"Question 3.) For the function f(t) = 'your life', show that f(t) converges to 'bitter loneliness'."

I probably would have moved on and kept doing my homework had I not made the mistake of taking one last look at her. She was resting her perfect cheek bones against her hand as she read. When she would blink, her cute little eye lashes would bat in the air bashfully. It was just too much. I know I had to say something to her, even if it was, "I don't have any poor people."

The next thing I knew, I was standing up, walking towards her. My hands were sweating, my heart was beating furiously, and my sphincter was clenched tight enough to fuse the atom. I didn't have a game plan or any game, but I just had to try. This was it. I walked up to her and tapped my shaking finger against her shoulder. She turned her absolutely perfect face towards mine and smiled.

"Excuse me ma'am. Did you know that the barnacle has the biggest penis to body size ratio of any animal?"

---

[4] not of barnacle proportions.

Maura Hanley

Tears of Purpose

I came to the realization that I had a unique talent at a prime age. Sure, I had missed numerous opportunities to use said talent but at least I had found it before it was too late.

The Realization

I was in Girl Scouts like many young girls my age and once a week we would have our troop meetings. On this particular week we were role playing how to help a friend in need. At this point I had aspirations of becoming a famous actress so I volunteered and was ushered aside and given my role. I was to play the role of someone grieving over the loss of their dog. How is an eight-year-old supposed to get into a role when given so few details? These are the details I came up with to play my role more convincingly: (1) Since I didn't have a dog I picked the dog I was most familiar with, Scooby; (2) I pictured him running from all the ghosts and monsters but ultimately choking on a Scooby Snack (I just learned CPR in Health Class but it didn't cover dogs); (3) My mom and I were going to bury him in my backyard just like we did the rabbit my cat decapitated. As I turned around to face the rest of the troop I put my hands up over my face and started making sobbing noises. To my dismay they started laughing, so I knew I had to fine-tune my art. I stopped the sobbing and moved my hands away from my face and to my surprise they stopped laughing. Tears were streaming down my face and a girl in the troop asked me what was wrong. As I wiped some tears away I explained about my dog and carried out the rest of my act flawlessly and all the while I was thinking, Hollywood here I come.

The Capitalization

Sure, growing up I was able to get that ice cream cone or seat at lunch I really wanted after shedding a few tears, but it really came in handy when I was a teenager. In Middle School, girls traveled in groups and so did the boys and everything involved a lot of drama. The best way to get it all to stop was to shed a few tears. Once everyone's attention was turned towards me, they would continually ask me what was wrong and I would keep shaking my head like I couldn't speak because I was so upset. When the drama was completely over I would reveal that I thought I had something in my eye and acted like my behavior was completely normal. Another situation it would come in handy was when I was being pestered by a boy I didn't want to talk to. The next best thing to mentioning my monthly friend to a teenage boy was crying. They would run back to their huddle of friends wondering why they risked ever leaving it.

The Culmination

This technique worked right through high school and college. It even got me off jury duty during my senior year. I was beginning to get the feeling that all this practice was building up to one final performance. I was interviewing for jobs and I headed into an interview for my dream job. I've wanted this job ever since I realized I wasn't going to Hollywood. I walked into my interviewer's office and he said, "How much does a polar bear weigh? Enough to break the ice! Hi, I'm Dave." I started laughing hysterically and since I'm not great at fake laughing, I started crying to add to the sincerity. Later in the interview Dave told me a gripping story of how the company softball team beat the rival team at the last second and I started tearing up again to show how much the story moved me. Finally, the interview ended and I was leaving the building with a bad feeling about how the interview went when I slipped on some water in the main lobby. I started to get back up when everyone converged on me and I heard some woman who worked for Human Resources mention the company getting sued. I started sobbing, tears streaming down my cheeks; a few minutes later I was told I got the job.

David Fairfield

Separation of Church and Speech

The beginning of the First Amendment of the United States Bill of Rights reads:

Congress shall make no law respecting the establishment of religion, nor prohibiting the free exercise thereof, or abridging the freedom of speech or of the press. (Amendment. I, Sec. I). The freedom of religion and speech were major purposes for the creation of the early American nation. Despite this, the freedom of speech has become less important than religion. As Americans strive to be tolerant of all religions, it is beginning to erode our freedom of speech To prove this we will be looking at four events that have recently occurred in which the freedom of speech and expression was limited so words and actions would not insult certain religious groups

In 2010 Imam Rauf announced plans to construct an Islamic cultural center mere blocks away from the site of the September 11th attacks. While this announcement was met with some criticism from media figures, the matter was debated rather peacefully and even defended by New York Mayor Michael Bloomberg and President Barack Obama as a freedom of religion protected by the First Amendment. In response to Imam Rauf's mosque construction, Reverend Terry Jones of the Dove World Outreach Center told the press that his Christian church would honor September 11th by burning copies of the Koran. His actions, however, were not defended under the same Amendment that afforded Imam Rauf his liberties. Countries of the Middle East region staged mass protests in which many people were killed and hundreds of churches destroyed. Even in the United States, politicians and military personnel scrambled to diffuse what they called a threat to national security. President Barack Obama and members of his administration criticized the Koran burning as "un-American" (Reuters). Eventually Reverend Jones called off the Koran burning due to great pressure put on him.

It is clear that building a mosque less than one mile away from Ground Zero may not be the wisest choice but it was honored as a liberty that we possess as Americans. However, when a Christian minister uses a liberty given to us in the very same Amendment to respond to the mosque's construction, he is judged by a different set of standards. Why are Americans allowing the free expression of one religion but limiting the freedom of speech of another?

Seattle Times cartoonist Molly Norris declared May 20, 2010 to be National Draw Mohammed Day in response to Comedy Central's *South Park* announcing that they will no longer be mocking the prophet Mohammed after the incident drew death threats from around the world. The response to National Draw Mohammed Day was overwhelming. Protests from all over the world took place calling for the death of Norris and the destruction of America for allowing such cartoons to be drawn. Yemeni cleric Anwar al-Awlaki even placed Norris on an international assassination list (Meeks and Nelson). National Draw Mohammed Day drew such a fierce reaction that Molly Norris, with the help of the FBI, changed her name and is now in hiding (Vancouver Sun).

In July of 2010 veteran White House reporter Helen Thomas resigned from her post after making what was deemed anti-Semitic comments. In response to a question about Israel, Thomas replied, "Tell them [the Israelis] to get the hell out of Palestine." Thomas went further and stated that "the Jews should go home, back to Poland, Germany, America, and everywhere else." While her statement was directed at the citizens of Israel, many asserted that her statement was aimed specifically at the predominately Jewish majority of the nation. Immediately after a video of her statement surfaced, calls were made to fire Thomas for her anti-Semitic statement. Rather that being fired, Thomas resigned her White House post shortly thereafter. While her conduct may have been out of place for a White House journalist, does it necessarily mean that she must lose her job? Why must stating her opinion cost Thomas her career just because it might insult a certain religious group?

Opponents argue that while some people may have faced censorship, Congress has yet to pass any official legislation restricting what can be said when it comes to religion. Second, some argue that our freedom of religion means that we are protected from insult via the words and actions of others.

While there may not yet be any laws, we as a society have already begun to limit our scope of expression The main reason we have done this is out of fear; fear of insulting someone, losing our jobs, terrorism, or even death threats. We do not need laws to limit our freedom of speech when our neighbors have already begun to do so without them. Second, our freedom to worship whatever deity we like does not protect us from verbal assault, only acts of physical violence and legal restriction.

But to curtail a civil liberty because of a few hurt feelings contradicts not only our sacred Constitution but also the common laws of nature entitled to each person upon their entering of our American society.

While the evidence could fill numerous books, just these few examples have shown us that in our attempt to make sure no one's religion is offended we have not only stifled the freedom of speech in America, but we in fact offended other religions even more. People's safety and careers should not be demanded in response to them saying something that has insulted a certain group of people. The liberty to worship and speak as we freely wish are the core values of the American way. Even though we may be offended, it is just a part of our freedoms that we must deal with. I close with a saying of Thomas Jefferson: "I would rather be exposed to the inconveniences attending too much liberty than to those attending too small a degree of it."

Works Cited

"State Dept: Church Koran Burning Plan "un-American" | Front Row Washington | Analysis & Opinion | Reuters.com." *Reuters.* 07 Sept. 2010. Web. 24 Feb. 2011. <http://blogs.reuters.com/frontrow/2010/09/07/state-dept-church-koran-burning-planun-american/>

Anonymous. "Cartoonist Behind 'Everybody Draw Mohammed Day' Prank Forced into Hiding." *The Vancouver Sun:* B.5. Print. 2010.

Nelson, Katie, and James Gordon Meek. New York Daily News. "Cleric Anwar Al-Awlaki Puts 'Everybody Draw Mohammed' Cartoonist Molly Norris on Execution Hitlist." Daily News, 11 July 2010. Web. 24 Feb. 2011. <http://articles.nydailynews.com/2010-07-11/news/27069689_1_awlaki-al-qaeda-christmas-day-bombing-attempt>.

United States Bill of Rights. Amendment I. Print. 1789

Dario Rainone

Multitasking: Addictive to You, Profitable to Them

In the fast-paced world of today, people find the urgent necessity to become increasingly efficient in every aspect of their lives. They not only attempt to perform tasks quickly, but even conduct multiple tasks simultaneously. The latter is known as multitasking. It can take many forms, for example driving and talking on the phone or reading while surfing the Internet. However, if one of the two activities requires only a minor degree of thinking from a person, such as walking while talking, he or she is not actually multitasking (Malone and Bastian 1). Multitasking is proven to be inefficient, economically unsound and even addictive. The consumer electronics industry takes advantage of its addictive effects by persistently offering this feature to its consumers.

Multitasking is defined as managing various tasks simultaneously, however recent research shows otherwise. Earl Miller, professor of neuroscience at MIT, published a study in 2008 focusing on a person's ability to multitask. The study showed that, rather than performing multiple tasks at the same time, people quickly switch from one task to another. "You're not paying attention to one or two things simultaneously, but switching between them very rapidly," Miller stated ("Think You're Multitasking? Think Again"). The brain only fools itself into thinking it performs many tasks at once.

Other researchers, such as Daniel Weissman, a neuroscientist at the University of Michigan, arrived at the same conclusion. Dr. Weissmen used an MRI scanner to analyze the behavior of subjects' brains as they were performing different tasks. He observed that the brain pauses between tasks to replace information about the previous task with information about the next one. The study concluded that even if the tasks are simple, multitasking can overwhelm the brain and lead to error ("Think You're Multitasking? Think Again"). The common impression of successfully multitasking is nothing but an illusion, and yet the consumer electronics industry continues to sell products that enable consumers to multitask.

Multitasking is not only a cause of error, but it also slows down the process of performing a task. Eric Horvitz, a Senior Researcher at Microsoft Research, and scientist Shamsi Iqbal of the University of Illinois, conducted a study in 2007 investigating the quotidian work of a group of Microsoft employees. They reported that when checking their email or instant messages, workers took on average 15 minutes to return to work (Lohr 1). This phenomenon at Microsoft, where multitasking leads to an inefficient use of time, is not an isolated case. Basex, an IT research firm that focuses on knowledge management, conducted a series of interviews and surveys over a period of 18 months, showing that interruptions and distractions due to multitasking represent 28% of a knowledge worker's day (Spira and Feintuch 4). This percentage of lost time results in billions of dollars in costs to businesses countrywide every year. Clearly, legitimate scientific evidence proves that multitasking benefits neither efficiency nor the quality of the work performed.

Current empirical research provides the basis to believe that multitasking is not only counterproductive, but also addictive. Doctors Ratey and Hallowell, psychiatrists at Harvard Medical School, carried out a study in 2003 to determine how modern technology can affect focus and distraction. They discovered that people who constantly multitask by checking their emails or answering the phone between tasks become more easily frustrated with long and mentally demanding tasks than those who do not. Drs. Ratey and Hallowell coined the term "pseudo-attention deficit disorder" to refer to a condition where a person has developed a shorter attention span due to the influence of technology (Richtel 1). To better explain this condition, Dr. Ratey compared the consumption of drugs to the irresistible necessity to multitask by stating, "It's like a dopamine squirt to be connected. It takes the same pathway as our drugs of abuse and pleasure. It's an addiction. Without it, we are in withdrawal" (Richtel 2).

This type of addiction for multitasking reflects itself in the increasing usage of electronic gadgets that allow this very practice. Smart phones let users multitask more than any other electronic gadget. A study from the British media regulator Ofcom reported an evident rise in the use of smart phones, such as iPhones (Midgley 2). According to the survey, people send text messages four times more than they did six years ago and roughly 13.5 million people surfed the Internet on their mobile phones in 2010, compared to the 5.7 million from 2008. An article from *The Telegraph*, discussing the Ofcom study, reports that, "People are also using several media at the same time...," which indicates the link between smart phones and multitasking (Midgley 2). Addicted to the latter practice, a growing number of consumers have been using and purchasing smart phones.

The consumer electronics industry answers these high demands with products that enable users to multitask. For instance, although the previous iPhone 3G did not have multitasking features, Apple's current iPhone 4G and iPad 2 devices are able to run multiple programs at a time, "an ability that phones from Apple's rivals already offer and that iPhone owners have long sought" (Metz 1). The recently launched Windows Phone 7 smart phone too allows multitasking. Its major developer, Charlie Kindel, said that Microsoft will continue to improve the ability of the device to simultaneously run applications in the future (Foley 1). To satisfy the increasing multitasking trend, the majority of smart phones on the market today have this ability.

Rising scientific evidence has shown the negative effects of multitasking. It impairs the quality of the works performed and slows down the process of performing them. Multitasking in the workplace leads to considerable monetary losses to the national and, possibly, the global economy. Constant multitasking can decrease one's attention span (i.e. pseudo-attention deficit disorder), thus damaging the psyche. Despite these complications, the consumer electronics industry does not hesitate to take advantage of the addiction induced from multitasking. It persistently offers new ways to multitask, deluding the consumer that it will improve his productivity.

Works Cited

Foley, Mary Jo. "Can Windows Phone 7 multitask?" ZDNet (2010): 1. Web. 04 Nov 2010. <http://www.zdnet.com/blog/microsoft/can-windows-phone-7-multitask-and-other-microsoft-mobile-questions-and-answers/5565>.

Lohr, Steve. "Slow Down, Brave Multitasker, and Don't Read This in Traffic." *New York Times* (2007): 1-2. Web. 26 Oct 2010. <http://www.nytimes.com/2007/03/25/business/25multi.html?pagewanted=1>.

Malone, Laura A., and Amy J. Bastian. "Thinking About Walking: Effects of Conscious Correction Versus Distraction on Locomotor Adaptation." *Journal of Neuropsychology* (2010): 1. Web. 15 Nov 2010. <http://jn.physiology.org/cgi/content/abstract/103/4/1954>.

Metz, Rachel. "iPhone to get long-awaited multitasking ability." Msnbc (2010): 1. Web. 28 Oct 2010. <http://www.msnbc.msn.com/id/36268647/ns/technology_and_science-wireless/>.

Midgley, Neil. "Britons spend half their waking hours using technology, finds Ofcom." *Telegraph* (2010): 2. Web. 29 Oct 2010. <http://www.telegraph.co.uk/technology/news/7952091/Britons-spend-half-their-waking-hours-using-technology-finds-Ofcom.html>.

Richtel, Matt. "The Lure of Data: Is It Addictive?" *New York Times* (2003): 1-2. Web. 02 Nov 2010. <http://www.nytimes.com/2003/07/06/business/the-lure-of-data-is-it-addictive.html>.

Spira, Jonathan B., and Joshua B. Feintuch. "The Cost of Not Paying Attention: How Interruptions Impact Knowledge Worker Productivity." *Basex*, 2005. Print.

"Think You're Multitasking? Think Again." NPR. 02/10/2008. Radio. 01 Nov 2010. <http://www.npr.org/templates/story/story.php?storyId=95256794>.

Faculty
Writing

Introduction

Writers render their perceptions from far off places and times; rarely do they live close to us, and rarer still do we know them or have the opportunity to know them, if only because they have died. They're almost always strangers with disembodied voices to whom we have no easy access. This can be a source of frustration to anyone who has wanted to ask a writer to elaborate on a particular point or share their experiences with the nuts and bolts, from conception to execution, of a written subject.

In the following section, examples of the work by Drexel faculty have been included in *The 33rd* as representations of fine writing. The authors are alive and kicking and on campus; some may be your teachers now or in the future. You can see from the pieces that the approaches and subjects range from original works of poetry, fiction, and personal essay to book and movie reviews to scholarly articles on topics like education and Harry Potter. You can assume that each subject presented particular challenges that the authors had to grapple with in the same way that all writers must, including, of course, those in a composition class.

Genevieve Betts

Review: *Fault*

This fourth poetic work by Katharine Coles layers motifs of disaster, love, and science using numerous arrangements. The book opens with the section *Accidental,* and as the title suggests, investigates life's misfortunes. The speaker of these poems testifies to catastrophes like bombs and fires. In the poem "Good Eye," Coles allows the audience to peer out the window of her witnessing eye, and the speaker's gaze eventually rests on an earthquake in Turkey: "Across the ocean, fault will turn a city: / Shaken, it undoes us, wall by wall" (15). What naturally follows these dangerous events is an examination of life's brevity. In the last lines of this poem, she writes, "Another breath, another day. / Short on miracles, what else can I do / But count them down to measure my long luck" (15). These lines illustrate our brief existence and the accidents or good luck that make the difference.

The second segment of poems, *The Double Leash,* explores human relationships and a love between each other, animals, and nature. Many times, she uses forms like ghazals and pantoums, weaving slant rhymes into intricate rhythms. Starting with human relationships, Coles turns her focus first to marriage. In the poem "Marriage: Ghazal," she opens with the inquiry, "What's lost in love? What retrieved? It could be / we lose ourselves to make love what could be" (42). Here, the push and pull of romantic relationships chafes against individual identity. Coles portrays a similar movement between humans and animals. The poem "The Double Leash" examines this connection as the speaker walks her dogs. They tug against each restraint as she concludes:

> Mediums between
> foreign principalities, they're tied
>
> to me, to each other, by my will,
> by love; to that other realm
> by song, and tooth, and blood. (50-51)

Again, the nature of bonds oscillates between a give and take, never moving in a straight line.

In *Alchemy,* the final section, Coles continues her play with forms, but rather than sonnets and ghazals, she pulls inspiration from scientific theories. In "Outside Newton's House," the speaker examines her experience of visiting Newton's house after hours in the form of the scientific method. She imagines Newton inside and asks, "Could he change his fortune? / In this room I peer at, hands cupped to glass, / He dreams on" (68). Here, Coles returns to themes of fate and sets the reader's gaze on Newton's pacing ghost. These poems also move between the scientific and the spiritual, and she blends the two, rather than seeing them as opposites.

In an era where large-scale disasters abound, these poems speak to those with their eyes fixed on life's urgent unfolding. A glance through this window reveals moments where relationships, tragedy, and invention collide in the course luck allows. In the final poem, "Middle Ages," Coles emphasizes the interplay between the past and fortune one last time: "History cannot be left to chance. / Our histories won't leave us, though even chance / fails in the end" (91).

Works Cited

Coles, Katharine. *Fault*. Los Angeles, California: Red Hen Press, 2008.

Paula Marantz Cohen

Counter Argument

I was strolling through a department store recently, killing time before meeting a friend, when I became lost in the maze of cosmetic counters. I was not literally lost, of course. I could make my way past the makeup into the shoe department blindfolded. The problem is when I'm *not* blindfolded. That's when my head gets turned. Although I know, intellectually, that the makeup sold in this labyrinthine space is the same as what I can buy in the drugstore for a fraction of the price, I am unable to resist the fancy packaging and the placards advertising free gifts and special enzyme action. I am seduced into believing that these products will make me, in the immortal words of Oprah, "as cute as I can be."

So there I was, loitering among the age-defying moisturizers, when a young woman in a white smock smiled seductively in my direction. The come-hither look of a cosmetic saleswoman could mean only one thing: She wanted to make me over.

The term "makeover," as used here, would take a flight of feminists to unpack, so I won't even try. Suffice it to say that it entails, first, that you climb onto a very high stool so that your legs dangle foolishly. Once perched on said stool, you then succumb to the ministrations of the white-smocked saleswoman—the white smock providing a vaguely medical aura to the proceedings—who will daub and brush your face for the purpose of making you look as unlike yourself as possible. This dubious disguise will last all of about 20 minutes, a window during which you will be sold a truckload of products you don't need.

I knew all this, but still, it is the nature of the cosmetic counter to erase memory, not to mention logic and common sense. So there I was, perched on the stool, as the cosmologist (OK, cosmetologist) took out the products in her line. I had not bothered to notice what line this was, and now fearfully glanced over to see. Fortunately, it wasn't one of the European lines with austere packaging (the more austere, the more expensive) that would bankrupt me with the purchase of a lip gloss. It was instead one of the fun, wannabe lines that would bankrupt me more slowly. I thus relaxed into the experience.

The products had now been aligned in military formation on the counter, awaiting deployment on my face. As anyone who has visited a cosmetic counter knows, these products constitute an intricately interlocking system: buy one and the others must follow as the night cream the day cream. I have to tip my hat to the marketing genius who came up with the cosmetic system;

it not only helps the company's bottom line, it also helps its female consumers live in hope. If in purchasing the foundation and the pressed powder, you still don't look like Halle Berry or Gwyneth Paltrow, you can always rationalize this by the fact that you did not buy the moisturizer or the blush. Elaborate the system enough and there's always something you haven't got. As new products get added or changed, flawless beauty always remains an under-eye cream or pore-minimizer away. Makeup, in this regard, is a metaphor for desire. It keeps us women convinced, as we grow old and decrepit, that we can still look like supermodels.

But to return to my makeover. The saleswoman who had smiled at me a few minutes earlier now grew stern as she peered at my face. Having been made over before, I was ready for what was coming: the ritual of trashing my current appearance to prime me for a massive investment in something new.

"I see you don't wear makeup," said the white-smocked saleswoman, as though I were a hillbilly lost in the big city.

"Well, actually..." I stumbled. Of course I wore makeup. I had spent at least half an hour that morning slathering it onto my skin. But the tack among makeover saleswomen is to pretend you have nothing on your face, thereby suggesting that you are wasting your time with your old system. I knew this ploy, but knowing doesn't help. If you're insecure about how you look (and who isn't?) you're still going to be suckered.

The white-smocked cosmologist (sic) now continued, sensing her advantage: "Do you take care of your skin?"

This was a trick question. Or rather, a question in which the answer was already implied. If she thought I took care of my skin, would she ask? No, she would say: "What lovely skin you have. You must take good care of it." Which would in turn imply: "Why in hell would you want to mar your lovely skin with this product line that will cost you an arm and a leg?" Needless to say, this was not the reasoning she was after, especially in a recession.

The fact is that she'd hit on a sore point with me. I'm self-conscious about my skin. Ever since suffering from mild acne in the seventh grade, I have spent a lot of time scrubbing my face, and I know that those in the skin care business do not consider scrubbing a good technique. You are supposed to dab lightly in the way you would in cleaning an Old Master painting.

Knowing that I had been remiss in my curatorial duties, I murmured apologetically. But the saleswoman was not interested in what I had to say. She was engrossed in cleaning off my face, occasionally looking down in disgust at the engrimed wipe so as to reinforce the notion that whatever I'd been doing before had been wrong. She then began to coat me with the various emoluments displayed before her, until Voila!, she tilted the mirror in my direction to reveal my new appearance. I squinted at the reflection. The effect, if not exactly prepossessing, was colorful. My cheeks, for example, were very rosy, as though I'd just been climbing a mountain on a windy day. Although climbing a mountain is not my thing, it's nice to know that I can look as though I climbed one.

"You see how I've erased the laugh lines and minimized the jowls," the saleswoman pointed out (jowls, I assume, are something one needs at all costs to minimize). It was true: My face looked as though it has been covered with spackle.

"And look at how your eyes pop," she added. This was true, too. My eyes, which are small and deep-set, now looked like those of a mildly crazed beetle. I gazed at my sparkling little eyes in wonder and some fright.

"And you see what the right gloss will do for the lips." (Please note how cosmetic marketers dissect the face into self-standing parts that can thus be evaluated as though they belong to someone else. This allows them to sell you an entire system devoted to a singular part: the eyes or the mouth—or, once these major sites have been taken care of, lesser ones like the neck or the eyebrows.)

I inspected my lips, which, bathed in a sticky substance, looked like ripe plums. (The question, of course, is whether one wants one's lips to look like ripe plums.)

"The lips are fabulous!" exclaimed the white-smocked saleswoman, putting an end to doubt. "Bodacious berry is definitely your color."

I was not sure about any of this, but the high stool, the lights on the little mirror, and the white-smocked expert's air of authority all combined to cloud my brain. I was under a spell, my will entirely obliterated so that I purchased $100 worth of products. It's a good bite (though far from all) in the product line, for which I was rewarded with a cartload of free samples so as to entice me to buy more.

When I got home, my daughter said I looked like a clown and my husband said I looked the way I always do—two extremes that, opposed though they are, suggested that the system I had just purchased might not be worth it. As it happened, I was allergic to the foundation, thereby toppling the product system of which the foundation was, literally speaking, the foundation. I was relieved that the store was willing to refund my money—the red patches on my face possibly convincing them that a lawsuit would not be worth the trouble. But I did keep the lip gloss. It turns out I like having lips like ripe plums. Bodacious berry is definitely my color.

Valerie Fox

Teacher

In the next room my teacher, smoking and trying not to listen to me playing her good guitar. Her mentioning the musical tastes of the boy whose lessons overlapped mine now and again (who forgot briefs under his cut-offs). Her pride telling stories about her mongrel show dog, Hap. Being proud of him. Her hinting that even though I ought to practice the Tarrega more, she understood how I only played for myself. Her lying dead for a while. It was the weekend and no one to check up on her. Only a few years after I'd gone. Now and again I think about her when I'm trying to teach something to some of these people.

Valerie Fox

how the river had invited her down for a serious talk

We went down there because it was high
It was a natural disaster and we wanted to get closer
We talk about it now and again
By the little league park and the small pier

We go down there to the place that feels natural
It's clean
We are clean when you compare us to dirty things
Tires and dangerous vapors

We never see her any more
It's a shock because you think a person's image cannot fade
The face of someone twice removed
gets replaced by someone else's face
The mind's eye always seemed to grow keener,
it's not doing that any more

Down there we can sit in the car and talk
Don't get out
Don't get out you can see everything
you need to see
from here

Cassandra Hirsch

Ghosts

When I was ten and my brother, Colin, eight, my parents bought an old schoolhouse in a northern corner of Ontario, just north enough to be away from home; too far away for me. It sat on an acre of grass with trees all around it on the outer perimeter, and it was one hundred years old. At first, we went there on weekends and lived in it just as it was, with its pit toilets right inside the house, its one remaining wood and wrought iron desk nailed to the floor, its one large room filled with our bedraggled furniture.

I hated it there. When I wasn't playing on one of the two puckered wood swings, their thick, rusty chains gritty in my hands, or trying to keep my brother up in the air on the sea saw, I truly hated it. In between charming the garter snakes out of the nest they'd made under the house or climbing the barbed fence to go groundhog spotting in the neighboring field, I wanted so badly to go home that I refused to betray any fleeting interest I had in the place with a smile.

Right from the first, I began to imagine children who must have gone to school at our weekend home when it was built in 1875. In my mind, it was mostly girls who played in the yard, wading through the thick, uncut grass with their long dresses, coming toward me with smiles and a plan to rescue me from my crippling boredom. I wanted them to exist and daydreamed them into the lonely days I spent with my brother who annoyed me as much because he seemed to like the schoolhouse as for his speed and agility.

Tree climbing was effortless for him, though I managed somehow to clutch the limbs that would take me high enough to look from that silver maple out onto the other fields and the houses and farms and think of jumping in one free-flying leap toward the farthest one just to see if I could. But rather than jump from tree to swaying wheat, we climbed over the barbed wire to plod through the adjacent fields.

While our parents read and napped, we got to know the McDermotts up the road, whose farm boasted pigs and cows, dogs and cats. If the pigs were out, we rested against the fence, our arms dangling over it while the pigs lay around, their muddied backs cracking in the sun.

Sometimes we headed for the barn and Colin scrambled up into the loft, his little blond head rising almost indistinguishably from the hay bales stacked high as he grabbed onto the rope and swung into the heap of straw below.

It was fun to watch him, but I wasn't tempted. The smell of the hay, its ends brushing against my clothes and prickling my bare legs, was enough for me.

Our parents knocked the ceiling out after the first year, in 1976, and put in three bedrooms, leaving the first floor open after they took out the makeshift walls and moved the beds upstairs. The railing at the top was one person wide between slats, the stairs gapped wide enough for an errant foot to slip through. My room had a map of England covering one wall. In love with England through books, I looked at that map every night, running my finger along it, imagining the patchwork of fields brought into focus past the grid lines.

Attached to the schoolhouse was, and still is, a small barn, with a door leading into the house that was sealed shut. Inside were cobwebbed remnants of the building, covered in dust. It was the smell of things forgotten that I still equate with death, not knowing what death smells like, not making sense even then of my longing for the ghosts of children who'd lived a century before me and what they would have smelled like if I could have met them in my own stultifying reality.

When we were old enough to venture further away from the schoolhouse, Colin and I took to the unpaved road that led to Glen Huron, a tiny town with a water wheel and a general store, two or three miles away where there was salvation in candy.

We didn't talk much on the way, united only by our boredom and the appalling lack of kids our age, a persistent problem through the years we'd spent there so far, removing ourselves from our friends most weekends from June through August. Fingering the few dollars entrenched in my pocket, I imagined the chocolate bars I'd buy that would see me through the rest of the weekend. My brother, more private by the time he was 11 or 12, might have been thinking anything; maybe thinking he'd rather be playing with his friend Martin than poking along a country road with his older sister. I never asked him that question, never thought to.

I don't remember when I was first allowed to stay home while my parents went up North. I must have been about 17 and possibly Colin stayed with me. A few times in my college years I took a girlfriend up for the weekend without my parents there and we went to the beach, to the shores of Georgian Bay, went out to dinner, or cooked at the house, its one room filling with whatever our botched efforts yielded. Colin would go up on his own often later, in his late teens and twenties, perhaps preferring his own company.

I never talked to him about why he liked the schoolhouse so much; likely, I connected it with his inclination away from the family, his pronounced need to spend time apart from us even as he treated us all with a kind of acquaintance-level respect. He and I got along well enough when we reached our teens, but I don't think we found a mutual pass-through until our thirties when we revealed the work we were both doing, the writing we'd both chosen that would define our lives, shape them and, for Colin, ultimately rob him blind of the life he'd chosen to pursue as a writer.

After my late teens, I didn't go up to the schoolhouse for years, forgetting the ghosts I waited for who never came, audibly grateful for my autonomy as soon as I had it. Being allowed to stay home while my parents were up there was a power I didn't even know how to use, or abuse, since for most of 17 I didn't have a boyfriend. At 18, I brought my then-boyfriend up and his very real allergies to old things made him ill, so we never went again.

Not long after, I was engaged to a man plagued by an allergic reaction to the mold that inhabited unmined corners of the house. We weren't a fastidious family, my mother content to leave things coated in dust, smeared with grease, dotted with crumbs so she could gather fiddleheads or milkweed to make edible. It drove my father mad, but I didn't know this until long after I moved away and kept my own house. They would visit Joe and me and out of her earshot my Dad would remark to me how much neater I was than my mother. I'd smile, aware of the truth, that my husband was a far more exacting housecleaner than I would ever be, or want to be, that I kept a reasonably clean house more to sidestep his scrutiny than to counter what I'd grown up with. And anyway, though I didn't say this to my father, I'd always admired her unusual lack of accountability to anyone. I still admire this about her even as I poke a little fun which has the effect of making her laugh at herself.

When our children were small, they loved the schoolhouse. They loved the supernatural quiet of it, the remove from everything they thought of as natural. On drives up to Toronto to visit my parents, we would ogle the indolent cows lying in the sun, the horses grazing near the roadside, and clutch our guts on the roller coaster of the Hockley Valley road. (Just the name of that highway still summons queasiness.)

When we were there with the kids, I would look up at the night sky and wish I'd looked with less fear as a child. Then, one August, when our youngest daughter was a baby and the older two children were still awake, a brilliant light undulated across the sky and I felt certain something terrible was going to happen. It lingered for hours, soundless and graceful, and we stood under it. Beneath that brilliance, I could see where the ground was scarred where the sea saw and swings used to be. The bats had the good sense to stay in the eaves, away from light. Occasionally, I'd go inside and stand behind the screen willing the terror out of me, finally half-convinced that we were all experiencing a close encounter. I pictured our family clawing at the ground with feeble fingers as we struggled against being beamed onto a mother ship and I still laugh at how that single protracted sighting of Northern Lights could stir such panic in me when my mother stood fearless most nights of my childhood under the night sky, beckoning me out because I couldn't sleep. And I would join her and my father for a few minutes only to scurry back inside, favoring a lonely house with a maddeningly sleeping brother over a star-clouded ceiling.

In late 2003, my brother told me that part of his plan to write and teach English and Drama the way our grandfather had involved the schoolhouse. He wanted to live there for several months with his dog Gabby who loved it there as much as he did. He would do so in winter, the loneliest time up there, waiting it out until he could earn his teaching degree in Australia the following year. Most years our parents had rented the place to skiers, the sport popular up there with the swells of Blue Mountain and other runs nearby. So, it was winterized and ready to receive him.

I had looked at him in disbelief and possibly admiration when he filled me in. Yes, I knew he liked it; I even felt a certain jealous prickle that he was free to chase his dream, that he could make a decision to change his life and be truer to himself, and that part of his scheme involved a cross-Canada cycling trip that would begin his new life.

But what resonated when he first told me about his plan during an October visit to Philadelphia, and asked me not to tell our parents yet, was the idea that he would hole up at the schoolhouse when the earth was dead and the trees bare, the wind shrill at the windows, the people...well, that last didn't matter because people were not what he was after.

I didn't tell my parents. When he finally let them know what he'd be doing, from selling his home, to cycling across the country, to staying at the schoolhouse writing away the months of autumn well into winter and then attending school, I recall that pride stuck in my throat, displacing envy. I hope I told him that what he was doing was hats off incredible.

In the summer of 2004 on that summer-long cross-country cycling tour, Colin lost his life to a man driving on a Western Canadian highway as if he had the right-of-way all over the road, as if my brother were merely a decoy he could plow over. Yes, the man and his driving companion stopped afterward, but by then Colin was broken and gone from me, from everyone.

I didn't tell him that I'd started to write a play about our earliest years at the schoolhouse and that the characters of Carrie and Mitchell were composites of my two older children, him and me, or that there was a prominent ghost in the story. In the play I have yet to finish, Penelope, a girl who had been a student in the schoolhouse 100 years earlier, comes to Carrie in her dreams and lulls her away from her belligerent need to hate the place. She shows Carrie clues to a lush legacy in the town, relics in the barn adjoining the schoolhouse, mends fences between Carrie and her vexing younger brother. Finally, Penelope helps them hatch a plan to keep the schoolhouse when their parents find it's much more than they'd first thought they could handle when they plucked their children from city life to show them that quiet wasn't just when the lights went out at night.

Rebecca Ingalls

The Trilemma Revised: Harry Potter and a Landscape of Moral Uncertainty

In his discussion of the religious controversy that has orbited around J.K. Rowling and her *Harry Potter* novels, Andrew Blake (2002) makes the case that—unlike the books of C.S. Lewis and J.R.R. Tolkien—*Harry Potter* is devoid of "allegorized Christianity." Citing the books' lack of attention to Christmas as a spiritual event, the absence of a "superhuman power" that might protect the souls that Dementors are trying to devour, and the relativism of morality in the texts, Blake asserts, "Harry Potter isn't anti-Christian—the faith just isn't there" (2002, p. 95-96). The faithlessness of the novels, he argues, is what bonds them with others of the "post-Christian context" in which texts "work...precisely to stress the presence of the irrational and inexplicable in the contemporary world" (2002, p. 98-99). Blake posits that Rowling's books—while frightening to Christians—are reflections of today's "general crisis of faith" and are applicable to all people in that they dare to "deal with fundamental questions of human existence" (2002, p. 99).

While Blake makes an important argument about the novels' arrival in a cultural context that is rife with the questions, doubts, and disorder of postmodernism, he fails to recognize the uncannily similar thread of Christian rhetoric in the stories of Narnia and the Wizarding World of *Harry Potter*. Specifically, the "trilemma"—the three-part rationalization (Liar, Lunatic, Or Lord?) that Jesus was the Son of God, which Lewis illustrates in *The Lion, the Witch and the Wardrobe* (1950)—is ubiquitous in the adventures of *Harry Potter*. The multivalent question that haunts Narnia (Aslan's existence and resurrection as a Christ-figure) also winds its way through the unfolding plot of the *Harry Potter* series, showing a flicker in the first book, emerging full force in Book Five, complicating itself further in Book Six, and reaching its culmination in Book Seven.

What is particularly striking about the trilemma in the *Harry Potter* series, however, is that it is revised and leads the narrative down a different rhetorical path than the one found in the explicitly Christian stories of Narnia. Defying and confusing some traditionally stark boundaries between good and evil, mortal and immortal, *Harry Potter* is not Lewis's tidy story of clear ideological divisions or a clear rationalization of who-is-God and who-isn't-God. In Narnia, Lewis brings to life the story of Christ in terms easily translatable: Christ (or, Aslan), as the symbol of unconditional love and forgiveness, has died, has risen and will rise again. Edmund is the Judas character who turns himself around, and Aslan's (Christ's) identity as Lord is easily deduced in his sanity and honesty. Within the *Harry Potter* series, however, the narrative illustrates that Evil, too, in its myriad forms, can die, rise and return again; and no one is immune to doubt, mortality, or the temptation of "unforgivable curses."

Amid the texts' continued popularity (especially on the brink of the release of the last two films in 2010 and 2011), Christian resentment for the texts, and the ruins of Rowling's last book, we are compelled to ask, what is the message of *Harry Potter*? I argue that this rhetorical thread of the trilemma is critical to the composition of the Potter books as postmodern texts, and as tools to draw their readers into a conversation about what it means to negotiate today's social world outside of the texts. Indeed, as Blake (2002) suggests, the texts represent the "irrational" and "inexplicable" state of the world today. However, I assert that even amid such turmoil, there *is* faith to be found in the rhetoric of their message.

Lewis's Trilemma: A Rational Argument

We find C.S. Lewis's assertion that Jesus Christ was indeed the Son of God in his book *Mere Christianity* (1952), in which he writes:

> A man who was merely a man and said the sort of things Jesus said would not be a great moral teacher. He would either be a lunatic—on the level with a man who says he is a poached egg—or he would be the Devil of Hell. You must make your choice. Either this man was, and is, the Son of God: or else a madman or something worse. You can shut Him up for a fool, you can spit at Him and kill him as a demon; or you can fall at His feet and call Him Lord and God. (1952, p. 56)

Lewis's three-part rationalization for Jesus-as-Lord is otherwise known as the "trilemma," as articulated by Josh McDowell in his 1980 book *More Than a Carpenter*, in which he cites Lewis's *Mere Christianity* as he builds his case for the argument that Jesus is the Son of God. Leaning heavily on logos, McDowell asserts that the "liar, lunatic, or Lord" "trilemma" should lead a potential believer to see that Jesus was not deliberately telling people un-truths (based on his lifestyle, his "teachings," and his eventual crucifixion), and he was not insane (based on the profundity of his teaching), so 'logic' would suggest that he was who he said he was (1980, p. 25-35).

It is no secret that C.S. Lewis was, as Bruce Edwards (2005), C.S. Lewis scholar and author of *Further Up & Further In*, articulates it, a "pioneer of faith" (p. 1). A convert to Christianity after a series of personal losses and a great distancing from his father during school-aged years spent in miserable boarding schools, Lewis sought to "pursue with a pure heart his real vocation of communicating the gospel in fresh and refreshing ways in multiple genres for a diversity of audiences" (Edwards, 2005, p. 5). Lewis's closing remarks in *Mere Christianity* encompass his larger message to readers: "Look for yourself, and you will find in the long run only hatred, loneliness, despair, rage, ruin, and decay. But look for Christ and you will find Him, and with Him everything else thrown in" (1952, p. 190). In inviting his readers to "look for Christ," Lewis endeavored to write Christ in accessible terms into his narratives. Edwards illustrates how in *The Lion, the Witch and the Wardrobe* Lewis constructs "inherently a spiritual world, a world informed by C.S. Lewis's Christian convictions and wise understanding of our fallen planet" (2005, p. 12). In his book, *Jack: A Life of C.S. Lewis*, George Sayer (1988) asserts that Lewis's "idea, as he once explained [to Sayer], was

> to make it easier for children to accept Christianity
> when they met it later in life. He hoped that they
> would be vaguely reminded of the somewhat similar
> stories that they had read and enjoyed years before.
> "I am aiming at a sort of pre-baptism of the child's
> imagination." (1988, p. 318)

Using children's fantasy as his device, Lewis aimed to argue for what he believed to be the very reality that Jesus Christ was "man (just like you) and God (just like His father)" (*Mere Christianity*, 1952, p. 162). He hoped that—along with the myriad other memories implanted into the mind of the child in his youth—his stories would embed themselves and become part of the child's emerging and devoted faith.

The Potter Controversy

Though J.K. Rowling openly admits to no such religious agenda, since their debut the books have been contested between fundamentalist voices who believe them to be anti-Christian and even evil; those who partially defend the books as potentially evil but useful in preaching to children against evil; those who believe the books to be laden with moral teachings (though coinciding with Christian doctrine but not necessarily overtly Christian) and suitable texts for children; and those who argue that the books are obviously—and even deliberately—rich with Christian themes. Such a debate opens the door for rhetoricians to closely examine these texts and to unearth not only the potential messages they may be sending to a range of audiences, but also to identify the textual strategies that are used to send those messages. In a heated debate about banning books and teaching children about God—or not—it becomes not only intellectually interesting to compare and contrast the compositions of these texts, but also critically important to the ways in which we think about marketing them, teaching them in our classrooms, and using them to think seriously and meaningfully about how they might represent the context in which they have been written.

We might begin, then, with a look at some voices in the debate. Citing "good magic" as inherently evil in the Potter series, Jack M. Roper (2007), whose writing is largely dedicated to cult research, argues, "Periodically in our society, mystical heroes penetrate our culture. Harry Potter, an orphaned witch, is one such hero who has captured the innocent heart of many children. When such a hero uses evil as a problem solving tool, we need to be warned" ("Harry Potter: The Hero for Modern Witchcraft"). This article, which may be found on the Christian Broadcasting Network's web site in a section called, "The Harry Potter Controversy," is also accompanied by slightly contrasting arguments for the Potter novels as conduits for teaching the Christian Gospels. For example, even though she, too, believes that the books may be dangerous for those readers who are "easily led astray," Connie Neal (2007) attempts to find a middle space with the novels. In her article, "What Would Jesus Do with Harry Potter?" she suggests, "Jesus might read the Harry Potter stories and use them as starting points for parables. He might use kids' interest in the battle between good and evil to explain the ultimate battle between good and evil."

On the other side of the 'definitely-evil' and 'potentially-evil' spectrum, there are others, though perhaps not as numerous, who see Rowling's books as thematic representations of Christian teachings. Some even believe them to be driven by a Christian agenda and suggest that the books are appropriate for children because they help to tell the Christian story. John Granger (2006), author of *Looking for God in Harry Potter*, is "convinced that the fundamental reason for the astonishing popularity of the Harry Potter novels is their ability to meet a spiritual longing for some experience of the truths of life, love, and death taught by Christianity but denied by secular culture" (2006, p. 2). While he admits that he initially would not let his own children read the books (2006, p. 4), Granger has come to believe through his own reading of them *"that the Harry Potter stories 'sing along' with the Great Story of Christ is a significant key to understanding their compelling richness"* (2006, p. 2, emphasis his). His position on this issue suggests that the novels fill a gap in faith that mainstream culture didn't even know it had.

Rowling and Lewis: A "Kinship," a Departure

Though fewer in number, scholarly and religious voices have emerged to assert that there are Christian links between Rowling's and Lewis's narratives: some draw comparative parallels, while others find critical points of departure. Indeed, Granger (2006) refers repeatedly to C.S. Lewis, and aligns his own Christian beliefs with those found in *Mere Christianity* (2006, p. *xiii*). In some similar ways, Joy Farmer (2001) cites myriad religious parallels between Rowling and Lewis. Sharply contrasting Blake's (2002) claim in the introduction to this article, she argues, "Given the moral and spiritual dimension of Rowling's books, it is no surprise that they contain almost as much religious allegory as The Chronicles" (2001, p. 58). Acknowledging their shared appreciation for "both benevolent and malign" magic, Farmer suggests that each author links magic back to the miracle stories of healing and replenishment in the Bible. She writes:

> Jesus changes water into wine, feeds a multitude with five loaves and two fish, and restores a blind man's sight with spittle. Because the context is religious, these events are deemed miracles, not magic. Yet Lewis and Rowling both deliberately blur the distinction in such examples as Aslan's Table, whose feast is daily renewed and daily cleared away; the dishes in Hogwarts' Great Hall, which fill and empty (seemingly) by themselves; Lucy's "cordial which would heal almost every wound and every illness" [qtd. in Farmer]; and the tears of Fawkes the phoenix, which have similar curative powers. (2001, p. 54)

Such examples of magic/miracles, Farmer argues, acknowledge the existence of the Divine, but do not take away from the fact that suffering and evil exist, as well (2001, p. 55-56).

Further, Farmer draws a direct link between Aslan and Harry Potter in their mutual representation of Christ. Citing his "mixed parentage," the rhetoric of chosen-ness that surrounds him, his instincts to protect his friends, and his "unique and miraculous survival of Voldemort's attack," Farmer argues that Harry, like Aslan, is meant to be a Christ-figure (2001, p. 58). Moreover, she suggests, Harry's mother's sacrifice of her own life so that he could live (a scene that might also bring to mind Mary's self-sacrifice), and the subsequent scar left on Harry's forehead from that life-saving act, recalls the rhetoric of death and resurrection, and God's ultimate protection from evil, in the New Testament. Such a parallel, Farmer argues, constructs Harry to be "like Christ the Second Adam [who] represents all humanity" (2001, p. 59).

Likewise, in "The Search for 'Deeper Magic': J.K. Rowling and C.S. Lewis," Griesinger (2006) argues against the fundamentalist belief that the Potter novels are inherently evil, and instead asserts, "Paradoxically, while drawing on imagery and symbols associated with witchcraft and the occult, Rowling nevertheless incorporates into the magic of her vision ideas that are neither occultic nor pagan but *decidedly* Christian" (2006, p. 318, emphasis mine).

Citing Lewis's discussion of the "Deep Magic" of Aslan's self-sacrifice in *The Lion, the Witch, and the Wardrobe*, Griesinger, like Farmer, argues that Rowling, too, implements her own version of "Deep Magic" with Lily Potter's sacrifice to save her son from Voldemort, and Harry's risking of his own life for the sake of others (2006, p. 326-327).

These parallels between characters and twists of the plot, I argue, are important similarities that should draw a reader in for a closer look at the way in which the texts grapple with and make arguments about more complex issues, like morality. Indeed, the conversation among scholars about how Rowling and Lewis take on Christian morality is divided between those who believe that the two series represent clear moral boundaries, and those who believe that Rowling's texts make such distinctions far less clear to readers. Griesinger stands with the former camp on this issue. In her response to those Christians who rail against the books for being "morally confusing, without clear boundaries between evil and good," she writes, "I do not see this confusion," outlining the myriad lessons in the book that demonstrate "learning and playing by the rules" and the reality of having to "struggle and make right choices" (2006, p. 324). She refers to Harry's first experience with the Sorting Hat as a dilemma that illustrates such a struggle: "Harry has to decide which group to follow. Who will his role models be, honest Gryffindors or conniving Slytherins?" (2006, p. 325). Griesinger's suggestion is that while Harry himself may struggle to find righteousness, binaries in "the battle between goodness and evil" (2006, p. 331) are clearly delineated. Matthew Dickerson and David O'Hara (2006) agree that the Potter texts reflect an "objective morality," and they point to Dumbledore as "the great hero of the books" (2006, p. 249). Specifically, they assert that "Rowling's Dumbledore is in the same company as the heroes of Lewis and Tolkien when he says that there is a battle and that everybody is on one side or the other" (2006, p. 247).

Contrasting these authors' claims about the presence of distinct moral coding in the Potter books, Rebecca Stephens (2003) argues the very opposite and, as I will illustrate, helps to set us up for a critical rhetorical analysis of the ways in which the texts utilize the trilemma as a device. In her discussion of the similarities and differences between the Wizarding World and Narnia, Stephens asserts that in Narnia, "the reader always knows where one world ends and the other begins" and the righteous Aslan seems to be in control of everything (2003, p. 55-56). In the Wizarding World, however, the "limitations" of Dumbledore suggest that he "is clearly no Aslan" (2003, p. 57), and the lack of a clear, morally righteous authority figure makes it so that "all of the forces of the good in the book are decentralized" and "power seems horizontal" (2003, p. 57). As such, anyone could take up either the reigns of good or evil, and "traditional power structures are actively subverted" (2003, p. 57-58). It is this lack of authority and moral unity, argues Stephens, that is likely the cause for many Christians' vehement opposition to the texts. Like Blake, Stephens asserts that "in a world where traditional rules are not working" *Harry Potter* is an artifact of a society that is morally and culturally fragmented, and the many modern readers who are drawn to the texts may find themselves represented in them.

Indeed, what we have in the *Harry Potter* series, I argue, is a world that is unraveling. While early books in the series may suggest either-or questions of rightness or wrongness that will ultimately be answered, the progression of the series reveals a critical departure from such clear binaries all the way to the last book and beyond. Lewis's work is especially helpful in this rhetorical examination of Rowling's texts because, like those of Lewis, Rowling's books utilize the trilemma as a rhetorical tool. However, while the trilemma works in Lewis's books to edify morality, it works in Rowling's to splinter it. The dilemmas of honest-versus-conniving, good-versus-evil that the *Harry Potter* novels present become part of a critically complex—even unanswerable—trilemma that asserts that it is not always easy or even possible to decipher righteousness from wickedness. Reflecting in many ways the "Liar, Lunatic, or Lord?" rationalization about who is ultimately the most benevolently and malevolently powerful, the *Harry Potter* texts employ a trilemma of a larger scope that invites Harry, the other characters, and the books' readers to ask, "Good, Bad, or Somewhere in the Middle?" This trilemma not only exists in an underlying question about faith and doubt as we seek to understand who Dumbledore, Harry, Voldemort, Snape and even the Wizarding World itself represent in Christian terms, but also in the ongoing, perhaps even nondenominational, question about who is fighting for which side of morality. By the end of Book Six, readers still don't know, and neither does Harry. By the end of Book Seven, the reader sees a mess of moral confusion, and an argument about "Deep Magic" that transcends the boundaries of Christianity into a more universal inquiry into the postmodern condition of today.

Deciphering Ultimate Good: Echoes of Lewis's Trilemma

The foundation of this comparative/contrastive analysis of the religious rhetoric of Lewis's and Rowling's series begins with the critical parallels between characters, which eventually help to illustrate how their roles translate from Hogwarts back to Narnia. It's important to note, from the outset, that the books are similar in ways that may not directly relate to religious rhetoric at all; such similarities lead a critical reader to look for places where the books are connected beyond the surface level. In understanding the ethos of *Harry Potter*, we find that parallels between characters in Lewis's and Rowling's work lead to important shared—and perhaps divergent—values.

We can begin with the nebulous portals (perhaps, even, characters unto themselves) from which characters leave the real world to enter the magical worlds: the ordinary wardrobe, and the illusory "barrier between platforms nine and ten" (Rowling, 1997, p. 93) that is Platform Nine and Three-Quarters. Guarding these borders are two similar gatekeepers: Hagrid and Mr. Tumnus. Both are messengers that lead the child across the boundary between the real or Muggle world and that of Narnia or the Wizarding World. Certainly, too, we can compare the main child characters of the books—Lucy, Edmund, Susan and Peter, and Neville, Ron, Hermione and Harry—who as a foursome soldier on into the magical world as its preservers. We see definite parallels between Lewis's White Witch and Voldemort, both of whom represent a wickedness that intends to cleanse the world of goodness with an immortal evil. And we may compare Aslan to Dumbledore, both omniscient, God-like and serving as the core of righteousness, or "Deep Magic" (as Lewis articulates); or we may compare Aslan to Harry, who survives Voldemort's attempts to murder him and seems destined to fight against "evil" and to risk his life to save his friends.

Despite what seems to be ultimate destiny, however, the unfolding drama in the Wizarding World is far more morally cluttered than the mindfully organized Narnia that Lewis has constructed. This critical difference, however, may be found on common ground. Analysis of character parallels gives way to an even more compelling similarity between the narratives of Lewis and Rowing—the use of the "Liar, Lunatic, or Lord?" trilemma as a rhetorical device. First used by Lewis in *The Lion, the Witch and the Wardrobe* (1950), the trilemma works to help him communicate the story of Christianity. Narnia falls literally and figuratively under the burden of evil marked by eternal winter, no Christmas, and living beings turned into stone by the White Witch, and has a chance to be redeemed by Aslan and those who fight with him on the side of morality. In order to execute this redemption, however, Lucy, who first ventures through the wardrobe to Narnia, must convince her siblings that such a place exists. When Susan and Peter reject Lucy's story, they go to the Professor for advice. It is through the words of the Professor that we see Lewis's rationale most clearly. We read:

> "Logic!" said the Professor half to himself. "Why don't
> they teach logic at these schools? There are only three
> possibilities. Either your sister is telling lies, or she is
> mad, or she is telling the truth. You know she doesn't tell
> lies and it is obvious that she is not mad. For the moment
> then and unless any further evidence turns up, we must
> assume that she is telling the truth" (1950, p. 51-52).

The Professor's words, as it turns out, amount to much more than the suggestion that Susan and Peter should merely have faith that Narnia exists.

Having faith, in Lewis's book, extends beyond the boundary between the wardrobe and Narnia, for Lewis's trilemma may later be seen in the character of Aslan. His first appearance to the children is by way of the Beaver's utterance, "They say Aslan is on the move—perhaps has already landed" (1950, p. 74). With the introduction of this character, Lewis constructs Aslan's ethos and turns directly to his readers to say,

> And now a very curious thing happened. None of the children knew who Aslan was any more than you do; but the moment the Beaver had spoken these words everyone felt quite different. Perhaps it has sometimes happened to you in a dream that someone says something which you don't understand but in the dream it feels as if it had some enormous meaning—either a terrifying one which turns the whole dream into a nightmare or else a lovely meaning too lovely to put into words, which makes the dream so beautiful that you remember it all your life and are always wishing you could get into that dream again. It was like that now. At the name of Aslan each one of the children felt something jump in its inside. Edmund felt a sensation of mysterious horror. Peter felt suddenly brave and adventurous. Susan felt as if some delicious smell or some delightful strain of music had just floated by her. And Lucy got the feeling you have when you wake up in the morning and realize that it is the beginning of the holidays or the beginning of summer. (1950, p. 74)

Such is the rhetorical power Lewis infuses into Aslan's character; the utterance of his name seems to bring each child's truth to the surface. Of course, as we see in the responses to Lucy's story, popular perception of Aslan is divided. Though his presence brings Spring to Narnia, there are many who fight for the White Witch against him and who believe, as the White Witch does, that Aslan is "the fool" (1950, p. 166). But Aslan is Lewis's messenger; he constructs Aslan as a Christ figure who sacrifices himself to save the traitor Edmund and, though humiliated, tortured, and killed by the White Witch and her masses of followers, dies gazing "up at the sky" (1950, p. 170) as if it were the Heavens, and is not long after resurrected. To Lucy's proclamations of "Oh, you're real, you're real! Oh, Aslan!" (as if she herself doubted), Aslan explains the "deeper" magic that has brought him back to life and proceeds to breathe life back into all of the creatures that the White Witch has turned to stone. By the end of the novel, the trilemma has been logically resolved. He is no liar, he is not a lunatic. He is Lord.

So, too, do we find the questions of the trilemma woven throughout the Potter series. In Book One of *Harry Potter*, Rowling first introduces readers to the disappearance of Voldemort after Harry's mother protects her son from his powers (and thus sacrifices her own life). Hagrid reflects, "Somethin' about you finished him, Harry" (1997, p. 57). From the very beginning of the first chapter of the first book of the series, Rowling has constructed Harry as a boy much more extraordinary than either Muggle or wizard. Through this branch of the narrative, and quite like Aslan, Harry is constituted as a kind of immortal figure who once survived death at the hand of ultimate evil. After Harry is delivered as an infant to the doorstep of the Dursleys, we learn that his survival has inspired a great wave of belief, and the rhetoric of celebration echoes the arrival of the Christ child. Harry, also wrapped in swaddling clothes, is exalted as a blessing to all: Rowling writes, "...at this very moment, people meeting in secret all over the country were holding up their glasses and saying in hushed voices: 'To Harry Potter—the boy who Lived!'" (1997, p. 17).

However, not everyone in the Muggle or magical worlds is certain of Harry's extraordinary nature. While his reputation as an exceptional child precedes his own knowledge of his history, there are many who doubt or resist what Harry represents. Certainly, the Dursleys are essential in the construction of doubt; Mr. Dursley's absolute rejection of the onslaught of messenger owls and his subsequent retreat to "the broken-down house" (1997, p. 44) in the middle of the sea suggest his disbelief that Harry could be anything other than ordinarily mortal; indeed, he is perceived and treated as much less. Furthermore, Harry arrives at Hogwarts to mixed reviews. Draco Malfoy is far from impressed by Harry (though we might see his treatment of him as pure envy), and the Sorting Hat itself seems uncertain about whether Harry is, as Griesinger articulates in her article, an "honest" Gryffindor or a "conniving" Slytherin (2006, p. 325). If the Sorting Hat represents an all-knowing revealer of 'true' identity, then the question of whether Harry—so lauded by so many in the Wizarding World—is truthful or deceitful about who he is certainly invites one part of Lewis's trilemma into play. Though many rejoice unto Harry, as if he were indeed a savior, doubt about his genuineness is invited early on in the series. Perhaps he is a liar.

Sanity—the other piece of the trilemma—is called into question when we first meet Albus Dumbledore, who is believed by many to be the most powerful and righteous of all wizards, and the only one that Voldemort fears. Upon hearing Dumbledore's first words—"Before we begin the banquet, I would like to say a few words. And they are: Nitwit! Blubber! Oddment! Tweak!"—Harry asks Percy Weasley, "Is he—a bit mad?" to which Percy replies, "Mad? ...He's a genius! Best wizard in the world! But he is a bit mad, yes" (1997, p. 123). The significance of sanity as it applies to Dumbledore and not to Harry may, at first, seem unclear. However, we soon learn that Harry and Dumbledore have an indelible bond that begins in Book One and is carried all the way to the end of the series. Dumbledore becomes a father-figure for Harry, giving him James Potter's invisibility cloak, directly instructing him more than he does any other child, and defending him above all (even when Harry has broken rules). Before his death, Dumbledore has taken it upon himself to guard Harry with his own life, and to give him one-on-one lessons about the history of turmoil in the Wizarding World and wisdom about further unrest to come. By the end of Book Six, Harry has become not only the leader of Dumbledore's Army, but he has also set off to avenge Dumbledore's mysterious death at the hand of Snape and to challenge Voldemort himself. The relationship between Harry and Dumbledore recalls that of God and Christ—separate and the same. Thus, if Dumbledore himself is perceived as mad, Harry's intimacy with Dumbledore calls his own sanity into question.

But questions about Harry's sanity are not simply associated with Dumbledore, for the state of his own mental wellbeing is often subject to the scrutiny of his community. For example, in Book Two, Harry learns that he speaks Parseltongue, a form of snake communication that Slytherin and Voldemort also know. This knowledge is, perhaps, Harry's first introduction to what he will later learn is a kind of shared consciousness with Voldemort. Harry's scar blinds him whenever Voldemort is near or when he is doing evil deeds. Even more critical is Voldemort's breaking into Harry's mind in Book Five, which leads Harry to dream, and thus predict, Voldemort's evil doings, and which prompts Dumbledore to ask Snape to teach Harry Occlumency, "the magical defense of the mind against external penetration" (2003, p. 519). The fact that Harry is now sharing his mind with Voldemort begs questions not only about his mental health, but also about his trustworthiness.

Moreover, we see other evidence in the transition from Book Four to Book Five of the "Liar, Lunatic, or Lord?" question as it applies not only to Harry's immortal power, but also to the resurrection of Voldemort himself: Is Harry a liar? Is he a lunatic? Or does he really know that Voldemort is *back*? At the close of Book Four, only Harry will attest to Voldemort's murder of Cedric Diggory, and into Book Five we learn that doubt about his testimony is popular opinion. It is not until well over halfway through Book Five, when Harry agrees to an interview for *The Quibbler* in which he explains everything that happened the night that Voldemort "came back," that we see the public doubt lift. In response to the article, Fred reads Harry one of the letters that a member of the community has written in to the newspaper: "Says you don't come across as a mad person, but he really doesn't want to believe You-know-Who's back..." Another letter: "Little though I want to think He-Who-Must-Not-Be-Named has returned, I am forced to accept that you are telling the truth." And another letter, read by Ron: "...this one says you've got her converted, and she thinks now you're a real hero" (2003, p. 579-580). Harry is neither a lunatic nor a liar... then it must be true that the Dark Lord is back.

Still, many continue to doubt the legitimacy of Harry's word. Questions about whether Harry is mad or lying seem to morph into one, as the entire community is stricken by the dismantling of what were once clear truths. Wizards from all over experience the paranoia that "the boy who lived" could be an evil-doing lunatic, as well as the possibility that Harry is actually right about the doom to come. Rita Skeeter calls him "Disturbed and Dangerous" (2000, p. 611), the Ministry works to shut him up altogether, and after Voldemort murders Cedric Diggory at the end of Book Four, Harry's belief that Voldemort is back throws the community further into a tailspin of panic and disbelief that is uncannily similar to the conservative Christian panic about the books themselves. Harry is tried in Book Five for using magic outside of school to fend off dementors (which moves many on the jury to believe he is lying). Dolores Umbridge tortures Harry by forcing him to carve into his own skin, "'I must not tell lies'...as long as it takes for the message to sink in" (2003, p. 266), as if Harry himself doesn't even *know* that he's lying. And, by the time we get to Book Six, questions about one boy's identity are large enough to permeate the media of the entire community. One newspaper reads, "Harry Potter: The Chosen One?" (2005, p. 39). Here, the rhetoric of chosen-ness links back to the Christ narrative.

Such controversy over who Harry is—is he a liar? Is he mad? Is he Chosen?—seems to create a clear parallel with the rationale that Lewis presents to his own readers: a reader knows that Harry is not lying about Voldemort's return; and a reader is led to see that even when Harry doubts his own sanity (as when he has peculiar dreams that leak into reality), he is not really insane. So, "logically," he must be the Chosen One. Certainly, one could argue that Harry is indeed a Christ figure, and that his struggle to figure out his identity does not suggest anything "morally confusing" about the books, but rather a series of either-or questions that he—and those in his community—will come to resolve. Perhaps, even, it could be argued that, like Lewis's texts, the *Harry Potter* books clearly delineate g(o)od and evil, presenting to the reader a world that is certainly in a state of unrest, but one that can be brought to right as cleanly as Spring comes to Narnia with the return of Aslan.

And yet, while the trilemma's questions may exist in *Harry Potter*, they are not so clearly answered.

Morality and Methods: The Trilemma Revised

Further rhetorical analysis shows that the clear parallels between Rowling and Lewis become significantly blurred as the *Harry Potter* books progress, and ultimately revise the argument of the trilemma. This instability between good and evil, I argue, helps the texts to spin the trilemma in such a way that the question becomes less about whether or not Dumbledore is God or Harry is the Chosen One, and more about fundamental morality as it applies to anyone and everyone in today's society. While Lewis's power of elimination—indeed, his logos—aims to clearly name the ultimate good (if ___ is not true, and ___ is not true, then ___ must be true), the trilemma Rowling's texts employ invites the reality of uncertainty: it could be ___, it could be___, or it could be ___. All are possible. As clearly as the trilemma works in Lewis's texts to make an argument for Christian morality, it works in Rowling's texts to question morality in general.

The tidiness of binaries in the *Harry Potter* series is complicated by several destabilizing factors. First of all, we should address the fact that Harry escapes from death with the Dark Lord in his blood. Harry's lightning-shaped scar is symbolic for parts of himself that he cannot reconcile; the mark, in many ways, is a smaller scale version of a Harry Potter he hardly knows. Dumbledore explains to Harry that in surviving Voldemort's murder attempt, Voldemort "transferred some of his powers to [Harry] the night he gave [him] that scar" (1998, p. 333). In the books, Harry must come face to face with Voldemort on several occasions (much like Luke and Vader), and in the process must confront his own mortal identity. In being so much "like" Voldemort, Harry is quite unlike Lewis's Aslan; Harry's character is constructed to be much less purely good. Despite the fact that Harry seems to fight for righteousness, above the narrative hovers the question of whether or not Harry actually is as powerful as many have believed him to be. Such questions are further illustrated in the less pure parts of Harry: he copies Hermione's homework, he often breaks rules while at school and sneaks around using the Marauder's Map, he lets his anger get the best of him and "accidentally" practices magic on the Dursleys and Aunt Marge in the beginning of Book Three, he frequently gets into tussles with Draco and his cronies, and he acquiesces to adolescent lust and engages in a physically romantic relationship with Cho Chang and Ginny Weasley. Perhaps most significantly, at the end of Book Six, Harry vows, "I'm the one who's going to kill [Voldemort]" and alludes to hurting Snape "along the way" (2005, p. 651), a pledge that leads him on the deadly mission of Book Seven. While most of these traits might be considered simply mischievous and simply "human," Harry's decision to murder Voldemort and/or attack Snape are not in line with Christian doctrine. These departures from the path of righteousness complicate Harry's character significantly, and invite the idea that he is, in many ways, both "good" and "bad."

Returning now to the rhetoric of chosen-ness, we can go back and re-examine Harry's role as the Christ figure. Recalling the "Harry Potter: The Chosen One?" newspaper article, which foreshadows a mysterious "prophecy [that some think] names him as the only one who will be able to rid [them] of He-Who-Must-Not-Be-Named" (2005, p. 39), we may find that, despite Dumbledore's certainty that Harry is chosen, the identity of "Chosen" may not completely belong to Harry. We have learned in Book Five, for example, that the prophecy partially suggests that Neville Longbottom may be a candidate. And even though Dumbledore assures Harry that Voldemort "chose [Harry], not Neville" and has paid the price for choosing the boy that has "power the Dark Lord knows not" (2003, p. 842-843), Dumbledore's credibility begins to waiver soon thereafter.

Later in Book Six and mainly in Book Seven, Rowling turns the trilemma toward the God-figure, Dumbledore, who has since Book Five slowly become the subject of popular doubt. His public ethos has been in jeopardy since he took Harry under his wing, defended him (despite his rule-breaking) against his professorial colleagues and in the presence of the jury in Book Five, and became his mentor. Numerous attempts made by the Ministry of Magic aim to take Dumbledore's headmaster authority away from him because many believe he is "getting old and losing his grip" (2003, p. 95), and the government itself seems torn between just and unjust practices. By the end of Book Six, disempowered and murdered like Aslan, like Christ, Dumbledore becomes the subject of the sacrificial death as the protective strength of Hogwarts and its headmaster falls into ruin; and the "dark and twisting path [Harry] saw stretching ahead for himself" (2005, p. 652) comes into view. In Book Seven, Dumbledore's core identity is called into question when his personal history with Grindelwald becomes public knowledge. Harry's confusion surfaces in the words, "Some inner certainty had crashed down inside him.... He had trusted Dumbledore, believed him the embodiment of goodness and wisdom. All was ashes" (2007, p. 360). By this point, Harry's connection to Dumbledore has weakened, and Harry is less of a Christ figure and savior to his community now, and more of a mercenary. This revision of the trilemma works to underscore Stephens's argument about conservative Christian panic over the texts: to many, the moral relativism of the texts represents an "assumed lack of control [that] stems from the idea that our world is crumbling because the proper order of things—the hierarchy of power with God and Christians on top—has been disturbed" (2003, p. 61). With so much unrest in the authoritative body of the Wizarding World, Harry's fight is, in many ways, personal, confused, and doubtful, which may drive some Christian readers away from seeing him as any kind of hero.

But certainty about Harry, his connection to Dumbledore, and the world he's trying to save has "crashed down" long before we are privy to Rita Skeeter's *The Life and Lies of Albus Dumbledore*. The events of Books One through Six reveal to us characters deemed "good" or even good-enough who use less-than-righteous tactics or even appear to assert less-than-noble values, which further destabilizes the clear binaries of good and evil. We have, for instance, seen the Ministry of Magic employ dementors—morbid creatures that guard Azkaban and injure their prey by sucking their souls out of their bodies—to patrol and protect Hogwarts. It is the Ministry of Magic that begins to doubt Dumbledore's wisdom and authority, and we see evidence of its crumbling ethos in employing Percy Weasley, who stops communicating with his family and sides with those who are trying to unseat Dumbledore and expel Harry. Moreover, it is the Ministry, too, that sends Dolores Umbridge to Hogwarts to be the new Professor of Defense Against the Dark Arts in Book Five; she gets pleasure from torturing Harry to write lines with a pen that makes his skin bleed. While the Ministry itself, perhaps, has not yet turned "bad," there is anxiety about its agenda that begins in the early books and creeps over books Four, Five and Six like a storm. Every issue of Hermione's *Daily Prophet* suggests a new transgression, and the one reality that becomes clear in Book Six is that it is entirely possible that those who were deemed good may now be less so, if at all. In fact, many who fear the disconnectedness and destruction that is befalling their world are the ones who are helping to make it more fragmented.

Giving material and contemporary structure to this looming distrust is Hogwarts itself. Built to withstand evils wanting to enter from the outside, Hogwarts is intended to be a fortress. As Hermione explains, the school is "...bewitched... If a Muggle looks at it, all they see is a moldering old ruin with a sign over the entrance saying DANGER, DO NOT ENTER, UNSAFE" (2000, p. 166). However, we learn that there are many ways for evil to permeate its walls: by leeching onto a Hogwarts professor (Queril), in the form of an Animagus (Peter Pettigrew), by sneaking into one of the Tri-Wizard Tournament tasks (the Death Eaters and Voldemort), by working for the Ministry of Magic (Umbridge), or by being one of Dumbledore's loyal colleagues for many years (Snape). The school itself, rhetorically constructed as a fortress of protection for the children—its walls and staircases have a wisdom of their own, and Dumbledore has long been its headmaster and guardian—proves to be as porous as the morality of those who inhabit it, and here we see the fragmentation that is characteristic of a post-911 world outside of the book. Perhaps most symbolic of the castle's frailty is the scene following Dumbledore's murder, when Harry finds his dead body lying outside in the castle yard: Hogwarts has grown so weak that it can no longer protect its headmaster (2005, p. 608). When Harry, Ron, and Hermione return to Hogwarts in Book Seven, the castle is a battleground, as much a victim to the tyranny of corruption and Voldemort as any of the wizards who have been weak enough to give in to Dark Magic.

In the midst of this devastation, the reader—and Harry—are left with core moral questions at the close of Book Six. Was Dumbledore, "the greatest wizard Harry had ever, or would ever, meet" (2005, p. 608), misled in allowing

Snape to work at Hogwarts for so long? Was he simply not as wise as so many students and wizards thought? Could it be that Snape really is as evil as he seems? Will the Ministry find its way back to just practices in overseeing the Wizarding World? Is Harry really going to commit the murders of Voldemort and Snape? Will Draco Malfoy, whom Harry now pities rather than hates, really fall to Voldemort? How do we know who is Good? Who is Bad? Such are the ambiguous questions that sit with Harry, with much of the Wizarding World, and with readers. Certainty about characters' morality has dissolved in the contested space between the monstrous and the seemingly innocuous. And while the pendulum of morality does not always swing so dramatically from one to the next, the narrative demonstrates that sometimes it does, and it isn't always clear when that shift will happen.

In Book Seven, these questions linger as the revision of the trilemma works to draw the narrative to its culmination, and as Dumbledore's ethos continues to dwindle even after his death, even after the close of the book. Harry is the secret keeper and leader of the "mission" Dumbledore has sent him on. Certainly, the mission itself and the Battle of Hogwarts would be a sham without the help of his peers, but Harry is the mental vessel in which scenes of past and future appear, and he is still the one who must defeat Voldemort, who is made to critically question Dumbledore's love for him, who is made Godfather to Tonks and Lupin's child, and who is "not supposed to survive" (2007, p. 691) Voldemort, but then lives to meet Dumbledore at and then descend from King's Cross, the books' metaphorical Heaven. Even with this certainty about Harry's chosen-ness lingering, however, the questions of the trilemma are unanswered by the one who we might have thought could answer them. In this Heaven we see Dumbledore as decidedly human: he has a past that is marked by his desire for "glory" and a Wizarding World that dominated that of Muggles; and, despite the wisdom that has so much been a part of his ethos as a great genius wizard, Dumbledore himself is not altogether certain about Harry's fate or about the future of his world.

Redemption in Uncertainty

However, this analysis of a trilemma revised offers some illumination, an answer to our question—what is the message of *Harry Potter?*—that does not attempt to force a happy ending, but rather acknowledges a unity among readers and a sense of hope. We see the culmination of the trilemma and of the argument of the texts after Dumbledore's admission of uncertainty. Before Harry leaves King's Cross and Dumbledore, he asks the old wizard, "Tell me one last thing. Is this real? Or has this been happening inside my head?" Dumbledore responds, "Of course it is happening inside your head, Harry, but why on earth should that mean that it is not real?" (2007, p. 723). And in this exchange there is an expression of faith. In the last chapter in the series is

Rowling's own articulation of "Deep Magic," which Lewis sought to ingrain in his young readers' minds. Aptly titled, "The Flaw in the Plan," the last chapter before the epilogue presents a scene reminiscent of Obi-Wan's fight with Vader, and Harry seems to know in this last battle *after* the battle that he must take on Voldemort alone. What is revealed in the exchange between Harry and Voldemort, however, is not Harry's chosen-ness per se, but rather the power that has fueled Harry's survival—love, remorse, faith. In today's society, such words are fluid, and intimately defined and redefined by those who use them. In fact, in an online post to readers asking about Neville's possible chosen-ness, Rowling assures her readers that Voldemort chose Harry, but that this act should not be looked upon as an act of fate. Rather, she argues, "destiny is a name often given in retrospect to choices that had dramatic consequences" ("F.A.Q. About the Books"). In other words, the paths of good and bad are up to us as humans to decide, we cannot predict the paths that we or others will take, and we cannot necessarily define for others what is "good" and what is "bad."

At the close of the series, Voldemort has unexpectedly murdered himself, and Harry has chosen the path of mortality. The cheery epilogue, which depicts Harry's life with Ginny and the happy, successful adulthoods of the series' characters, doesn't quite mollify the melancholy of what has happened only pages before; there is very little victory in the disappearance of Voldemort, and the inquiry of the trilemma still hovers. It is not altogether certain that his Dark Magic is gone for good, as the weight of the seven books sits heavily in its own questions about what will become of the Wizarding World. The books' characters, like its readers, are very much steeped in the uncertainty of today's world, and neither the end of battle, nor the tying of knots, nor the healing from loss will order the disarray.

But there is redemption to be found in the rhetoric of the revised trilemma. Though they may offer readers a darker, less certain world than the Narnia that Lewis creates, *Harry Potter* does present us with a world that is current, human, and, perhaps, more applicable to its vast audience of today's readers. Stephens suggests that "the Harry Potter debate is a microcosm of our cultural debates about how to live with diversity and change," and that the debate itself has created "a point of connection" for people of all kinds (2003, p. 63). I argue that the big questions that the trilemma poses, and that *Harry Potter* seeks to address, problematize, and leave open, help not only to give people something to argue about together, but also to offer some hope in the face of uncertainty.

The revision of the trilemma also underscores one of the tenets of Christianity: faith despite struggle. In *Mere Christianity*, Lewis asserts that the Christian life is not easy, and that those who seek it "must not be surprised if we are in for a rough time...the process will be long and in parts very painful; but that is what we are in for" (1952, p. 174-175). In the Christian life there are many obstacles to walking that path. This doctrine, however, need not necessarily be seen as solely Christian. While Griesinger argues that Rowling's narrative "sets the stage for the Christian gospel and provides readers a 'real though unfocused gleam of divine truth'" (2006, p. 331), we might also see *Harry Potter's* stage as humanity itself. In negotiating the trilemma of Good, Bad, or In Between? we are all navigating a moral landscape, regardless of its religious specificity. In many ways, *Harry Potter's* characters ask specific questions about the existence of God and the ultimate truths of right and wrong, but more broadly, they invite us all to ask ourselves how we know goodness or evil when we see it. In so doing, they acknowledge that sometimes morality does not answer to logic.

Works Cited

Blake, Andrew. *The Irresistible Rise of Harry Potter.* New York: Verso, 2002. Print.

Dickerson, Matthew, and David O'Hara. *From Homer to Harry Potter: A Handbook on Myth and Fantasy.* Grand Rapids, MI: Brazos Press, 2006.

Edwards, Bruce. *Further Up & Further In: Understanding C.S. Lewis's* The Lion, the Witch and the Wardrobe. Nashville, Tennessee: Broadman & Holdman Publishers, 2005. Print.

Farmer, Joy. "The Magician's Niece: the Kinship between J.K. Rowling and C.S. Lewis." *Mythlore* 88 (Spring 2001): 53-64. Print.

Granger, John. *Looking for God in Harry Potter.* Carol Stream, IL: Tyndale, 2006. Print.

Griesinger, Emily. "The Search for 'Deeper Magic': J.K. Rowling and C.S. Lewis." *The Gift of Story: Narrating Hope in a Postmodern World.* Eds. Emily Griesinger and Mark Easton. Waco, Tx.: Baylor University Press, 2006. 317-331. Print.

Lewis, C.S. *The Lion, the Witch and the Wardrobe.* New York: HarperCollins, 1950. Print.

---. *Mere Christianity.* New York: Macmillan Publishing Co., Inc., 1952. Print.

McDowell, Josh. *More Than a Carpenter.* Wheaton, Ill.: Tyndale House Publishers, 1980. Print.

Neal, Connie. "What Would Jesus Do with Harry Potter?" *Christian Broadcasting Network.* 2007. Web. 27 July 2010.

Roper, Jack M. "Harry Potter: the Hero for Modern Witchcraft." *Christian Broadcasting Network. 2007.* Web. 27 July 2010.

Rowling, J.K. *Harry Potter and the Chamber of Secrets.* New York: Scholastic Press, 1998. Print.

---. *Harry Potter and the Deathly Hallows.* New York: Scholastic Press, 2007. Print.

---. "F.A.Q. About the Books." *J.K. Rowling Official Site.* Warner Brothers Enterprises. Web. 3 May 2009.

---. *Harry Potter and the Goblet of Fire.* New York: Scholastic Press, 2000. Print.

---. *Harry Potter and the Half-Blood Prince.* New York: Scholastic Press, 2005. Print.

---. *Harry Potter and the Order of the Phoenix.* New York: Scholastic Press, 2003. Print.

---. *Harry Potter and the Prisoner of Azkaban.* New York: Scholastic Press, 1999. Print.

---. *Harry Potter and the Sorcerer's Stone.* New York: Scholastic Press, 1997. Print.

Sayer, George. *Jack: A Life of C.S. Lewis.* Wheaton, Ill.: Crossway Books, 1988. Print.

Stephens, Rebecca. "Harry and Hierarchy: Book Banning as a Reaction to the Subversion of Authority." *Reading Harry Potter: Critical Essays.* Ed. Giselle Liza Anatol. Westport, CT: Praeger Publishers, 2003. 51-65.

Miriam Kotzin

Collection

Crimson
carmine
vermilion
today's trash, plastic bags, in artless
imitation of that sculpture
at the Modern,
basic black bulging chic,
charcoal green shade of the fifties,
and one shocking translucence
in reds and pinks
scarlet cardinal

sins of lipstick stubs
drying in a box of souvenirs:
Persian Melon
Tahitian Sunset
Vangogh Sunflower
Tangee Natural
all but Luvlee
which we pubescent literalists
crooned Loo-vlee.

Lou, Lou, skip to my Lou
when we could do anything
we wanted to our faces:
eyelids enameled blue, green,
lids lined thickly
with thoughts of kohl
and Cleopatra who on her barge floated
down the Nile of our fantasies.
My lips are rarely pale these days.
My body makes its own bloom.

Together we are new;
Unshared memories arrive
unsolicited as a chain letter.
We cannot empty ourselves
like houses of the deceased
cleaned by distant relatives
who bundle everything
to the curb.

Miriam Kotzin

Magic Act

With care I write your name
out of my life into my past
where like other memories
you will languish, in a slow
vanishing act, a neat trick.
I write this sentence
as though with a few
strokes I might banish
you from the present tense
with possibilities.
            Once, love,
you were not an abstract
noun; you were a wild cyclist
urging me to ride; you were
a dancer whose moves made
me dizzy, you were a sleeper
whose dreams summoned me.
When I entered your world
we stirred a field of flowers
into life as startled white
butterflies took flight. I
was air, I was sunlight on water;
together we were wind filling
a sail. We were at our best
disembodied.
            Now I roll a cabinet
onto stage, mirrored sides
flashing in the spotlight.
I fold down the panels,
reassemble the rig. Obliging,
you step inside while everyone
watches. I tap all six sides.
Drumroll, please.
            When I open
the door, you are gone, my
last, my best illusion.

Scott Gabriel Knowles
Phantom of the Fair

If Shanghai isn't really China (as I was repeatedly told by Shanghainese), and the Expo isn't really Shanghai (in but not of the metropolis, they also insisted), then I really have no clue where I spent 10 days last month. I ate Swiss fondue, bought a Kyrgyz felt hat, and had my passport stamped "Trinidad" by a young Chinese woman who never looked up from her text messaging. It was thrilling to visit North Korea and pretend the guard watching me was compiling a surveillance report on "the American with straw hat and a digital camera." I think he really was. The replica of the Trojan Horse was undeniably creepy, hovering in the ominous blue light of a well-sacked mock-Troy. There was a parade every night and lines all day and the staff drilled and marched in military display. I was encouraged to consider the universality of 21st-century urban life by wax figure families from six different cities around the world. Disoriented and sweaty, I walked from one end to the other and back on this two-square-mile microplanet. Making sense of it all was impossible. All I really wanted to find out, in true world's fair tradition, is if the future is going to be more interesting than the present.

Creatively confusing the visitor defines the core work of world's fair designers, and much of the attraction for world's fairgoers. You are meant to be off balance and thus receptive to persuasion, expansion of view. Ever since London's path-blazing Crystal Palace of 1851, world's fairs have served as bazaars for new products and showcases for mind-bending architecture and design innovation. Over the years fairs evolved into overlapping planes of temporary existence: corporate showrooms for consumer appetite cultivation like the legendary GM Pavilions of '39 and '64, techno-utopian fantasylands exemplified by Chicago's 1893 Columbian Exposition, and pavilions for nationalist posturing like Cold War Brussels in 1958. None of it works without a crowd, ideally a slightly bored crowd hungry for the spectacle of the new. With a month to go Expo 2010, Shanghai has hosted 59 million visitors, and officials are prepared for more than 70 million—only Osaka 1970 comes close with its 62 million attendees. That's as many people as you will find in Shanghai, Beijing, and the next four largest cities in China plus New York City combined. A great world's fair also needs a resonant theme, a reason to call the meeting in the first place. In "Better City, Better Life," Expo 2010 expounds its reason to exist—an exploration of "the common wish of the whole humankind for a better living in future urban environments." The symmetry is perfect: the future of sustainable urban living on display to the world, in one of the world's fastest growing cities.

A Chinese friend patiently explained to me after I enthused about all of this that "Better City, Better Life," rendered into Mandarin, means something more like "The City Will Improve Your Life." "What's the difference?" I asked him. I considered this as I waited almost two hours (considered short) in line for the China Pavilion with several thousand of the 340,000 people at Expo that day. Architect He Jingtang's "Oriental Crown"—a green-energy advertisement in immaculate "Forbidden City" red (the escalator handles glisten like red licorice)—hovered over me like a lacquered UFO until I was at last summoned inside to learn the mystery of the Chinese Urban Future. Here I learned about the improvements on offer for the modern Chinese family. An ambitious 8-minute film follows a day in the life of the Chinese city; it is cross-cut with sweeping scenes conjured to render heroic the drama of 300 million people caught up in the meteoric Chinese urbanization of the past 30 years. The city comes alive, it swirls and makes money, it creates and walks down green park lanes, it sweeps up its mess and goes to sleep. The proto-typical family comes together in a tiny apartment and children enter the picture, work and sacrifice tender expanding numbers, both of children and square feet. Multiple generations celebrate life together amidst the material accumulations of a life well spent in the city. Then the lights come on, the crowd blinks, and shuffles out to see a football-field long scroll painting, "Riverside Scene at Qingming Festival," alive with animation and set behind a real-fake flowing brook. The quiet comforts of the 12th-century village festival provide a palliative to the shock of the urban new.

Shanghainese I talked to told me that the city has not improved their lives. Everyone speaks of housing prices quadrupling in the past decade and of speculators growing rich. This rapid urban cramping has led the government to propose the need for a "Harmonious Society," an acknowledgment that the minting of Chinese billionaires and glimmering skylines do not exactly square with the revolutionary ideology. In material ways, though, the Expo does seem to have improved life in Shanghai, or it has at least made its own temporary contributions. In a trick of Chinese federalism that might remind Americans of our own inter-governmental squabbles, it seems that the central government impressed on Shanghai the necessity of the world's fair. Boosters in the city took this order and made the best of it, building new subway lines faster than the U.S. Congress can vote down a transportation bill. In addition, savvy Shanghainese planners selected an Expo site on the Huangpo River where the country's largest and oldest steelmaking and shipbuilding facilities resided. Here is the site of the Chinese industrial miracle, the Chinese version of Homestead, Pennsylvania or the Chicago rail yards. Ordinarily, the status of these state-owned factories would be decided in Beijing, no matter the value of the land for local development, and without appeal. But the Shanghainese insisted that this was the best site for Expo and they won the argument—when

Expo closes next month they will studiously go about disassembling the pavilions and start building high rises in their place. In real estate terms it was a tour-de-force of urban renewal, with the old and rusting packed away to the outskirts and the new and gleaming already drafted, funded, and ready to rise. Visitors to the fairgrounds next year will recognize the street grid, and the China Pavilion and a few other buildings will remain, but the rest will be merely The City, for better or worse, depending on whom you ask.

As I moved through the African Pavilion just before closing time, it occurred to me at last that I was merely a phantom at this fair. It's a strange moment for an American abroad—and when it happens you wince and surrender your non-existent birthright: the realization that this is not all here to entertain me. In fact, though, all world's fairs up to this one have in one way or another been there to entertain westerners, even Osaka. With Chinese nationals making up the overwhelming majority of the visitors to Expo 2010, though, I was really witnessing the creation of Chinese elites packaged and presented to the Chinese masses, a tour of the world as the elites want China to see itself, and as participating countries want to be seen by the Chinese.

This explains why the U.S. Pavilion—with its suburban corporate architecture, cowboy hats and basketballs for sale—is focused on bland ideas like teamwork and the victory of the little guy, with no mention of democracy. Certainly if more Americans or Europeans had been expected in the audience it would be unacceptable to show a feel-good film with a Chevron executive lecturing the world on environmental sustainability. This also explains why pavilions from Venezuela to Mozambique to Uzbekistan featured huge portraits of the nation's leader smiling and shaking hands with Hu Jintao. This explains the appeal of the startlingly large globe over which you stand in the Urban Planet Pavilion. As a latter-day John Glenn (or 21st-century Chinese astronaut?) you orbit and watch helplessly as the blue planet turns brown and withers before your eyes. Global warming is real in Expo, it must be confronted, and China will be part of the solution. Chinese carbon emissions are not much up for discussion. Neither are U.S. carbon emissions, or Australian carbon emissions for that matter. That is impolite and definitely bad business. Instead, the focus in Expo's version of contemporary history is a world with its hands open to China in gestures of friendship and free trade. The troubles of the world are the troubles of China, and the way forward cruises effortlessly through the Chinese city in the sustainable car of the future. This nifty little car, by the way, is on display at the hugely popular General Motors/SAIC (Shanghai Automotive Industry Corporation) Pavilion; performers in colorful future-driving-suits sing and dance around them while you gaze.

The Better City of the future is full of people of good will and good ideas who will render the Better Life of green industry and international harmony.

Expo 2010 may be the first world's fair ever to balance the enthusiasm of an emerging nation with the temperance of international concern—in this case concern over the environmental impacts of the history of emerging modern nations. Toward the end of my visit I asked an Expo official over lunch if the success of the fair meant that Beijing would be next, Hong Kong, Xi'an? Once Chicago succeeded, I ventured, St. Louis had to have one, and so on. He laughed and said no, there will never be another world's fair in China. Having done it big and correctly once, and at enormous state expense, there was no need to do it again. It wasn't exactly the competitive spirit of the free market, I thought, but it was telling of a culture trying to balance reverence for tradition and rapid urbanization. Expo 2010 Shanghai will serve as a reminder of this conflicted moment in time for modernizing China; presumably the website will at least remain. But as for the site itself, well, in a month it will all be gone, replaced by cranes and returned to the mundane, no more confusing than the average city of 20 million.

Jeffrey Ethan Lee

After she said, "You can work around me"
somehow he knew

(his side)

                                                        (her side)

she kept peeling carrots like nothing had changed—

                                                then it was as if

I kept soaping and rinsing the restaurant plates

                                             my whole body

like it was all the same,

                                             was standing by

but I had to stand so near her

                                            a shower door

to share the hot jetting water

                                        that had just opened

I almost felt her inhale,

                                      with cascading steam

and she felt my exhales down her back

                                            flowing out

like warm waterfalls—

                                        around me like

leaning on the deep sink

                                        a subtler body,

she'd asked me to work behind her,

                                    touching all of me

my long arms encircling her

                                        down my sides,

as though she were much smaller

                                  then my back and front—

and clasped in a tango only we could hear—

                              it was more than his warmth

the fresh ribbons shooting down

                                      breathing on me

and the dishes oozing suds

                                  or his torso almost

made the rhythm of her hands stammer—

                                      grazing me—

her carrot grew wobbly,

                                  it was how he'd refrained

her peeling stopped,

                                      from touching me

and my arms swam through air like honey

and forgot themselves all around her.

that broke me open,

and somehow he knew—

Lynn Levin

On Going to the Playboy Club with My Father

When I was a student at Northwestern University during the mid 1970s, my father visited Chicago for medical conferences a couple times a year. On these occasions, he would make it a point to treat me to dinner at a white tablecloth place downtown—usually $$$ in the AAA Tourbook. I would take the El down from Evanston. Dad and I would indulge in stylish seventies dishes like Steak Diane or Chicken Kiev. Shrimp cocktail first, of course. I was the envy of the girls in the dorm who were forced to fork their way through the mystery meat in the Willard Hall cafeteria.

My parents' marriage had fallen into the dumpster at this point, and our father-daughter dinners felt vaguely like dates. I'd guide the conversation along a light path—my French and English classes (très boring to Dad), my job at the library (a little more interesting since it earned me pin money), and my volunteer work at NU Legal Aid (definitely helped me rule out law as a career). Avoiding the subject of Mom, Dad would update me about my brother, who was learning how to live an organized life at sleep-away military school, and my sister, apparently a normal high school senior: she went out on dates, talked on the phone a lot, and didn't like homework. My father would remind me that I needed to slim down, said diet to commence directly following our splendid meal. Then he would bring up the dreaded topic of my post-college plans. Of this I had no solid notion, merely a vision of myself in Europe attending garden parties with famous literary types. I was careful to agree with Dad on all things. He had a famous temper, and you never knew how many cranks it would take to make him go jack-in-the-box. Two issues classically unhinged him: not getting his way and not receiving enthusiastic demonstrations of love from his children. Although he did not realize it, the jack-in-the-box thing could sometimes strain the quality of affection.

Now retired, my father was an extremely dedicated doctor and often received notes of thanks—once even a live chicken—from his grateful patients. He studied voraciously, rose before dawn to make his hospital rounds, and with office hours and research meetings often did not arrive home until late at night. He loved golf, ice skated like a pro, considered himself a wine connoisseur, and when out to dinner with other couples battled for the check. His taste in clothing ran from mod to odd: he grooved on bold colors and big stripes. Maybe it was the golfer in him; maybe it was the belated influence of the swinging London and Carnaby Street style. When it came to trends, our hometown of St. Louis lagged behind other cities; the sixties didn't reach us until the seventies.

Clothes and appearance mattered a great deal to Dad. One of the worst fights my parents ever had erupted over a brand-new black-, brown-, and white-striped shirt that Dad wished to wear to a party. Mom said he looked like a clown or a carnival barker and wouldn't let up on her criticism. A rampage resulted. My parents, now long divorced, were like two tornados loose in the house. Small wonder that Dad looked forward to business trips.

One night Dad called me at school to say that he was coming to town for a research conference and directed me to meet him at the Playboy Club on East Walton. "Someone at the meeting," confided Dad, his voice thick with secrecy and excitement, "has a key to the Club. This is very VIP. Strictly big time. Only special people have keys to the Club."

The Playboy Club! The hair on my unshaven legs hackled up. I was a budding feminist and hated Hugh Hefner with the best of them. He was a seedy old perv who reduced women to sex objects and peddled the myth of the modern liberated girl, on the Pill and ready to ball (that awful word from the sixties and seventies) with whomever, no regrets, no aftermath. Sure I knew *Playboy*. It arrived at our house in St. Louis every month like an evil period, its slick pages scattered with bare-breasted gals slithering around on silk sheets or, in the winter issues, lounging bare-cheeked before an open fire. Fantastic figures, no zits, no cellulite. Talk about making a woman feel embarrassed about herself by comparison.

I knew that the consequences of resistance would not be calm, but I sallied forth anyway. I was a college girl. I was a protester. I believed in speaking up for what I believed in.

"Dad, Hugh Hefner's a male chauvinist pig and a creep. He makes me sick. I don't want to go the Playboy Club."

"Don't worry," said Dad, humoring me. "Hefner won't be there."

"That's not the point. The point is that Playboy exploits women. It's against my principles to go there." I knew I was turning the crank, but the faint hope flickered that Dad would see things my way.

Thankfully, the Playboy Clubs have gone the way of the powder-blue leisure suit and the eight-track tape. The last old-school American club closed in 1988, and the final international holdout in Manila mixed its last cocktail in 1991. In 2006 Hefner opened a new Playboy Club in Las Vegas, and I was hoping that what had happened in Vegas would stay in Vegas, but now there's buzz about new clubs in Cancún and Miami. In any event, back in 1974 Playboy Clubs were a pasha-land for guys of a certain cast of mind, men who fancied themselves swingers even if they never really swung. The sales magic was in the tease. The turn-on was the fantasy, the promise of sex. And Bunnies had, er, strict rules of conduct. They were not allowed to date customers or, when serving drinks, heave their cleavage in a fellow's face. To prevent such a spill, the girls had to perform a straight-backed, curtsey-like maneuver called the Bunny dip. Whatever. While other marketers were using sex to sell toothpaste and cars, Hefner was using sex to sell sex ... and booze in the clubs and ad space in the magazine. Hefner's marketing genius did not redeem him. My feminist sisters and I deplored everything Playboy. The whole concept degraded women. It was exploitative, objectifying, sexist, lookist.

My conversation with my father had been taking place on the hall phone in my dorm, Chapin Hall, which happened to be an all-women's residence. Normally, the girls gave whoever was on the phone a lot of space, but with "Playboy Club" and "Hugh Hefner" springing out of the conversation like champagne corks, I attracted a crowd, a sort of Greek chorus in bathrobes and curlers. Jan, always a cut up, made bunny ears behind Jill. Linda, the biggest women's libber on campus, raised the power salute. Karen and Nancy listened as they munched from a freshly popped bowl of popcorn.

I was militant to begin with, but the more the women watched, the more emphatic my advocacy became.

"Dad," I tried to bargain, "why don't you go to the Playboy Club with your friends, and I'll meet you for dinner afterward."

No dice. He wanted to introduce me to his conference friends. This made me feel like a specimen; furthermore, I knew I was no match for their sons and daughters who were already in or headed for med school and law school and grad schools of various types. The conversation juggernauted on. I mentioned one more thing about feeling weird around the half-naked Bunnies, and Pop popped. I had flunked his test of love and loyalty; his inner King Lear sprang to the surface.

"I will NEVER ask you to meet me anywhere else again!" I could hear him slamming the top of his desk. "Goddamnit, stay in the dorm and do your homework." A bruise spread through the air. My Greek chorus melted away.

My father paused. His anger required a second wind.

"I pay a goddamn fortune to send you to Northwestern, and this is the thanks I get?" His voice was shaking with what I thought was rage, although it might have been something else, something more desperate. Then he fired his best shot. "You can pay your own way through college."

My father knew that I wanted to stay in school more than anything else, and this was not the first time he had threatened to stop paying for Northwestern. So I caved and agreed to do the filial thing, if you can call a date with your father to the Playboy Club the filial thing. I was practical if nothing else.

I dressed in protest. This was not too difficult as I was cultivating the communist factory worker look at the time. I donned a shapeless polyester jumper the color of dead leaves, a yellow oxford shirt with stains on the frayed cuffs, black tights, and oxblood brogues, which I coveted for their strangeness and clunkiness. Pretty much my usual clothes, but in a worse-than-usual combination. As I dressed, visions of Hugh Hefner bubbled in the alembic of my mind: a middle-aged man in his all-day pj's always ready for a go-around with one of the nubiles, his hawkish male gaze smoldering over his pipe, on the lookout for fresh girl. Near at hand, a glass of Pepsi. There was only one way to deal with the situation; I would act as anthropologist. I would observe and report back to my cohorts. I thought of Gloria Steinem and her famous Playboy Club exposé.

The late spring sun still blazed as I emerged from the odorous El, and I found my way to 116 East Walton Street. A door Bunny let me into the club, and I was mildly surprised that she did. It took a while for my eyes to adjust to the gloom—for some reason the atmosphere felt draped in black crêpe. Every other person appeared to be smoking; I knew that I'd come back to the dorm hair and clothes reeking of cigs. The scents of booze and men's cologne spiked the air, and the room bubbled with animated chatter like a house party. Friends were meeting friends. Alone and out of place, I felt more self-conscious than ever.

The room was furnished with upholstered square booths and dark wooden tables with wooden chairs. Everyone was drinking. No one was eating. Patrons, I understood, dined in restaurant rooms upstairs. I noticed a few groups of guys in their upper twenties, dateless but looking. For whom, I didn't know. I saw very few single women, and I certainly didn't count as game. Carrying a drink tray on which sat a stack of glass ashtrays, a voluptuous Bunny would sidle up to a stag table and welcome the men in a sultry voice. To impress her, the guys would try to outdo each other with displays of cool sexual charm, but behind the show of bravado I perceived shakiness and a sinking sense of unslakable desire.

In your dreams, fellas, I said to myself.

I'll say one thing for the Bunnies, at least on the floor of the club, they did control the men.

But stag guys were only part of the mix. Among the patrons, I also spied older businessmen on the town and Midwestern guys with their dates, many of them regular gals in their office-worker skirts and blouses. Only one woman appeared the paragon of chic femininity. Slinky in a sleeveless black sheath, about thirty, she held a glass of white wine and inclined to her man. Near the bar perched a less glorious dame, feverish with blush-on, apparently snozzled; she seemed to scan the room for the date who might or might not be standing her up. This was not my scene. My scene was hairy, down-home, Chicago folkies in jeans.

I saw far fewer Bunnies than I expected. Every so often, one would float by, drink tray in hand, cinched into her tiny-waisted satin corset, breasts pushed up so that she seemed to be carrying two cups of pudding on her chest. The Bunnies wore headbands with satin bunny ears, flesh-toned stockings, high-heeled pastel pumps with pointy toes, and that odd male tuxedo touch—bow ties and white cuffs with cufflinks. Sure enough on her rear, each girl sported a big poufy cottontail, like a giant powder puff. The Bunnies were pretty, the way cheerleaders and certain sorority girls were pretty. So there I stood, a groundhog among the Bunnies, a sack of potatoes in the confectionary. To the patrons, the Bunnies smiled their pressed-on smiles. Most appeared not to see me, though one cast me a suspicious eye. Like I might go Carrie Nation on the place or start a protest chant.

Drawn by the sound of jazz, I squeezed through the crowd to a little stage area where a black jazz trio—a drummer, a pianist, and a man on a upright bass—was playing "A Lot of Livin' to Do." I joined the small audience around the combo. Thank God, I thought, I could stand there and appreciate the music while waiting for Dad. After a couple songs, the small audience drifted away, but having nowhere to go I hung around watching the guys swing into "What Kind of Fool Am I" and then "Someday My Prince Will Come." The bassist nodded my way. Maybe I was making too much eye contact or something, and just as I figured I had overstayed my welcome in front of the combo, Dad approached beaming with his group of conference friends. He wore a green jacket that made him look like he'd won the Master's Tournament. We embraced. Then taking in my get-up, he grew glum. "Did you have to come here looking like this?" he asked.

Nevertheless, Dad introduced me to his colleagues. I wondered which guy possessed the famous Playboy Club key.

"Comparative literature, what's that? What do you do with that?" pressed one associate who smelled like English Leather and still sported his conference tag.

"My sentiments exactly," rejoined Dad merrily.

America was in the post-oil embargo recession. People with Ph.D.'s were cleaning zoo cages. But as I suspected, the progeny of my father's business associates were forging forward. The colleagues bragged about their sons and daughters in medical, dental, and law school. How surprised I was when one of Dad's colleagues drew me aside and told me that I was a very good sport to meet my father here. He said that his daughter would never set foot in a Playboy Club. "She'd scream bloody murder if I asked."

A Bunny in a tan corset came up to take our drink order, and when my dad put his arm around her waist she pressed on a smile and removed my dad's hand. Then she pretended to see a customer across the room and slid off into the forest of patrons.

"You're not supposed to touch the merchandise," admonished one of the colleagues, his voice dry as a martini.

"These girls? It doesn't mean anything to them. That's part of the game," Dad replied.

The other guy shrugged with a suit-yourself look.

It look a long time before another Bunny came up. And the one who appeared was slightly less glamorous than the rest. She wore a blue corset. Her ears drooped. Her gray eyes looked a little weary, but behind her frosted pink lipstick and pressed-on smile, she also seemed more serious. When she took my drink order (a gin and tonic) she met my eyes with a knowing sisterly look.

Returning, the blue Bunny had only one drink on her tray and that drink was my G&T. She asked me if I were in college and told me that she was at Circle Campus, putting herself through school, studying social work. The Bunny job really helped. The money was decent, and she could go to classes during the day. I wondered when she had time to study, but I didn't ask.

"Your plan is super," I told her. "You're so independent."

"I have to be," she replied.

I admired her. I was in awe of her self-reliance. I thought of how she would be helping others in her future job as a social worker. Most of all, I considered how tough things were for her. How easy they were for me. I glanced over at my dad in his green jacket. He was listening closely to something an associate was explaining. I felt mercenary and somewhat ashamed of it. I thought of what a small price I had to pay for money. How steady, if imperfect, was my father's love.

Harriet Levin Millan

Swimming in a Glass

Hardly anyone can stop looking through
the oversized martini glass made just for the disco.

It holds a swishing girl in mermaid fins,
her breasts still sunlit and sparkling

with every eye riveted onto her, eels or hair
flickering in oscillation

under strobe and ultraviolet light,
black box and laser burst ball.

Like the yawkyawk, her story will travel
from one country to the next.

An entire culture will spring up, initiation rites constructed
around how long a girl can hold her breath,

lips puckered, that practice kiss, and heroically
reemerge, crooknecked against the glass toward a shore

of outstretched arms. It's easier to grow a culture
under glass. The most hermetic sound in techno

is percussion, not a hand drum made of skin,
but one that's forged with prerecorded sounds

like a fake ID, repeated on cue. Thank goodness
her story doesn't involve a raft,

machine guns, crossfire, a bloody massacre.
She can hedge death, flash like a gem

in glittering scales, the salt in the air, the spray
kicking back. She will always seek

as water seeks, a level, which, lacking confines
of a mortal life, ridiculously overflows,

a condition Hans Christian Anderson blamed on the mermaid's
attraction to drowning men,

their storms, endlessly battered loves.
Dancing with you, the hem of my jeans hits bottom.

Besides the threads of my clothing fraying,
my skin exposed, your fingers run a surge down my body,

so electric the current carries me.
I grow fins, numb and cold.

The low-pitched booms dolphins make
mouth to mouth fill up the universe.

Harriet Levin Millan

You Walk In Late

to class, dressed early instead,
sharp shoulder blades buckled
up through flesh.

To have followed your walk in stiletto heels
from a room overlooking the skeletal view
of an isthmus' oil fields
caged flames, is to hear the fricatives of your native Kwa
crack in our ears as you read: "This is how I am loved."

A choice? You give your grandfather these words:
Not one of my children is here. There is nothing for them.
They sucked the oil until it was dry. Then they abandoned us.
Now like cocks we scratch the ground for a living.

When paws dip into bowls of cream, they leave tracks,
but hands wield instruments: spoons, bellows, shackles, drills.

Your chair scrapes against linoleum,
against the awkward silence.
Your loose-leaf notebook open
on the table, paper bound
in the tightening grip of metal rings,
a grip held equally as tight
as when you string arms against bedposts,
and dig spikes into flesh,
as you wait for praise.

Tongue-tied, we also wait
at the corners where you meet men
to use you, slick and rich,
an abundance of crude.

The blackboard seeks to erase
eye shadow on lids,
the flower with cat-o'-nine tails stem delicately
tattooed in the crevice between your breasts,
carried from the Delta. So close
to the heart, it blooms,
releasing fragrance into stunned air.

Kathleen Volk Miller

A Haunted House

I grew up in a haunted house. We would each hear thumping behind our headboards; my sister would sit up in bed laughing in a strange voice; the two of us would wake in our four-poster twin beds as they shook. People sometimes came out of our closet, talking to one another.

When my parents finally acknowledged that we were not having nightmares, there were not raccoons in the chimney, my father threw away the Oujia board, and no one said much.

The back door slammed open on its own; the dog barked at nothing we could see; we stayed.

Catholics, we had the house blessed; the priest went room to room, praying in Latin, sprinkling our walls and rugs and furniture with holy water as his arm slashed the air.

That night, the thumping rocked the house. I was nearly 12, and I was just so sad that it didn't work. During the thumping—that's what we called it then and what we still call it—"the thumping"—each time I'd think—"This is the worst time." I still think this time really was. The thumping kept thumping, then, it stopped.

I remember the silence. Then my father said, "I think it's over now."

So, when the Virgin Mary's face appeared over mine in the mirror as I cried, when Jesus appeared at the foot of our beds when my sister was sick with pneumonia, when I woke up in a hospital croup tent and there was Jesus again, when crayon scribbles appeared on the walls and the ringer was always shut off on the phone, and I later found out children had died in a fire in my first-ever apartment, and when lights dim in series of three, and channels change on the television, and on, and on, I've been able to shrug.

This acceptance of the unexplainable inured in me was little help when my oldest brother died of a brain aneurism, suddenly, stunningly, while watching a Monday night football game at a local pub. We were told that he stood up from his stool, said, "I need help," and fell over, brain dead.

This acknowledgment that the ground we walk on is tissue paper was little help when my husband died from a cancer that was not supposed to kill him. The nuns, the priests, the holy medals, the prayers, had not worked.

But, belief in the window between worlds was necessary the morning after he died, when I woke to the feeling of his hand in my hand, warmth, pressure, and realization that he had died was coupled with the acknowledgement that he wasn't actually gone.

The coin has two sides, joy and terror co-exist. My mother's death on Christmas Day is not tolerable, but the yellow light, the warmth in my core when I held her and breathed her in a last time, must be what made me return to my children, watch them open gifts, put a turkey in the oven; go on.

Anne-Marie Obajtek-Kirkwood
American and French Voices
Telling/Re-telling September 11

On September 11, 2001, two planes crashed into the Twin Towers of the World Trade Center, starting thus a tragedy of un-witnessed proportions yet on North American soil, with worldwide repercussions. The euphoria of the year 2000 was quickly buried in this ensuing tragedy which was to shake and upset the data and references of this new century as World War I had done for the preceding one, according to Jürgen Habermas.[1] Alain Finkielkraut would simply call it, in his journal of September 23rd, "the event," the absolute of the definite article reinforcing thus its specificity, its exceptional character in the history of terrorism. To circumscribe a phenomenon where imagination and understanding fell short, he wrote: "Words failed on September 11 2001 when watching the two civilian planes crashing one after the other into the twin towers of the World Trade Center. And words are still failing. Precedents and concepts which first come to mind are all strangely defective"[2] and furthermore: "We knew that the worst could happen. We held ourselves ready for anything. We were wrong. This was not all, it did not encompass the event that had just happened. There is worse than the worst. There are limits that emerge to consciousness only when they cross over into reality" (252).

This unthinkable, too horrible to be imagined, and totally unheard of, had also been conjured up by Marguerite Duras about World War Two and the Holocaust in particular, in alike fashion: "One looks for anything equivalent elsewhere, at other times. There is nothing."[3] Frédéric Beigbeder referring to Claude Lanzmann for whom the Shoah is a mystery, adds that for him "September 11 is too", and he pursues: "It was an event which was unforeseeable because it was impossible. It is, quite, literally, incomprehensible, by which I mean it passes human understanding."[4] For his part, Paul Virilio stressed war: "Let us make no mistake about it: with the 11 September attack, we have before us an act of total war, remarkably conceived and executed, with a minimum

---

[1] Derrida, J. et J. Harbermas. 2003. Le 'concept' du 11 septembre. Dialogues à New York (octobre-décembre 2001) avec Giovanna Borradori. Paris: Galilée, 2003. 55.

[2] Finkielkraut, Alain. L'Imparfait du présent. Paris: Gallimard Folio, 2003. 251.

[3] Duras, Marguerite. La Douleur. Paris: Gallimard, coll. Folio, 1998. 64.

[4] Beigbeder, Frédéric. Windows on the World. A Novel. Trans. Frank Wynne. London & New York : Fourth Estate, 2004. 268.

of resources. [...] On September 11 2001, the Manhattan skyline became the front of a new war."[5] As for Claude Lanzmann, "9/11 is the extreme of understatements", "like an immense horror secret and shameful joy in front of horror, which defied enunciation, forbade commentaries, condemned thinking. 9/11 is a spectacular discovery which will enter human history and will stay forever in the history of bloody euphemisms just like "the final solution."[6] In a similar vein, Baudrillard, the sociologist, called 9/11 "an absolute event", "an event that defies... any form of interpretation."[7]

This tragedy which seems to have no end through its consequences or the consequences that are grafted on it by force has deeply shaken the commonly admitted generalities and certainties up to then and generated a new world. It has also produced a massive live world television coverage, documentaries, written analytical, political, critical works and also fictional work, on film and paper, to try and make sense, to somewhat elucidate in parts this devastation. In the French language, there have been more than a dozen literary works published, of various genres (science fiction, novels, poetry, short stories, travelogues, and plays). It seems that next to more or less scientific explanations, there is also a need for fiction to grasp this phenomenon, or as Nancy Huston puts it, there is a need to go beyond the "Ur-Text", the "primitive narratives" to reach for fictional art which brings something else: "What fictional art can do, on the other hand, is to give us another point of view on these realities. Help us put them at a distance, dissect them, see through them, criticize the underlying fictions."[8]

Writing a fictional work on 9/11 appears nevertheless a real challenge to some writers due to the specificity of the event. If Frédéric Beigbeder in his *Windows on the World*, a novel that came out in French in 2003, claims that "the only way to know what took place in the restaurant on the 107th Floor of the North Tower, World Trade Center on September 11th 2001 is to invent it," he also recognizes the difficulty of using fiction in his own work: "Writing this hyperrealist novel is made more difficult by reality itself. Since September 11, 2001, reality has not only outstripped fiction, it's destroying it. It's impossible to write about this subject, and yet impossible to write about anything else.

---

[5] Virilio, Paul. *Ground Zero*. trans. Chris Turner. London : Verso, 2002. 82.

[6] Lanzmann, Claude. Bonnes feuilles : *Nouvelles mythologies* :. http://bibliobs.nouvelobs. com/20070910/296/le-11-septembre-2001 Retrieved September 2009.

[7] Baudrillard, Jean. *The Spirit of Terrorism*, trans. Chris Turner . London : Verso, 2002. 41, 13.

[8] Huston, Nancy. *L'espèce fabulatrice*. Arles: Actes Sud. 2008. 185.

Nothing else touches us" (8). Our two authors here under consideration, Michel Vinaver and Luc Lang in their respective works, *11 septembre 2001/11 September 2001* and *11 septembre, mon amour* seem reluctant to use a great deal of fiction in their writings.

Both works, published shortly after 9/11, in 2002 for Vinaver, 2003 for Lang, share a few points in common but also diverge totally or seemingly so in their approach to the U.S.: they let immediate witnesses or voices, totally with Vinaver, partially with Lang, occupy the narrative space, in bilingual form (English and French) for Vinaver. Vinaver's libretto, as he calls it, was first written in English a few weeks following the destruction of the towers, then translated into French by the author. One hears unidentified voices from the cockpit of American Airline Flight 11, air traffic controllers, the pilot of United Airline Flight 175, male, female voices, some characters identified as Madeline, Lisa, Michael, a chorus, a journalist, Rumsfeld, instruction sheets given to the hijackers, impersonal voices narrating their harrowing escape from the towers and the ordeal of some friends who did not make it, and then Bush speaking followed by Bin Laden, replica after replica. This polyphonic mingling of voices, victims, survivors, terrorists, leaders and various elements engenders confusion, ambiguity, chaos, misunderstanding and one wonders whether confronted by such an event one can really write on it, or rather, as Vinaver states, aim at a musical object, cantata or oratorio.

Lang's *11 septembre, mon amour* is also unusual: not a libretto, but a hybrid text, somewhat of a chronicle, partly autobiography, partly reportage, that Lang himself calls both a "road-storie" (sic) and "a political narrative."[9] It also entails a polyphonic opening, which gives back intense life to the voices of the people who perished in United Airlines Flight 93 that crashed in Pennsylvania and closes with them. He lets us hear the vibrant, tragic, last words of love of those who know they will perish, words that tell the impossibility to act when there is still time, voices that talk of regrets and hopes still, and thus Lang pays homage to the victims of this tragedy. In his work, after a polyphonic opening akin to Vinaver's, Lang chooses instead an autobiographical narrative combined with historical analysis. He describes his trip to the Blackfoot Indian

---

[9] Lang, Luc. « Travailler à obtenir une voix libérée ». *Le Monde*, Rencontre, 22 septembre 2006.

reservation in northern Montana, where he learns of the September 11 terrorist attacks on CNN. Contrary to Vinaver, he takes a strong position about the event and the U.S. in general, characterized by a sense of solidarity for the victims and for an alternative America, antithetical to the official one, which is harshly criticized.

Vinaver, a playwright who wrote seventeen plays before his *11 septembre 2001/11 September 2001*, is faithful to himself. He started with *Les Coréens* in 1955, a play about the Cold War that was threatening to evolve into a Third World War, then wrote about the Algerian War and has now written about what has led the U.S. and other countries to an ongoing war against terrorism. His method of putting his text together has also not much varied since he was 17. He cuts and pastes press cuttings into big copy-books and can still show one of Pétain's trial with his comments that he did in 1945 when he was 18. Vinaver describes himself as a written press addict,[10] needing his daily fix. This is the very same method he used to create *11 septembre 2001*, as he states in the foreword, in bilingual form, and we'll choose the English version here: "Text written in the weeks following the destruction of the Twin Towers in Manhattan. Written in English (more precisely in American), no doubt because of the location of the event and because English is the language of the words taken from daily newspapers."[11] It must be added that Vinaver has not chosen to translate the chorus into French in the French version and has no explanation for this, other than his love for the English language, which he prefers to French,[12] maybe because they add to verisimilitude, and because some puns were untranslatable.

He did not wish to write a play about 9/11, thinking that "because of this event, one could not write theater." In the meantime his publisher published his libretto as a text, and since it has started a life of its own as a theater play rather than a musical piece.

In a foreword to R. Cantarella's staging of his work, Vinaver explained his rejection of fiction for this particular opus, contrary to his preceding works where imagination intervened more:

> *September 11, 2001* is an imitation of the event that
> happened on that day. [...] One cannot imagine starting

---

[10] Darge, Fabienne. « Michel Vinaver, dramaturge du réel ». *Le Monde* 01.23. 09.

[11] Vinaver, Michel. 11 septembre 2001 11 september 2001. Paris : L'Arche, 2002. 8.

[12] A propos du 11 septembre de Michel Vinaver. Ecrire sur les événements récents. www.theatre-contemporain.net Retrieved September 2009.

from the event of September 11 because the event
surpasses imagination. What I tried to do was to fix it.

The whole world, or nearly, attended the event live. The
shock was unprecedented, the reflections were blinding.
And then rivers of comments, they were necessary, to try
and see clearly, and it is not over.

What motivated me was the need to establish the event
outside of any comment, naked, in its immediacy. Maybe
against the bloating of memory, against oblivion.

To reflect the event rather than to ponder on it.[13]

Such are Vinaver's reasons here for shying away from fiction as it would
have betrayed the event, hence his choice of mimesis to approach reality. But
if fiction is denied, art or access to a special form of representing the real is
privileged: voices identified by names and functions utter words. No character
is fully developed among these anonymous, or famous, victims or survivors,
witnesses or actors of the event. The drama unfolds chronologically with
the various terrorists in the four planes, the crash of the two planes into the
towers, the impressions of those who die, those who have survived, those who
remember, and those who confront each other.

Characters are skimpily outlined, because Vinaver aims at some
detachment, refusing compassion as he says: "There is a double movement in
the writing: go towards and at the same time, not go as far as fusion."[14]

What makes Vinaver's work so arresting, in its representation of 9/11,
is his use of voices and words, of dialogue, and how it flows or does not
flow. His work approaches the form of a cantata or an oratorio, minus the
very music, with the use of repetitions and the chorus, and of a journalist
as reciter. Characters and their utterances follow in very rapid succession;
some are paired by twos and are thus easy to follow, others are interlaced
and broken into groups of three, four or more, which renders comprehension
difficult, fragmentary, if not chaotic, all the more as one is left suspended for
end of thoughts or sentences that at times never come (46-54 for example).

---

[13] Vinaver, Michel. Mimésis. http://www.theatre-contemporain.net/spectacles/
September-11-2001/ensavoirplus/ Retrieved September 2009.

[14] Idem.

Dialogue or lack of it underlines superbly the chaos, confusion, and terror that ensued that day.

In rendering the reality of what was, through this multiplicity of voices, Vinaver does not take positions ideologically or politically throughout the exchanges, but when it comes to the last section, one wonders whether this still holds true as he willfully pairs Bush and Bin Laden in contrasted pronouncements of course, but also in parallel ones where both invoke fight and battle for freedom in the name of God, and finish thus:

BIN LADEN
May God shield us (68)

BUSH
May God continue to bless us (70).

The irony of this juxtaposition is obvious. To the question whether he was revealing his opinions in his text, Vinaver gave the following answer: "I am asking permission not to be in the dialogue, whose words constitute the theatrical object. This is a non-question for me. I am the master of the work, I am nowhere and I am everywhere. I do not have to identify myself. But I am in the editing, I am responsible for letting these voices that join to be heard."[15] Vinaver also confessed he felt some hatred towards monotheism in general compared to other religions which are way less offensive, especially the polytheistic ones, though that does not prevent them from being very cruel too, but less so than when one has God in one's camp, he said (*A propos du 11 septembre*).

Though Vinaver did not wish to write fiction on 9/11, and lots of his passages ring genuine, Bush's and Bin Laden's statements being totally original, he confessed that the very end of his *11 septembre 2001* about a young employee missing work because of being sick and thus saving her life is completely fictitious. The journalist character is also totally invented. And how are the chorus's interventions to be interpreted? Their meaning is totally lost in French as they remain in English; besides, some would not translate and that may be the reason they stayed in English. The chorus interventions are really a mixed bag. Some comment on the political or financial situation (20) with passages quoted straight from the written press, but then, after the crash of the second airplane into the tower, we get this ironical, mocking, humorous,

---

[15] *A propos du 11 septembre de Michel Vinaver. Ecrire sur les événements récents.* www. theatre-contemporain.net Retrieved September 209.

disruptive intervention with puns and reminiscences of the London Bridge nursery rhyme:

Hi
Jacked
Hi
Jacked Jets Jackety Jets
Hijacked Jets
Hi
Jets Hit Trade
World Weird
Worderly Trade
Pentagon
Twin Towers
Falling Down Falling Down Falling
Gone
The Twin Towers Are Falling Down Falling Down Falling Down (22, 24)

Evil genii, comic relief? How to explain the gist of this passage, how to square it with the overall Vinaverian purpose? It seems the playwright could not resist some humor, however incongruous it appears.

Reading *11 septembre 2001 11 September 2001* is a taxing, harrowing experience due to the form chosen and the content: the extensive and crucial description of that day, the uneasy understanding at times due to the various fragments, and short, alternating, incomplete exchanges. Yet Vinaver, just like Beigbeder for his *Windows on the World*, himself underlines:

> "Give an account of what is the height of horror, but in
> the end, it is something beautiful to see which brings
> pleasure. A total paradox" (*A propos du 11 septembre*).

Contrary to Vinaver who was in France when 9/11 happened, Luc Lang was in the U.S., and he wrote his book between 2001 and 2003. He had been invited to present his latest novel then, *Les Indiens*, to various universities and was in Montana, on the Blackfoot Reservation as CNN started broadcasting the traumatic news. His description of what happened, found roughly in the middle of the book, is therefore a transcript of what he saw on CNN along the day, and as the day wore on, he noticed the reports becoming more and more repetitive, the pictures more obsessively the same and less informative which prompted him in the end to vent the following judgment based on a denial of death of the event and its sordid and cruel realism:

> Remain nevertheless suspicious of these pictures
> that do not deliver any visual clue of reality more real

than Hollywood pictures. It is the same mold, these are the same shots, same framing, same viewpoints: close, far away, overhanging, tilted-up, with a bouncy, sweeping camera on the shoulder. This is the same noise: shouts, yells, urban emergency sirens. The same crowd movements hounded by a curse, the same terror, the same frantic running away of some, the same stupor and the same state of shock of others... Then, as hours fly, I start feeling uneasy, sensing a striking abnormality. And suddenly I understand what unexpected and unforeseeable absence and lack empty the pictures and above all strengthen texts and commentaries which say, non stop, that we are in front of reality. Death is everywhere but in no body to be seen. Lightly wounded people can easily be spotted among these grey ghosts appearing from nowhere, a bleeding face can be noticed here but death is never embodied. Barely is it possible for the informed spectator to distinguish these figures jumping into space, fleeing the encircling fire.[16]

The caution and distrust were shared by Beigbeder who, through the indignation of his main character, reproaches American media for not having shown the reality of things:

Why did the dead go unseen? It was not some ethical code of practice, it was self-censorship, maybe just censorship, period. Five minutes after the first plane crashed into our tower, the tragedy was already hostage to fortune in a media war. And patriotism? Of course. Knee-jerk patriotism made the American press swagger about, censor out suffering, edit out shots of the jumpers, the photographs of those burn victims, the body parts. You could call it a spontaneous *omertà*, a media blackout unprecedented since the first Gulf War. [...] And it was thus that one of the greatest postwar campaigns of media disinformation was perpetrated. [...] When a building collapses, feel free to repeat the footage endlessly. But whatever you do, don't show what was inside: our bodies" (266).

---

[16] Lang, Luc. *11 septembre, mon amour.* Paris : Stock, 2003. 111. All translations of Lang's text are mine as it does not exist in English.

Vinaver expresses the same, though less precisely: "What does one finally know about September 11? What does one know of the reality of this event which has certainly deeply affected the minds but remains for the immense majority as something improbable, the picture of which was seen non stop on the screens?"

If Lang reacts so negatively to the televisual coverage of the event, he is nevertheless deeply moved by its audio aspect in the form of phone conversations and radio homage that open his book. Contrary to Vinaver who, for the most part, affirms to report true sayings, Lang does not let us hear the United Airlines Flight 93 passengers' last mobile phone conversations per se, but imagines them in context, callers and recipients at that time, where they were, what they were doing: we are thus presented with both parties in the unfolding drama. Contrary to Vinaver again, there is much affect in these opening pages, much pathos, compassion, fusion with each side, the passengers and the people they are calling and the manner both parties respond in these last crucial minutes. Lang depicts how people were just taken by their daily chores, absolutely unsuspecting of what was to come:

> People progressing along their ordinary day, with their
> wandering thoughts, more or less dark or grey or colored,
> with their hands, their bodies, their thoughts at work.
> People absorbed in their movements, advancing in the
> morning in their own labyrinth, against a background
> which is undoubtedly for nobody that of peace or social
> tranquility, but at least in the West a background where
> there is no projection of a shadow of violent death from
> war, no anxious intuition of being its possible victim (16).

And then these phone calls from loved ones, which made time stand still:

> It was the familiar voice of a beloved one simply mingling
> with the quiet flow of an ordinary day. Love words were
> spreading into the earpiece, final, unseemly words
> undoing the fluid coherence of the day, like pebbles, sand,
> flour, disintegrating continuous time-matter. And as these
> love words were no longer mixing with the flow, as they
> were hindering it, cumbersome like farewells, suddenly
> only the present existed, only the present, the sluggish
> and terrifying strength of the present that rivets body
> and mind on the spot. The day stood still, stopped, I fell
> into the void of this voice which tells me that it loves me
> forever since there is no future, only the eternity of death
> and love. And yet living and warm, it talks to me now, but

it talks to me as if it were in the hereafter, as if death had
already come, a present outside of time, the loved voice in
a moment beyond the grave (16-17).

This moving description in which time stops, in which love already
brushes death, is followed by a consideration of what technology can now allow
that did not use to be possible and thus also alludes to the crucial subsequent
human drama:

Here is what the cellular, the mobile, the wireless phone
invents this morning. The possibility of being called
anywhere by voices from beyond the grave, our loved
ones, our condemned ones, who have today the pathetic
power of suspending the flow of time by their tender
voices, shut in as they are in their aircraft-cabins or at the
summit of towers, nearly 400 meters high, already recluses
in the sky. When they touch the ground, they will absurdly
be no more, they know it, and talk to us from the point
of view of their own death as nobody before, carried away
in such a disaster, has been able to do: we are dying now
and we love you forever, our death will vouch for it, just
as your life will vouch for us, this is the condemned bet
from beyond death (17).

In a more theoretical writing of his, *Le Roman comme boîte noire, Notes pour
une poétique du roman (III)*,[17] devoted to this plane crash and its repercussions
on novel writing, Lang muses similarly on the cell-phone, and as has been seen
before with Vinaver and Beigbeder who wonder whether there is a possibility
of fiction after such an event, Lang sees that reality has overtaken fiction:

If this day of September 11 2001 had been imagined
by a novelist, if narrative immanence at work had
led him to write these voices who confide in their
relatives, free and unscathed, -sometimes absent and
in this case to the answering machine-, their sudden
imprisonment into an imminent death, the said
novelist could certainly not have gone much further
in the expression of cruelty and empathy.

Obviously reality preceded fiction, and Lang, in this first part of his work
entitled "The Voices" pays homage to the victims of this tragedy on American

---

[17] http://www.inventaire-invention.com/librairie/fichiers_txt/Lang_notes.htm#13 (15-16).
Retrieved September 2009.

soil but also beyond, as he specifies by the end of this section, adding all the innocent civilian Afghan victims of allied bombings during the 2001-2002 winter (26).

In this section, he alludes to another kind of homage rendered to the victims by a Montana radio station he hears while driving a pick-up Northwest of Waterton Glacier, and again he insists on names, voices and what they stand or stood for. Against a Mozart musical background, the names of newly disappeared people were pronounced, several days in a row, mornings and afternoons. This simple tribute touches Lang deeply:

> Thus other voices were answering the disappeared
> ones, they were simply telling of absence and loss,
> uttering a sonorous composition having disappeared
> too, since it consisted of each first name and family
> name that would no longer be pronounced. And music
> exhaled sorrow and mourning as it alone can do, an
> echo, a vibratory resonance. All this without raising the
> national flag, without barking a discourse on war or
> revenge, without big watery feelings. Besides I was no
> longer hearing Anglo-American, just the first names
> and names of those who should not have died and who
> had spoken to the living an unknown, universal and
> amorous language, separated from them by the infinite
> distance of their deaths (24).

In the middle of his book, when Luc or Lucas, Lang's alter ego, drives through Montana, he expresses gratitude to this radio program: "I wish now, at this moment, that I could thank the woman, the man, those who have thought of and realized this vocal event of remembrance, this compassion melody for the civilian victims, in the urgency of a time already saturated by the noise of war" (159). In part II of his book, entitled "The Names", Lang gives his own written tribute to some victims and their names by choosing from the 11 September Memorial those whose name starts with the letter L and lists six pages of them.

Part III and IV of the book relate Lang's trip to Montana proper, and are not devoid of deep criticism of some features of American culture and civilization, which has prompted a critic to call it "a strident anti-American screed."[18] He tackles what he calls the Indian genocide, Hiroshima, Vietnam but also today U.S. with its hamburgers, dollars, SUVs, preachers and more, and we have to wait for the last part, V "Amorous Epilogue", to understand the allusion of

---

[18] Versluys, Kristiaan. « 9/11 as a European Event : The Novels. » *European Review* : Vol.15, Issue 1, 2007. 65-79. 65.

the title *11 septembre, mon amour* to Duras's novel, as the writing parodies her *Hiroshima, mon amour*: "Yes, I saw the plane vanish into the skyscraper (235) [...] Yes, I saw all that, sometimes in slow motion, sometime frame by frame [...]" (237). The similitude with Duras's novel also lies at another level, by connecting this 9/11 tragedy to that of Hiroshima and in the deep love and compassion that Lang evidences for suffering mankind. In this last section, alluding to the deeply tragic aspect of 9/11, which so brutally annihilated lives, he stresses how much this tragedy has fatally affected us, partly so because of the media:

> Never has a collective drama been so lived and talked
> about in the present, individually, indivisibly, in the
> absolute solitude that makes each of us face his own
> death. Never yet has the technique of picture and sound
> been thus able to untie, undo, scatter, atomize collective
> tragedy into an endless addition of individual tragedies,
> that then come and hunt us down, question us in the
> intimacy of our lives and our time, so that we feel these
> individual tragedies like so many personal accidents. This
> does not save anybody and imprisons everybody in an
> unspeakable anxiety. Thus we no longer are a community
> confronted with a collective and historical event, we are
> as many distraught individuals, all carried away in a flow
> of pictures and sound which scatters us and gets us lost,
> then renders us contemporary to one another, renders us
> contemporary in isolation and separation (246).

Vinaver did not wish to deliver a committed narrative nor did he wish to write fiction on September 11 but "reflect" the event, thinking the best way to do so was to write a libretto with various voices "reflecting" our fragmented times. Lang also uses voices in his *11 septembre mon amour* but with a very different aim, out of compassion and love, far away from the distance maintained by Vinaver:

> Shouldn't we precisely give written shape to their
> shapeless, volatile, fugitive, scattered, accidental voices,
> brought to us on the air? Shouldn't we give meaning and
> permanence to these civilian and desperate, human, too
> human voices, to these voices from beyond death, which
> do not cry hatred, vengeance, war and murder of other
> women, other men and other children, no, which simply
> said: "do you hear me? I hug you, I love you." We won't
> see each other any more... because they occupy an ethical
> sound space, they draw its constellation, and because

we can't surrender them to the political mercantilism of the powerful, the cynical and the conniving who already recycle them in their false vengeful justice, who already invoke them to lead us into a real war and serve thus their truly hegemonic will. Yes, my love, we must accompany these lost voices, write them, so that the Innocents' massacre ceases, unconditionally, that of civilian populations who are the disarmed childhood, without power or flag, of all human societies (246-247).

Since we are a "fiction-loving species" (Huston), we need tales, stories to better grasp, understand reality, and Vinaver and Lang's literary works, among others, to realize that the horror of September 11 really took place. Their texts give us different perspectives through theater or narrative. In his French workshop, with deliberate detachment, Vinaver devised a collection gathering all the various aspects of the event, into a complex and fragmented mix of voices reproducing the real chaos of that day. Lang, travelling in the United States on that fatal day, chose the compassionate proximity of these voices that have become silent, gave a committed vision of the disaster which privileges the human aspect. Whatever their differences in approach or vision, one like the other strives to fight oblivion, do a witnessing work, Vinaver without any comment, Lang insisting on his deep sympathy for the victims.

Don Riggs

Inventio of Poetry

Where, and how, to start? That is one of the first questions that confronts me after I've already dealt with "Wouldn't you rather just skip today and not try to keep up this meaningless quota?" Actually, many of my better poems come out of the careless lines simply thrown on the page to get that daily sonnet out of the way. I'm not really sure how this happens; perhaps I don't have a heavy need to write on a certain subject or for a certain occasion, so things can slip in, unnoticed by my taste.

David Galenson distinguishes between artists who must plan everything out to the finest detail before setting pen to paper and those who just plunge in and find out where they're going by writing; I have come to identify myself with the second group over the years, partially as a result of Beat era poetics I read in the seventies. However, the question remains: how to start when the pen first hits the yellow pad?

Ancient rhetoric had a whole gallery of *topoi*, or *topics*—"places," literally, in which the orator would store an image to indicate talking points: a leash for the neighbor who was walking his dog at one in the morning and saw something, a glove for something with the victim's dried blood on it, found in the suspect's car. Robert Duncan's "Often I Am Permitted to Return to a Meadow" is a very beautiful example of a common place that is an archetypal source for him, and Adrienne Rich's "Diving into the Wreck" similarly gives her a place to start and a pathway down into a personal and possibly collective depth. Here, I reflect on the use of such a place in my own process:

What to write about? There are ways to find
topics for poetry, places to go
as art students go to the studio
where a naked human being lies down
in a position easily maintained
for forty-five minutes.
        Muscles relax
and bones shift until gravity opens
the body into a landscape that breathes
the model's mind into an alpha state
and the eyes vibrate behind drawn blinds.
Just like the art student, the poet's hand
trembles a simulacrum of the sea
bottom with geologic shifts, shipwrecks;
tentacles and anemones drift in slow motion.

One of the most topic-conscious poets I'm familiar with is that old curmudgeon of American Not-Quite-Modernism, Robert Frost. My father having been born in Dorchester, raised in Roxbury, and educated in Medford, I was raised on the knowledge that Boston was the "Athens of America," that Ralph Waldo Emerson was our foremost philosopher, and Frost our National Poet, reinforced by his reading at President John F. Kennedy's inauguration. As a sonnet writer, I have been additionally confronted with Frost, who wrote sonnets, some of them quite good, from his earliest volume on. I could envy Frost his proximity to Nature, his seeming ability to spend long walks in woods and fields, and the opportunities this proximity provided him for opportunities to read thematic significance into commonplace natural occurrences. Here is an entry for the Poetry of Envy:

Robert Frost, really, must have had it made.
All he had to do was walk out the door
and there he was, walking across the fields
and meadows, through abandoned towns, and woods,
where he could hunker down in the deep shade
and see the shadows on the forest floor,
assessing every movement for its yields
in poetry, rather than store-bought goods.
And who was the genius who took his book
and mass-produced it for men overseas
in the army and navy, World War II,
so while in Mindanao they could look
and recognize New England, like a tease
for death-familiar fighters: you come too.

Of course, this is a reflection on how I, living in the East Falls section of Philadelphia, do NOT have it made; I can walk out my apartment door and watch the traffic on Ridge Avenue leaving the city for Manayunk, or returning from Manayunk—"where the bear drinks"—to Center City, contemplate buying a slice of pizza from the pizza place next door, or watch the bikers and rollerbladers and power walkers on the asphalt path along the Schuylkill River several hundred yards away. Or, if I wanted to take the trouble, I could catch one of the buses to the Wissahickon Transfer Center and walk along the Wissahickon Creek, and attempt a Robert Frost-Henry David Thoreau communion with Nature. With my yellow pad in my pack, of course.

Again, I can be true to my own material context for writing poems: my bathtub. This is realism in its most concrete, direct form:

Before I step carefully into the wet
heat from which I feel the steam rising

beside me, I lean into the ball point
of the pen for one last bit of writing.
Undoubtedly, I will pick up the pad
once more when I have settled in the bath,
but I want to write down a final word
before the heat of the water has crept
through the skin of my legs and all the nerves
leading, like railways on a map of France,
directly to that control booth, the brain.
Perched there as in the Elysée Palace,
I will observe my extremities' pain,
the only counter to which is patience.

Dreams also provide a spur to write; for one thing, if I can recall a dream in the morning, I use the daily sonnet practice as a way of ensuring that I write it down, whether it makes for a good poem or not. Sometimes, as in this example from a few days ago, poetry itself enters into the dream:

Oneiric Accompaniment

His poetry was experimental,
which was all right with me, my own practice
notwithstanding, but I craved something more
musical in terms of experiment,
so I started rubbing against my shirt,
creating a leafy susurration
very subtly underneath the word sounds,
aleatory as the meanings were.
Soon some others, sandpapering also,
created complicated counterpoints
against my motion, not cacophonous,
but more like the whispers of sifting dusts.
We were all dreaming, in different places,
but we'd recognize each other later.

What had happened is that I was teetering on the edge between waking and sleeping through much of the dream, so that, on the one hand, I was aware that I was actually rubbing my bedclothes across my chest for a certain rasping sound, and that, on the other, I knew there were other people sleeping elsewhere who were joining me in this activity, a musical ensemble of isolated soloists simultaneously improvising. This kind of musical happening, by the way, I first experienced in the Modern Music Ensemble brought together in my college by Malcolm Goldstein, who now lives in the Vermont woods, taking the path less traveled by.

A final example of a poem's instigation, this time as a response to another poem. Frost's first book, *A Boy's Will*, starts with the sonnet titled "Into My Own."

Into His Own

Even in his thirties, he realized
the pines and maples of Vermont ended
somewhere, by a river or at a field:
something there was that made the darkness yield
to daylight before the old wood blended
with night. How pitiful the urban park
with its sycamores surrounded by streets:
extravagant nature economized,
day's simulacrum of sodium lights
mitigating the density of the dark.
He merely had to close his eyes to find
a remedy against the constant clearing,
the virgin forest's ceaseless disappearing:
snow sifting through the midnight woods of mind.

I can see, after going through these pieces, all done over the past week or two, that I tend to go over some fairly predictable, fairly repetitive concerns obsessively, writing from life, even if that life is circumscribed by a bathroom, writing from other people's poems, gleaned in part from memory and in part from stacks of paperbacks next to my bathtub, from traditional commonplaces, and from my own dreams—or lack of remembered dreams—and sometimes I go over these themes, or topics, or concerns, or questions like a dog gnawing at a bone, knowing that what is on the surface has been already cleaned to a shine, but sensing that, if I can only crack it open, then there will be some truly rich treat for me to savor!

Gail Rosen

Joan Rivers: Serious About Comedy

People may think she is the joke, but Joan Rivers is completely serious about being funny. Having never seen Joan Rivers perform live, I found her mildly funny (and sometimes annoying) when I would catch a snippet of her act on television. But I changed my opinion after watching this insightful and fascinating 84-minute documentary. Rivers is hilarious and to my surprise, inspiring.

Joan Rivers: A Piece of Work follows a year in the life of the then 75-year-old Rivers. Rivers candidly discusses her numerous cosmetic surgeries, the suicide of her husband Edgar Rosenberg, her relationship with her daughter Melissa, her relationship with Johnny Carson, who made her a star and then later blackballed her, and other professional triumphs and failures. The old footage of Rivers doing her act illustrates the success she deserves. Interviews with fellow comics Don Rickles and Kathy Griffin, daughter Melissa (she explains that her family referred to Rivers' career as "the career" and Melissa felt that the career was like another sibling), and business managers and staff add to the portrait of the complex Rivers. What struck me here was Rivers' astonishing hard work, her grounded sense of herself and her passion.

At the start of the documentary, Rivers points to the blank pages of her datebook and says "You want to see fear? I will show you fear." She wants to work all the time, and says yes to every offer if the money is right. She will hawk jewelry, give lectures and travel anywhere. Rivers explains this by saying that she lives an opulent lifestyle (she describes her ornate penthouse in New York by saying that "[t]his is how Marie Antoinette would live if she had money") and says that she prefers to work rather than retiring and living more modestly. One senses that this is only partially true. Her friends and business associates describe Rivers as a work addict. This would explain why she travels the country doing gigs, many in remote places with less-than-glamorous hotel accommodations (she sprays the toilet with Lysol in one hotel). Rivers has a huge file cabinet with jokes, each drawer meticulously labeled by topic, like "Melissa's Dates" or "My Sex Life." The documentary shows Rivers frequently creating and honing material. She tries an Obama joke on her staff, asking them if it is too much. "We used to call Jackie Kennedy Jackie O; can we call Michelle Obama Blackie O?" Her staff tells her it is too much.

Rivers is candid about her many cosmetic surgeries and allows directors Ricki Stern and Anne Sundberg to shoot her without any make-up, even though Rivers says she finds her naked face scary. She allows herself to be roasted on Comedy Central despite the fact that she knows there will be jokes about her age and her plastic surgery. She is right about that, and she says those jokes still hurt. But she smiles and takes part. One of the more powerful scenes shows a stand-up gig where Rivers is heckled by an audience member offended by her act. Rivers cuts him down and manages to keep the audience on her side. But after the show, she explains that this is not always easy to do. She expresses sympathy for the heckler.

My favorite scenes show Rivers working on an autobiographical play, *Joan Rivers: A Work in Progress by a Life in Progress.* The play was a big hit at the Edinburgh Fringe Festival and the film shows Rivers trying it out in London. The first-night audience seems to love it, but Rivers refuses to celebrate. She wants to wait for the reviews. She does not get carried away by her love for the play. The reviews are mostly bad. Rivers feels the pain of the bad reviews, but they do not affect her belief in the project. However, the reviews make her decide not to take it to New York. She knows that the New York press will be even tougher. Rivers seems to have arrived at that rare emotional place. Her belief in her talent is strong, but she is not deluded by her ego. She can look at each situation realistically. When she appears on a bill with other well-known comedians to honor George Carlin receiving the Mark Twain award, she assesses her own performance. "I was funnier than some and not as funny as others."

The film shows both the low points and the high points in what turned out to be a big year for Rivers. Despite having trouble booking gigs because of ageism, she goes on *The Apprentice* and wins. When doors start to open again, she is thrilled. She points to her datebook, which is now full. She reads the entries aloud by the time, followed by the activity. "That's happiness," she says. But she understands show business, and knows that she has to take advantage of whatever opportunities she has now. Towards the end of the film she reveals that she is "only really happy when she is onstage." She talks admiringly about comics like George Burns and Phyllis Diller who still performed when they were in their nineties. "I think I will outlast them," she states. I believe her.

Works Cited

Joan Rivers: A Piece of Work. Directed by Ricki Stern and Anne Sundberg. Joan Rivers (Herself), Melissa Rivers (Herself), Kathy Griffin (Herself), Emily Kosloski (Herself), Mark Anderson Phillips (Himself), Don Rickles (Himself) and Larry A. Thompson (Himself). IFC Films, 2010.

Fred Siegel

Doug Henning Can Fly

In 1975, on the most magical day of my fourteenth year, my father took me to New York. After a visit to Tannen's, the largest magic shop on the east coast, we went to the Cort Theater and saw a matinee performance of *The Magic Show*, a musical comedy starring the amazing Doug Henning.

How do you explain Doug Henning today? At a time in the 20th century when magic was all about men in formalwear doing classic tricks the way they had been done since the 19th century, Henning appeared out of nowhere—a hippie with long hair and a too-large mustache, who, in tee shirt and jeans, flew across the stage spreading joy and wonder. Henning seemed to be absolutely sincere—it was as if he believed in real magic and would leap tall buildings to make you believe it too.

The slight, silly show was built around Henning's large-scale illusions: a lady magically produced from a transparent box, ladies divided into halves, thirds, and fourths, a lady transformed into a mountain lion, and a lady levitated on the point of a sword. But despite the grand illusions, the dopey story, and a few charming songs by Stephen Schwartz (also composer/lyricist of *Godspell*, *Pippin*, and now *Wicked*), the scene I remember best centered around a newspaper. Henning displayed a section of the *New York Times* and pattered about reality and illusion. The newspaper was real, he explained, but his ripping of the newspaper was an illusion. As he said this, he ripped the paper very fairly and slowly and into many pieces, wadded them up and held them in front of his chest. Then, with no suspicious moves, the newspaper instantaneously restored to its original condition. The audience gasped.

Doug Henning did bigger tricks in that show, but I remember the newspaper best. It was the first time he spoke directly to the audience and it was as if he were speaking directly to me. It was as if he were saying, "Fred, someday YOU will be a magician!" The Doug who spoke to me in my imagination was correct; while I don't make my living as a magician I have performed magic, read about magic, and thought about magic every day for over 40 years. I don't think I'll ever stop.

In 1983, Henning returned to Broadway with a second show, *Merlin*, co-starring the fabulous Chita Rivera as an evil queen and featuring the foppish and funny newcomer Nathan Lane as the comic foil. The magic was stronger and more elaborate, but the magical Doug was lost in all the pageantry. Still, at the end of Act One, Doug Henning flew around the stage, very much like Peter Pan but apparently without the wires. This illusion would be perfected in subsequent years by David Copperfield, but still, what I saw there was magical and liberating and tear-inducing, perhaps because it is based on real desires to float and fly and soar.

This brings us to the ironic ending of the Doug Henning story. Henning could have kept his career going but his heart was no longer in it. Why? His involvement with the Maharishi Mahesh Yogi and the Transcendental Meditation movement became the primary force in his life. He ran for office on the TM political ticket and gave up his career to focus on planning Maharishi Vedaland, a theme park dedicated to enlightenment. After a career of simulating miracles on stages for the amusement of audiences, Henning sought real miracles. After creating the illusion of levitation on stages, Henning trained for "yogic flying." To the practitioner, this is an advanced technique by which a person floats in the air. To an outsider, however, the yogic flyer appears to be a blissed-out meditator in a lotus position hopping up and down on his or her buttocks. Look for "yogic flying" on YouTube and judge for yourself.

Towards the end of the 20th century, magicians heard tales of Doug Henning sightings in magic shops. Apparently, Henning was making a joyful return to magic—our kind of magic. Sadly, the joy did not last. Henning had been stricken with liver cancer and neither our kind of magic, the magic of medical science, nor the magic of the Maharishi could save him. Henning died in February of 2000 at age 53.

With the dearth of magic shops and the shortage of venues that feature live magicians, digital media have become the sources of inspiration for the current generation. What are most available are instructional DVDs and video clips of the latest tricks for sale in online magic shops. Also, creative young magicians record their magic using their Flips and webcams and share it with the world.

Like many people of my generation, I am wary of the digitization of magic. Nevertheless I imagine that a spirit, something akin to a digital Doug, floats through the ether, emerges from the screens of iPods and iPads and tablets and Droids, and whispers through the ear buds and into the imaginations of today's and tomorrow's fourteen-year-olds.

I look forward to their mysteries.

Elizabeth Thorpe
William Tell

Tell me, William, was it worth it? Do you remember the long shadows in that square, the way your shoes scuffed on the cobblestones, the way the multitudes cowered at the perceived authority of one man? Not you. You walked on by. So many of us work and work to make a legacy, but when push came to shove, doing nothing was your spark.

Of course, you had worked. Hours and hours in the woods with your bow had made you an expert in things of this nature. In shadows and light, with live prey and imagined, these skills were your greatest power. Your punishment tested what you did best.

And so you went to another square, another day, this time bound with your son in tow. Your son was scared, of course he was. You worried he wouldn't keep still. At the dinner table, in church, and with his own bow raised, he never kept still. This was a test of his bravery, maturity, as much as your confidence.

The crowd assembled, the same men and women in somber colors that had bowed not to the emperor, but to a symbol only, his raised hat. Did you wish at this point that you had just gone along with them, knowing it was stupid but doing it anyway? Did you see the way the sun shone on your boy's hair and regret your stubbornness? Or did you relish this chance to show your skill, to bite your thumb, as they used to say, at the powers that were?

The crowd went quiet, and you relied on them, too, not to distract you. Everything had to be just right, this golden moment: Boy, arrow, apple, string. Did you pause as you sized up the target? Were you proud of your boy for standing so perfectly still, still like the alpine air on that cool autumn day?

Yes. You pulled the string back, you took aim at the apple, just above the spot where your son shone brightest. You took aim, you let go.

The look on your boy's face when it was over, when he stood flecked simply with apple juice and not with blood. The pride you felt in him, in yourself. The way the crowd cheered.

Later Gessler shook your hand, and it seemed he had decided to make an ally of you. But you remembered those little indignities, the new things the teachers were told to teach, the unfamiliar lessons your son had come home repeating. The new colors on the castle walls and the new taxes at the farmers' market. They called Gessler a military man, but his hand was small and he shook softly. He smiled and asked about the second arrow in your quiver.

If he had been a sporting man, a working man, he would have known. Nobody relies on one arrow alone. Nobody gives himself only one chance. You looked at your son, gave him the old family signal, a nod of the head and he made himself scarce.

"If I had killed my son, so help me God," you said, still grasping Gessler's hand, "The other arrow was for you."

Scott Warnock

The Song Might Have Never Been: Zeppelin in the Age of Helicopter Parents

So a month ago my wife, in one of those heroic moves toward permanent marital stability, bought us tickets to the Jason Bonham Led Zeppelin Experience. The show tapped directly into my untouchable love of Zeppelin. I was awed not just by the talent of Bonham and his band but the emotion driving this tribute. Meandering home afterward, thinking about the grainy videos of Jason as a child that were part of the show, I wondered what if Zeppelin had tried to launch today, in the age of helicopter parents.

First off, Led Zeppelin's lead singer, the wild, wooly, poetic Robert Plant, demonstrated a love of singing when he was small. According to one biography, his dad, even though he disapproved, drove the teenage Plant to early jams. In 2010, dad would not just drive but likely would sit and watch, and however disapproving of the rock-and-roll lifestyle his youngster was pursuing, would make sure his young wailer was being treated fairly by the meager crowd. How would Plant have cultivated his rebellious, enigmatic musical persona while dad sipped a Shirley Temple in the back of the room and then laid on the guilt on minivan rides home: "My dear Robbie, I understand the good times, but what are all these bad times you're singing about? What did mother and I do wrong?" Too many rides like that, and a dispirited Plant might have had the germ of inspiration eradicated, following through on his accounting apprenticeship instead. I suppose he'd still be good for the occasional Black Sabbath song at local watering holes on karaoke night, where he might also sit and wonder, but, alas, only to himself, what is and what should never be.

Drummer John Bonham reputedly made his own drum kit at five. His dad apparently rigged up a mock snare to help the young banger, yet his parents didn't buy him his first full set until he was 15. 15! Nowadays, the moment that boy had tapped a rudimentary rhythm on a bath salts can, his parents would have rushed out to buy an armful of books about how to cultivate his obvious talent. On birthday three, Santa would have delivered a fully loaded youth drum kit. He would have begun intensive lessons, with his agent-parents plowing ahead to secure the finest instructors and seeking out elite academies. Fame and fortune would have beckoned. Forget "Four Sticks." By 19, Bonham—not Bonzo, for how do you get that nickname in a scrubbed-clean world of structured musical predictability?—would probably never want to look at a drum stick again.

John Paul Jones, Zeppelin's bassist, mandolin player, and keyboardist, grew up in a musical household. He started playing piano at age six, learning from his dad, who was a pianist and arranger for big bands. But six? In our day and age, no parent would have wasted that kind of time. The young John Baldwin (like Bonham, John Paul Jones too would have likely never picked up his performing name) would have been on the talent show circuit well before he was a wise, seasoned six-year-old. By then he'd have been on stage for years, clambering through reality shows like *My Kid's Bow Tie is Shinier than Your Kid's Bow Tie*. On his 18th birthday, a chilly January 3, instead of having been doing the session and arranging work that would be the precursor of one of the most versatile, brilliant rock careers ever, he'd step on stage at yet another talent show and wonder, despondent, how many more times he could do this sort of thing.

And what of Jimmy Page, the architect and guitar wizard of the band? Young Page was evidently a pretty good runner. So unfortunately for music, the 2010 Page ends up matched with sports-obsessed parents who see that glimmer of athletic talent and can't wait to get him on, say, a soccer field. Instead of growing up as a well-adjusted loner—Page said of his solitary early years, "...isolation doesn't bother me at all. It gives me a sense of security"—he would have spent weekends crammed in vans with a pile of kids rushing around to tournaments, games, and elite training sessions. He'd be playing year-round by the age of nine on different club teams. Alas, an overuse knee injury would end his career midway through high school. Since the real-life Page didn't meet up with a guitar until he was 15, maybe even this washed-up boyhood athlete would have a chance. But his parents, after the soccer debacle and eager to find the next route to that *scholarship*, at the first sign of plucking would have hustled him right into intensive guitar, before the knee was even healed.

The real Page recalls a key advantage to his early musical development: His high school teachers took his guitar *away* all day: "The good thing about the guitar was that they *didn't* teach it in school. Teaching myself was the first and most important part of my education... I enjoyed pure music because we didn't *have* to." Today that would be borderline child abuse. With sports and then music converted to seven to eleven occupations, young Page would have sputtered along, dazed and confused by his regimented life to the point of creative palsy.

Okay, these four were all so talented—you could argue each was the best rocker ever in his area—that despite growing up with overprotective, overinvolved, overindulging, meddling parents, the fates may still have aligned and the mighty Zeppelin might have risen. But even then, would we have heard its bewitching hum and throb over the rickety clatter of those helicopters?

Vera Wu

The Arizona Sheltered English Immersion Model: A Teaching Framework that Lacks Ethics or Care for ELLs

I recently attended a symposium at the American Education Research Association in New Orleans, Louisiana that drew attention to recent policy changes in Arizona that promote intensive Sheltered English Instruction (SEI)[1] or English Language Development (ELD) classes for English Language Learners (ELLs). I was both startled and shocked by what the educational policymakers in the state proposed as much-needed reform efforts to equalize education for children of immigrants. There were several aspects of this legislation that captured my attention right away. One of the presenters, Amy Markos,[2] from Arizona State University talked about certain "Super Strategies"[3] endorsed by the state, and the Department of Education required all of its ESL, bilingual, and SEI instructors to implement these practices in classrooms where they have ELLs. According to Markos (2011), one such strategy required teachers to require newly arrived and beginning ELLs to speak only English in the classroom, and to push them to do so to "their productive level of discomfort" (p. 2). Another strategy required teachers to utilize a 50/50 discourse configuration in their classrooms where teachers speak 50% of the time and then the students are required to speak 50% of the time. At one point during the presentation, Markos offered an illustration of how one of the SEI teachers she observed adopted this strategy of pushing her ELLs to speak only English in the classroom by encouraging other students to "out" any student who violates this policy.

Let me pause to explain how I was processing the information I heard from this presentation. I am currently a teacher educator at Drexel University, a large urban university in the Northeast. I teach both literacy and TESL courses for Drexel's School of Education. One of the courses that I teach is designed to help pre-service and in-service teachers understand the critical need for having a broad knowledge base about the intersections between language and culture and language and identity, and to view ELL teaching and learning through a sociocultural framework that honors and respects the cultural practices, histories, and traditions of these students and their families. This course is also required for students who want be certified as an ESL instructor in the state of Pennsylvania. To be completely frank, I was horrified when I attended this symposium and learned how Arizona was preparing the next generation of teachers to work with ELLs in the state.

During her presentation, Markos also offered useful analysis of the current policies regulating the SEI program in Arizona, as well as the lack of access to quality instruction that the "Super Strategies" afforded ELLs by presenting literature from the TESL field that forwarded the notion that teaching strategies should be guided by second language acquisition theories and "differentiation based on linguistic and cultural considerations" (p. 3). In her study of English Language Development teachers and classrooms, she discovered that some of the practitioners worked around these guidelines in an effort to create a more comfortable learning environment for their students. While I agree with Markos' argument that the ESL policies in Arizona and the endorsement of "Super Strategies" limit equitable access to education for ELLs, I also want to expand her argument and explain why these policies and strategies are ethically problematic and pedagogically unsound.

In the field of TESL, we have known for a while now that it takes anywhere from four to eight years to acquire academic literacies in English (Collier, 1987; Ovando, Combs, Collier, 2006; Suarez-Orozco et al., 2008). There is no way that a student who *just* arrived to the U.S. can be conversant in English, have the language "capital" required to be successful in all subject areas, or speak English "50% of the time" in class. Just as a way of comparison, in the state of Pennsylvania, beginning ELLs are recommended to have two to three hours of instruction per day, and they are not exited out of an ESL program unless they have met specific proficiency scores on the PSSAs (Pennsylvania System of School Assessment) and/or other standardized tests that are accepted by the state. However, according to the statutes of the ELL Task Force Committee in Arizona that were established on September 21, 2006, newly arrived ELLs are expected to be in English development classes for four hours a day with the goal of "mastering" the English language within one year so they can get pushed out of the ESL program as soon as possible.

These are fundamentally flawed policies and practices. TESL scholars have argued for years that effectively teaching ELLs requires extensive knowledge and understanding of students' cultural differences, educational histories, and parental involvement. A one-size-fits-all paradigm does not work with native-speaking students—it will certainly not work with the diversity represented within the individual and collective histories of ELLs. Teacher research studies such as the one conducted by Christina Igoa (1995) demonstrate how she used her understanding of her students' unique and individual linguistic and cultural backgrounds to find effective ways of developing their L2 (second language) acquisition and create a learning community in her classroom that was a safe haven and a "home away from home" (p. 129) for her students. Furthermore, Krashen (as cited in Peregoy & Boyle, 2008) argued that "social-emotional variables" are critical to second language development (p. 55), that ELLs need a "low-anxiety learning environment" (p. 55), and that beginning ELLs often enter a "silent period" where they are "listening and understanding" (p. 55) and developing some knowledge of the English language. It is also important to keep in mind that ELLs who have just arrived to the U.S. are not just adjusting to a new language, but they are also making difficult transitions culturally, socially, psychologically, and emotionally. Their teachers need to approach them with compassion, patience, and understanding of the complexities of the monumental changes that have occurred in their lives. The Arizona SEI policies ignore the holistic nature of teaching ELLs in order to promote a program that eerily resembles the old "sink or swim" philosophy of education in which immigrant children are forced into English-only classrooms with very little regard for "effective practices" in second language instruction or second language acquisition development theories.

The lack of recognition or acknowledgement of the importance of cultural differences among ELLs or the important role that the students' first language can have in the development of a second language was probably the most disturbing information to come out of the symposium presentations. As I scoured the Arizona English Language Learners Task Force circular that explained what the Structured English Immersion Models were supposed to look like in K-12 classrooms, there was a visible absence of any reference to honoring or supporting the students' cultural identities, languages, or histories in the classroom. There was a deliberate decision to remove any traces of culture or language in this report, as if to say that they did not matter, and the push for speaking English trumped any concern about considering the needs of the "whole child." In his article about the relationship between identity and language in ELLs, Jim Cummins (2001) made the following argument:

> When the message, implicit or explicit, communicated
> to children in school is "Leave your language and culture
> at the schoolhouse door", children also leave a central
> part of who they are—their identities—at the schoolhouse
> door. When they feel this rejection, they are much less
> likely to participate actively and confidently in
> classroom instruction (p. 19-20).

Culture and language are not arbitrary influences in the life of an ELL, but they make up integral aspects of their self-identity. Children will pull from what they already know, from their prior knowledge and experiences to "make sense" of what happens in the classroom. For many beginning ELLs, they already have a language foundation in their "Mother Tongue" as Cummins would describe it, and teachers of ELLs need to build upon this to help them learn a second language instead of punishing students for not speaking "English only" and forcing them to talk and write in a foreign language before they have the confidence or the ability to do so. When I used to teach the ESL sections of freshman writing at Drexel, my former international students used to tell me that they often felt frustrated with their writing because they knew what they wanted to say in their native languages, but when they wrote it down in English, the language barrier made it difficult to articulate the sophisticated and complicated ideas they had in their minds. I remembered having one student who was actually an accomplished fiction writer in China and had a good number of Chinese readers who followed his work. But when he was asked to write academic essays in English, it ate away at his confidence and he knew what he wanted to say, but the "code switching" from Chinese to English often masked what he really wanted to express in his writing.

Teachers of ELLs need to understand that it takes more time to learn English, particularly the academic kind that is needed to decode and comprehend subject area texts like science, math, and history, than what the Arizona SEI Program Models are mandating. These unrealistic and unfounded expectations, I believe, will create greater achievement gaps for ELLs because they are being pushed through the system much too quickly. Decades of Second Language Acquisition developmental theories and literature about why we need socio-cultural approaches to teaching ELLs are being tossed aside and the fundamental human and educational needs and rights of immigrant children are being blatantly disregarded in the name of monolingualism and monoculturalism in Arizona schools. What the field of education has fought so hard to do in the past 50 years in bringing issues of multiculturalism and diversity to the forefront of teaching and learning, particularly in light of the increasing numbers of ethnic- and linguistic-minority children in our schools (Branch, 2001; Cochran-Smith, 1995; Justiz & Kameen, 1998), has been trivialized by the recent ESL program changes in the state of Arizona. For those of us who care deeply and advocate for immigrant families and ELLs and believe in a democratic and equitable education for all children, we cannot afford to simply remain silent about the dehumanizing and unethical policies that are affecting a number of vulnerable children in this state.[4]

Works Cited

Arizona State Department of Education (May, 2008). Structured English Immersion Models of the Arizona English Language Learners Task Force [Online]. Available: http://www.ade.az.gov/ELLTaskForce/2008/SEIModels05-14-08.pdf.

Branch, A. J. (2001). Increasing the numbers of teachers in K-12 public schools. *The Educational Forum, 65*(3), 254-261.

Cochran-Smith, M. (1995). Uncertain allies: Understanding the boundaries of race and Teaching. *Harvard Educational Review, 65*(4), 541-570.

Cummins, J. (2001). Bilingual children's mother tongue: Why is it important for Education? *Multilingual Denmark, 19,* 15-19.

Igoa, C. (1995). *The inner world of the immigrant child.* Mahwah, NJ: Lawrence Erlbaum Associates.

Justiz, M. J. & Kameen, M. C. (1988). Increasing the representation of minorities in the Teaching profession. *Peabody Journal of Education, 66*(1), 91-100.

Krashen, S. (1982). *Principles and practices in second language acquisition.* Oxford: Pergamon Press.

Markos, A. (April, 2011). "Structured English immersion (SEI) super strategies": Are they really super? Unpublished paper presented at the American Education Research Association Conference, New Orleans, LA.

Ovando, C. J., Combs, M. C., & Collier, V. P. (2006). *Bilingual and ESL classrooms: Teaching in multicultural contexts (4th ed.).* New York: McGraw Hill.

Peregoy, S. F. & Boyle, O. F. (2008). *Reading, writing, and learning in ESL: A resource for teaching K-12 English learners (5th Ed.).* Boston, MA: Pearson.

Suarez-Orozco, C., Suarez-Orozco, M. M., Todorova, I. (2008). *Learning a new land: Immigrant students in American society.* Cambridge, MA: Belknap Press.

---

[1] The symposium I attended at the American Education Research Association (AERA) Conference was called, "A View of Arizon's Structured English Immersion: Offering Access or Creating Barriers to Education for English Learners?"

[2] The paper Amy Markos presented during the symposium is titled, "'Structured English Immersion (SEI) Super Strategies': Are They Really Super?"

[3] In her paper, Markos (2011) explained that the "Super Strategies" included "English-only in the classroom, students speak in complete sentences, teachers and students each talk 50% of the time, errors are corrected immediately, and students [are pushed] to their productive discomfort" (p. 2).

[4] I would like to thank Amy Markos for granting me permission to discuss her paper in this essay, and for generously sending me original copies of both her paper and the presentation she gave at AERA on April 9, 2011 in New Orleans, La.

Contributors

Tom Ben-David is majoring in architectural engineering and minoring in architecture. He was born and raised in Israel until summer 2007, when he moved to Commack, New York. Today he lives in Miami, Florida. In his free time he is an artist, working with pencil, acrylic and oil paint, origami, and mixed media.

Genevieve Betts received her MFA in creative writing in 2006 from Arizona State University, where she reviewed poetry for *Hayden's Ferry Review*. Recently, she was a finalist for the ABZ First Book Award and her latest work appears in *OVS Magazine*, *Western American Literature*, *Quarter After Eight*, *Midwest Quarterly*, and *NANO Fiction*. She currently teaches at Drexel University.

Kevin Biallas is an environmental science major from rural Selinsgrove, Pennsylvania. He owes his adventurous spirit and appreciation for history to his late father, with whom he shared many experiences and often went on the "road less traveled." He enjoys spending time hiking and camping in Pennsylvania's state parks and hopes one day to help work to protect them.

Chelsea Biemiller is a senior psychology major originally from New Jersey. In her free time, she enjoys scouring flea markets for antique clothing and books; reading; and playing with her dogs, Tallulah and Lucky. She is addicted to crossword puzzles, Coca-Cola, and calling out the answers on *Jeopardy*. Chelsea is the outgoing president of Drexel's undergraduate mock trial team, a position that's only fostered her natural inclination to argue. In the fall, she'll continue her education at Drexel by attending the Earle Mack School of Law.

Zach Blackwood began writing his freshman year at Drexel University while studying entertainment and arts management. He is now working toward the Certificate in Writing and Publishing.

Allison Brophy is a nursing major from Glastonbury, Connecticut. She attended Mercy High School, where she played four years of soccer and lacrosse. As a freshman at Drexel, she plays for the club soccer and lacrosse teams and serves as head of scheduling for Drexel EMS (Emergency Medical Services). Allison hopes to graduate from Drexel and continue her education, becoming a nurse practitioner specializing in neonatology and obstetrics.

Clinton Burkhart majored in biology and graduated from Drexel in the spring of 2011. After graduation Clinton planned to do a year or two of volunteer service with either the Peace Corps or AmeriCorps. One of Clinton's favorite authors is Isaac Asimov, and he was excited to be able to cite Asimov in his essay.

Alexis Burns is a freshman from the suburbs of Philadelphia. She is currently a four-year nursing BSN student. She enjoys reading and analyzing classic and modern literature and poetry when she is not busy with being a member of the Campus Activities Board and the Legislative Chair for the Drexel chapter of the Student Nurses' Association of Pennsylvania. Burns would like to thank her high school teacher, Ms. Laurie McBrinn, for imparting to her a love for literature.

Paula Marantz Cohen is Distinguished Professor of English at Drexel University. She holds a BA in French and English from Yale College and a Ph.D. in English literature from Columbia University. She is the author of four nonfiction books and four novels including, most recently, *What Alice Knew: A Most Curious Tale of Henry James and Jack the Ripper* (a Book-of-the-Month and Mystery Guild selection). Cohen is the host of *The Drexel InterView*, a cable TV show broadcast on 325 PBS, education, and community-affiliated stations across the country. Her essays, stories, and reviews have appeared in *The Yale Review, Raritan, The American Scholar, The Southwest Review, The New York Times, The Philadelphia Inquirer*, and *The Times Literary Supplement*. She is a co-editor of *The Journal of Modern Literature* and writes a regular column for *TheSmartSet.com*.

Abby Davis is a senior English/education major in Drexel's BS/MS program. She is originally from Columbia, Maryland, and is an active runner and player on Drexel's club field hockey team.

David Fairfield is from Croydon, Pennsylvania, a suburb of Philadelphia. He is currently in his sophomore year pursuing a Bachelor of Science in business administration with concentrations in legal studies and finance. His hobbies include golf, lacrosse, and reading works of literature and philosophy.

Charles Falone is an undergraduate physics major from Glenolden, Pennsylvania. He enjoys learning about the universe, in order to better understand humanity's place in it. His interests include helping people and having fun, ideally at the same time.

Valerie Fox's most recent collection of poetry is *The Glass Book* (2010, Texture Press). Her poetry has appeared in numerous journals, including *Hanging Loose, Sentence, Ping Pong, West Branch, Feminist Studies*, and *Six Little Things*. She is a founding co-editor of *Press 1*, a magazine that features fiction, opinion, photography, and poetry.

Zachary Geesey is a five-year electrical engineer major in the MS/BS program. He was born and raised in Maryland, where he attended Calvert Hall College High School and graduated in the top 10% of his class. His favorite subjects in school are physics and calculus. He became an Eagle Scout in the fall of 2010 and is currently contracted in the Army ROTC program at Drexel, and will commit eight years of his life to the Army once he graduates from Drexel.

Giby George graduated in 2011 with a degree in biology. She plans on writing, reading, and traveling during the upcoming year, after which she hopes to attend medical school.

Maura Hanley is a 2011 graduate of Drexel University's College of Engineering. She received a Bachelor's of Science in electrical engineering and a Certificate in Creative Writing and Publishing. Maura is commissioning in the Navy and serving on the USS Lake Champlain out of San Diego.

Cassandra Hirsch teaches freshman writing at Drexel University. Formerly a freelance writer, she now writes fiction and creative nonfiction. Her work has appeared in *Philadelphia Stories, Healing Lifestyles & Spas Magazine*, and *Parlor Journal*, among other regional magazines and periodicals. She has completed and is looking for a home for her historical novel, set in 1850s coastal Massachusetts, and is now turning toward writing a young adult novel. She holds an MFA in creative writing from Rosemont College.

Laurel Hostak is a junior in the screenwriting and playwriting major. She serves as president of the Drexel Players and participates in theatre on campus and in the Philadelphia community in various capacities. Her writing has been published in *Maya* literary magazine and *The 33rd* (2009).

Rebecca Ingalls is the director of the Freshman Writing Program in the Department of English and Philosophy at Drexel. She specializes in composition and rhetoric, and her work may be found in *The Review of Education, Pedagogy, and Cultural Studies*; *inventio*; *The Journal of Teaching Writing*; *POROI*; *Harlot*; and *The Journal of Popular Culture* (forthcoming). She is currently working with colleagues on an edited collection on plagiarism. She earned her BA at Cornell University, her MA at Boston College, and her Ph.D. at the University of Michigan.

Miriam N. Kotzin is professor of English at Drexel, co-director of the Certificate Program in Writing and Publishing, contributing editor of *Boulevard*, and co-founding editor of *Per Contra*. She is the author of five books, including, most recently, *Just Desserts: flash fiction* and *Taking Stock*.

Nisha Koya is an English major at Drexel University pursuing a career in medicine. Originally from Long Island, New York, she is the co-president of the Hindu Student Association on campus and enjoys dancing, traveling, and playing tennis.

Devon Laughlin is a history major from Houston, Texas. She enjoys singing in multiple choirs at Drexel and in Houston. She actively pursues her interest in human psychology through courses at Drexel.

Jeffrey Ethan Lee teaches at Drexel University, Temple University, and Community College of Philadelphia. His 2006 poetry book, *identity papers*, was a Colorado Book Award finalist and his 2004 book, *invisible sister*, was a finalist for the first MMM Press poetry prize. He won the 2002 Sow's Ear Poetry Chapbook prize for *The Sylf*, created *identity papers* (audio CD) for Drimala Records, published *Strangers in a Homeland* (chapbook with Ashland Poetry Press, 2001), and a new chapbook, *Towards Euphoria*, won an editor's prize from Seven Kitchens Press (forthcoming in 2012). He has a Ph.D. and MFA from New York University.

Lynn Levin is adjunct associate professor of English at Drexel and producer of the TV show *The Drexel InterView*. A poet, writer, and translator, she is the author of three collections of poems, most recently *Fair Creatures of an Hour* (2009), a Next Generation Indie Book Awards finalist in poetry, and *Imaginarium* (2005), a finalist for *ForeWord Magazine*'s Book of the Year Award. She holds a BA from Northwestern University and an MFA in Writing from Vermont College..

Nicole McCourt is an English major at Drexel University and lives in the Philadelphia area.

Chris McGuire is a Drexel computer science major who enjoys writing in his free time. He lives in Philadelphia with his cat and reality TV. His favorite authors include Douglas Adams, John Kennedy Toole, and whoever does the writing for Gossip Girl.

Harriet Levin Millan is the co-director of the Certificate Program in Writing and Publishing at Drexel, where she teaches poetry and creative nonfiction writing. In the spring she will be teaching a new topics course called *Your Immigration Story*. Among her poetry prizes are the Barnard New Women Poets Prize, the Poetry Society of America's Alice Fay di Castagnola Award, and a PEW Fellowship in the Arts discipline award. Her poetry has been featured on *Poetry Daily* and is widely published in journals, most recently in *Harvard Review, Iowa Review, Cerise Press,* and *Prairie Schooner*. She is the author of two books, *The Christmas Show* and *Girl in Cap and Gown*. She holds an MFA from the Iowa Writers Workshop.

Kathleen Volk Miller is an associate teaching professor of English, co-editor of *Painted Bride Quarterly*, and co-director of the Drexel Publishing Group. She writes fiction, personal essays, and articles. Her work has most recently appeared in *Opium*, and is forthcoming in *The New York Times* and *Drunken Boat*. She has spoken at various conferences on marketing, publishing online, working with student interns, and teaching with technology.

Tuyet-Nhung Nguyen is a biology major in the Pennoni Honors College. She graduated from Seaford Senior High School at the top of her class. She is planning on becoming a family practitioner.

Anne-Marie Obajtek-Kirkwood is an associate professor of French at Drexel. She co-edited *Signs of War. From Patriotism to Dissent* (Palgrave Macmillan 2007) and has published extensively on French authors like Simone de Beauvoir, Patrick Modiano, Marguerite Duras, Sophie Calle, and Viviane Forrester. She holds an MA in Elizabethan and Jacobean Comedy from the University of Lille III, France and a Ph.D. in 20th-century French literature from the University of Pennsylvania.

Dickens Omondi is an international student at Drexel University majoring in bsc. civil engineering. He lives in Kenya, in the small town called Homa Bay, on the shores of Lake Victoria. Among other things, he likes travelling and writing creative nonfiction pieces.

Dario Rainone is a freshman pursuing a degree in mechanical engineering, although he always likes to keep his options open. He emigrated from Naples, Italy in search of better educational and career opportunities. His top interests include languages, vegetarianism, traveling, and stand-up comedy, something that he hopes to be good at one day.

Don Riggs has been writing regular columns relating to poetry and his experience of living for the past decade for, first, the *Drexel Online Journal*, then *ASK*, and, currently, *Press 1*. He teaches courses in the Department of English and Philosophy at Drexel, including some that deal with poetry.

Gail D. Rosen teaches English at Drexel. She holds a BA from Temple University and a JD from Temple University School of Law. She has written weekly film reviews for *When Falls the Coliseum* <whenfallsthecoliseum.com>.

Arhama Rushdi is a political science major in the BS/JD program. She wants to become an international human rights attorney.

Andrew Seletsky is a biology major at Drexel University. He was raised in North Jersey and is loving life in Philadelphia. Andrew enjoys spending time with his friends and girlfriend and taking trips on his motorcycle. He hopes to work with synthetic biology in the future.

Stephanie Sendaula is pursuing her master of science in library and information science from the iSchool at Drexel. Previously, she earned undergraduate degrees in journalism and history from Temple University and was a freelance writer for a number of years. She enjoys baking and biking.

Kate Sherlock is a 3L at Earle Mack School of Law at Drexel University. She received her BS in Music Industry from Drexel University in 2006. Prior to attending law school, Kate worked as a music and media licensing coordinator for MTV Networks. She was born and raised in Marlton, New Jersey and currently resides in Cherry Hill, New Jersey with her fiancé.

Fred Siegel is a teaching professor of English at Drexel, associate director of the Freshman Writing Program, an actor in the improv group "Tongue and Groove," and a part-time magician. He teaches freshman writing, creative nonfiction, and Horror in American Culture. He holds a BA from Temple, an MA from Adelphi, and a Ph.D. from New York University.

Divya Sreenivasan is a nursing student at Drexel University. She is originally from Lansdowne, a suburb just outside of Philadelphia. Her main interests are dancing, listening to music, and photography. She hopes to one day become a pediatric nurse or family nurse practitioner.

Joshua Stolle is a senior at Drexel University, enrolled in classes for a concentration of marketing at the Lebow Business School. Originally from Waco, Texas, he joined the Navy immediately after 9/11. After training for a year in San Diego, he was stationed aboard the guided-missile frigate USS Crommelin in Pearl Harbor, Hawaii. He was a member of a narcotics seizure boarding team during his five years in Hawaii. Upon completing his service, he traveled the country looking for the perfect place to finish college and landed in Philadelphia.

Daniel Sullivan is studying computer science. During his freshman year at Drexel, he competed in the Microsoft Imagine Cup, and represented Drexel in the US finals, making one of only ten teams to earn the opportunity. He is passionate about technology and its uses in society, especially the global, universal impact it can have.

Kerri Sullivan studies film/video and is in her third year. She is the editor-in-chief of *Maya*, Drexel University's undergraduate literary magazine, where her writing and photography have been published. When she is not writing, she is probably photographing someone, reading, visiting a museum, or thinking about writing.

Elizabeth Thorpe's short stories and excerpts from her novel-in-progress have appeared in *Painted Bride Quarterly*, *Per Contra*, *Press 1*, *Puckerbrush Review*, and *The Maine Review*, among other publications. She teaches at Drexel University and in the Pre-College program at The University of the Arts. She earned her MFA in Writing from Goddard College.

Scott Warnock is an associate professor of English at Drexel and director of the Writing Center and Writing Across the Curriculum. His research and teaching interests include computers and writing, writing assessment, and writing in the professions. He is the author of *Teaching Writing Online: How and Why*, and he has contributed chapters to a number of anthologies and published his work in many academic journals.

Vera J. Wu is an assistant clinical professor for the School of Education at Drexel. She teaches courses in literacy and TESL. She was formerly an adjunct instructor for the English and Philosophy Department and taught freshman writing courses. Her research interests include examining the socialization and teaching experiences of teachers of color in suburban schools and utilizing practitioner research to investigate the pedagogy and practice of teacher educators who teach online courses focused on issues of diversity. She holds a BA in English from Boston University and an MS Ed and Ed.D. in reading, writing, literacy from the University of Pennsylvania.

Brian Zilberman is a student at Drexel University pursuing degrees in biology and history, with the goal of working in the medical sector. His forms of expression, other than writing, include cycling and dancing.

MEET & GREET

FUN, FOOD AND PRIZES!

The College of Arts and Sciences quarterly Meet and Greets allow all members of the CoAS community to meet and connect in a relaxed social setting. Students have the opportunity to make valuable contacts with faculty, establish new friendships, and win prizes!

DATES: Thursday, October 6, 2011
Thursday, January 26, 201
Thursday, April 19, 2012

TIME: 4:30 pm - 6:00 pm

PLACE: Paul Peck Alumni Center, 3142 Market Street

WHAT HAPPENS AT A MEET AND GREET?

1. Students and faculty mingle and enjoy a light reception.
2. Students receive raffle tickets from faculty members and enter into a drawing.
3. Names are drawn and winners receive prizes ranging from Barnes & Noble gift certificates to an iPod shuffle!

For more information, see the CoAS calendar: http://www.drexel.edu/coas/news/calendar/